07101035

GW00535915

THE OBELISK

A MONUMENTAL FEATURE IN BRITAIN

THE OBELISK

A MONUMENTAL FEATURE IN BRITAIN

Richard Barnes

FRONTIER PUBLISHING
2004

First Published 2004
Frontier Publishing
Kirstead
Norfolk NR15 1EG

British Library Cataloguing in Publication Data

Barnes, Richard, 1950-
The obelisk : a monumental feature in Britain
1. Obelisks - Great Britain - History
I . Title
725.9'4' 0941

ISBN 1872914284

Typeset in Cochin by T&O Graphics, Bungay, Suffolk.

PRINTED IN GREAT BRITAIN
by Biddles of Kings Lynn, Norfolk
and colour print by Crowes, Norwich.

CONTENTS

Obelisks in Britain need no introduction as they are in place throughout the land already. What I have attempted to do is to provide a wide picture of the feature. They are a big subject and this is inevitably a broad study. There are still many threads to gather up, but this book makes a start, particularly in commencing the gazetteer.

There are many ways to approach the subject and the one that I have taken is the result of my interests, which are in British history and landscape. Having written a book about the sculptor, John Bell, my curiosity was kindled by John Bell's lectures about the obelisk, and then spurred by the response to these lectures from an Egyptologist, who implied that British obelisks were of no account.

The method I have used is quite simple. I have considered the obelisk, century by century and added John Bell's lecture and some writing about cemeteries and war memorials. The chapter at the end, with all the theories of meaning, is quite conventional. I have left out some aspects. I have not listed the many obelisks in Britain's former colonies, or those in countries such as China, where British communities sited their own cemeteries. Nor have I entered into the endless debate about how the Ancient Egyptians erected their large monolithic obelisks. There are other writers who could have made a more complete work, but I doubt they would have started it, or known where to finish.

What I hope are my strengths are a general understanding of the British landscape and an open mind. I don't consider my character to be of relevance to this book, but like many, I veer between light-heartedness and gravity. As it happens, the subject is uplifting. I have been a retrospective witness to constant good intention - the desire of obelisk erectors to 'do it right ', even if the result turned out to be 'wrong'. As for gravity, the subject also calls for a practical outlook. Obelisks are bound to the earth and need foundations, levels, measures and plenty of power, both human and mechanical.

The quest to find out more about obelisks opened my eyes to skypiercing structures and the art within architecture. It took me along paths in beautiful gardens and wooded cemeteries where obelisks wait for sunlight. It led me up tracks into the hills, silent except for birdsong, towards an obelisk at the summit; (I still dream of this). It made me think about the British landscape again and placed me on the side of not just public sculpture, but monuments as well.

I hope that readers will take pleasure from these pages and that some may be motivated to raise 21st century obelisks. The national collection (see gazetteer) awaits additions.

Richard Barnes, August 2004.

I

The Sixteenth & Seventeenth Centuries

At his home in 33 York Street, off Portman Square, on the evening of 13th March 1860, Sir John Gardner Wilkinson sat down to his desk and began a letter which he had composed in his mind many times.

> With regard to the erection of obelisks in England, I confess I am altogether opposed to their adoption for monumental purposes. We attach no meaning to them; we have no association connected with them; we do not even appear to understand the use for which they were invented; and we employ them in places and positions diametrically opposed to their character and to the principle which led to their adoption by the Egyptians. Obelisks served as a vertical line to contrast with the long horizontal character of the Egyptian temple, where their effect and position were admirable. We place one by itself in some open space like some monster gnomon, we spoil the character of the obelisk by mounting it on a Roman pedestal, which entirely interferes with its general form and character, and we depress its apex as if we wished to deprive it of an important feature which constitutes one of its peculiar beauties.
>
> The mere imitation of an ancient monument, in no way suited to our wants, tastes or predilections, is a sad sign of deficiency of inventive talent; and unless an obelisk is so placed as to accord with the purposes for which it was originally devised, it is a false application of an ill-understood principle. The right application of it will, I have no doubt, be duly considered and determined by a sculptor of Mr Bell's great proficiency and taste, and we shall then no longer have to condemn obelisks as unmeaning objects.

This was Wilkinson's considered response to a lecture he had attended at the Royal Society of Arts, delivered by the sculptor, John Bell, who had talked at length about obelisks and their suitability for monumental works in England. The lecture was well received and Bell had been awarded the Society's medal for this work.

Yet it troubled Gardner Wilkinson for months and prompted the letter. England? What did he know? He had left the country for Egypt at the age of twenty-four and stayed there for twelve years conducting excavations around Thebes. His careful studies and drawings had been published in London upon his return in the 1830s. He was, in his time, acknowledged as the founder of Egyptology in England.

But it was far too late for his pronouncements. Obelisks had already arrived and found a home in Britain. They had been here two hundred years before 'Egyptology' and the import of one or two Egyptian obelisks. The feature had proliferated in Britain, not only as park and garden ornaments, but as important monuments. They were spreading as memorials in the new grave grounds which sprung up in the years while Gardner Wilkinson had been away in Egypt. The island race seemed to have a predilection for obelisks.

The story could begin in any number of places during four centuries of recorded occupation. It could even have begun in prehistory in Egypt or Britain itself. At various periods in history, the obelisk has been seen in different contexts.

Obelisks had started to arrive in the reign of Queen Elizabeth, in the form of exterior architectural and tomb decoration. The first known was a grand entry, whereby, 'Nonsuch in England received a marble obelisk, as high as the Palace'[1]. This was to King Henry VIII's Nonsuch Palace, which he had built from 1538 onwards at Ewell in Surrey and which was entirely destroyed in 1682. The Tudor heraldic gardens were still incomplete when King Henry died in 1547. The many finishing touches were made over a period of time from 1556 onwards by the 12th Earl of Arundel and his son in law, Baron Lumley. [2]

Lord John Lumley had visited and stayed at length in Rome, and it was he who introduced an Italian or Renaissance element to the gardens and terraces at Nonsuch. Among other items, including a marble Fountain of Diana, Lord Lumley brought the tall obelisk of streaked and veined Italian marble and had his his own coat of arms carved upon it, depicting a pelican feeding its young. The Palace was principally a two or three storey building, so the obelisk, which was put in position near the South-West tower, must have been somewhere between 20-30 feet in height. Elsewhere at Nonsuch, visible in a 1582 drawing, was a line of small stone obelisks, evenly spaced, forming the edge of the terraces behind the palace.

The inspiration and source for the obelisk was the imperial city, where as many as forty Egyptian obelisks stood or lay fallen, following the trophy hunting of Roman emperors in Egypt more than a thousand years earlier. The first books on architecture were being printed in Rome, borrowing from antiquity in their designs for tombs and mausoleums, including the use of obelisks.

The raising of the Vatican obelisk in 1586. Domenico Fontana, *Della Transportatione dell Obelisco Vaticano*

Successive popes had wished to enhance the city's architectural qualities. Sixtus V, who came to the papacy in 1585, was instrumental

Cavalier
Fontana,
"Nobelisco"

in the re-erection of five fallen Egyptian obelisks in prominent piazzas, circuses and squares. Sixtus employed Domenico Fontana to perform the task of moving Caligula's obelisk and raising it before St Peter's. The architect assembled a towering timber *castello dell obelisco*, which was moved and powered by the pull of horseteams. It carried and lifted the 83 feet long monolith into position in September 1586. The vista of poles and ropes and horses and men, with prominent detail, was engraved in Fontana's triumphant book, *'Della trasportatione dell' obelisco vaticano'*. Cavalier Fontana was honoured in every possible way: the pope ennobled him and joked that he was a 'nobelisco'. When the pope wanted more obelisks, agents searched the crumbling city of the Vatican, prodding the ground with long iron rods.

In England, the place for new designs in tombs and memorials was in the church. In 1591, twin obelisks, approximately 12 feet tall on pedestals and topped with spheres, were instated on the tomb of Sir Christopher Hatton, sculpted by Richard Stevens in Old St.Paul's Cathedral.[3] Two black marble obelisks standing on pillars were included on the elaborate monument to Sir James Harington (d.1591)and wife, to be seen in Exton church, Rutland. In 1592 the tomb of 1st Viscount Montagu and his two wives had four corner obelisks surrounding the tomb. Originally at Midhurst, it is now at nearby Easebourne, West Sussex, minus the obelisks. [4]

The Southampton tomb was raised in 1594 in Titchfield, Hampshire, and can be seen today. Three recumbent effigies of the 2nd Earl of Southampton, his mother and his son, are surrounded by four obelisks. These are about 7 feet in height, in black-veined marble, sited at the corners of the base, each topped with a small sphere.

The designer and sculptor of the tomb and obelisks was Garat Johnson. Garat, or Gerard, arrived from Amsterdam in 1567 and was assisted by his son, Nicholas. Their work took place in the workshops and stoneworking yards of Southwark, where there were numerous foreign carvers, principally from the Netherlands. As foreigners they were forbidden to be in the City of London itself, but Southwark was just across the Thames, the natural access for shipments of marble and stone.

It is thought that Johnson saw or picked up the idea of using obelisks in this way from newly printed books of architectural designs, which were referred to by those choosing a particular style when commissioning work. Du Cercau's *Second Livre d'Architecture*, published in 1562, had an illustration of a tomb with four tall obelisks, standing at each corner. [5]

The line of small obelisks along the terrace of Nonsuch had been admired and was soon copied. In 1598 Sir Edward Phelps set about the building of Montacute House, near Yeovil in Somerset. He had a row of obelisks along the parapet of the three-storey manor, forty feet above the ground. The obelisk finials on the roofline were impressive from some distance and started a fashion. The regularly interspaced line of obelisks continued in the garden along an outside terrace upon a balustraded wall. The obelisks, of local Ham Hill stone, were about four feet tall. Their appearance was marred by curvilinear dog-tooth bosses at the peak of the obelisks, in imitation of the pyramidion.

The novel manner of using obelisks among the turrets and parapets of a mansion roof had been used by the mason Robert Smythson in his work at Hardwick Hall and in his design for Sir Francis Willoughby at Wollaton Hall, Nottinghamshire, in the 1580s. A copy of du Cercau's *Premier Livre d'Architecture*, published in 1559, was known to have been in Willoughby's library. [6]

Thus, within a matter of a few years of its arrival, the obelisk had become an accepted and sometimes preferred feature in an architect's repertoire, in a variety of sizes, from 4 feet to roughly 30 feet tall. This could be either outside or under cover, freestanding or in conjunction with different features, or other obelisks. By 1603, the status of the feature was evident with the arrival of a new king. James I entered London through an archway, specially constructed for the occasion, topped by two obelisks on either side. [7]

The obelisk continued to be employed in memorials such as the 1613 Fettiplace Monument at St Mary's in Swinbrook, Oxfordshire, which exhibits Jacobean motifs of strapwork and obelisks crowning a conglomeration of ball finials, pillars, arched canopies, scrolls and ribbons, in marble and alabaster. The memorial of 1628 to Lord Chief Justice Tanfield and family at the church of St John the Baptist at Burford, presented obelisks above pillars and recumbent effigies.

In 1630, a different use was intended in the construction of a many-faceted sundial, topped by an obelisk. It was made by the king's master-mason, John Mylne III, for Lord Drummond, 2nd Earl of Perth, and sited in his garden at Drummond Castle, near Crieff in Perthshire. Although the garden was enlarged and redesigned in the 19th century, the sundial remained the focal point. It was extremely complicated with as many as eighty-five facets. As such, the mounted obelisk served only to give basic shadow readings along the radiating borders of clipped box and formal bedding. Its position in the view was central, drawing the eye beyond the formal garden to a straight uphill ride to the horizon.

It is thought that Scotland once possessed as many as seventy obeliscal stone sundials, amongst others those on Bute and at Tongue, Sutherland, inscribed with the date 1714. Although these were solar timepieces, Scotland could be overcast for weeks at a time, making the devices inoperable. There may have been other associations as the numerous incised shapes on the sundial were more than profiles to catch the sun's rays at different times. Heart-shapes, suns, moons, elipses and triangles abounded, and these are attributed to freemasonry. The unofficial society was relatively active in Scotland during the period. Freemasonry was to play a part in the story of obelisks, though to less of an extent than certain writers have suggested.

The obelisk feature was fairly dormant in the middle of the 17th century. There was little opportunity for art and architecture to progress while zealots raided churches and Cromwell purged landowners loyal to the crown. Britain would have to wait until the Restoration before resuming unfinished business with the obelisk.

Meanwhile, in Rome, the newly re-erected obelisks – or rather the hieroglyphic inscriptions carved on them – were causing developments. Sixtus and later popes had exorcised each obelisk as they raised them, marking many crosses about the base and fixing a metal cross at the top. However, this could not mask the obvious conflict of cultures suggested by these large non-christian items in the centre of Vatican city. There was a scramble for more information about the hieroglyphic texts on the obelisks. What did they mean? As long as nobody could read hieroglyphs, no interpretation could be refuted.

Within Europe, speculative theories encouraged the rise of secret societies, who saw themselves as the keepers of ancient knowledge. When these societies were later proscribed, as the church floundered in its defence against reformation and the power of European states, murderous persecutions took place. With the suppression of knowledge, further conspiracies abounded, borrowing myth and practice from all sources: Templar, Rosicrucian, Cabbalistic. With their mysterious glyphs, the Egyptian obelisks seemed to contain a lost code. In order to wrest control of the power of knowledge, that is to say, the meaning of the hieroglyphs on their obelisks, the church itself began to investigate.

Prominent in the offensive against heresy, sometimes referred to as the Counter-Reformation, was the Society of Jesus. Founded in 1541, the Society persecuted heretics, including learned scholars and even their own priests, whose studies had led them to question catholic dogma. In the 1630s, one Jesuit, Father Athanasius Kircher, had already conducted his own studies into languages and scripts before being consulted about hieroglyphs on one of the smaller Egyptian obelisks. This had been dug up and was destined for a Cardinal's garden, where it was to be placed on the back of a stone elephant, to a design by the sculptor-architect, Gian Lorenzo Bernini.

Moving in high circles in Rome, Kircher became the Professor of Mathematics at the Collegio Romano, a sort of private university and museum, owned and run by the Jesuits. The Society has an extraordinary history, full of high motivation and violence, which the present author is well acquainted with. In gainsay, they had other qualities, among which was their ability to acquire collections. In Kircher's lifetime, the museum at the Collegio Romano was transformed into a place with domed ceilings painted with planets and stars, and shelving heaped with Egyptian sculptures, mummies and curios. Seen in an engraving, as many as five Egyptian obelisks stood in a line down the marbled gallery.

In 1644, Kircher was asked by Pope Innocent X, to find out the meaning of scripts on yet another broken obelisk in Rome, destined for the Piazza Navona in conjunction with an elaborate fountain by Bernini. Since some of the pieces of the broken obelisk were missing, Kircher was expected to 'fill in' the missing scripts. When he had done this and the obelisk and fountain were completed, the pope asked Kircher to publish his research, which he did in *Obeliscus Pamphilis*. (Pamfili was the pope's family name). Kircher had men copying scripts in Egypt and from all directions came symbols and hidden meanings. Getting a taste for publishing, in 1652, he next produced a much larger work, *Oedipus Aegyptiacus*, with charts and engravings.

He was favoured by the next pope, Alexander VII, a scholar and poet who helped Kircher to pursue some very interesting studies, including symbolism and every possible aspect of linguistics, even Plato's essays on the effects of the sound of a word, or words. Kircher retired and spent the last few years of his life among his collections.[8] The German Jesuit was a typical encyclopaedist, but this was the inevitable direction for people who tried to decipher the hieroglyphs on Rome's obelisks. And what had all this study told about the obelisks themselves? By concentrating on the inscriptions only, practically nothing.

In Britain, the floodgates to the flow of cultural and scientific ideas were reopened with the return of the king in 1660. Nevertheless, Parliament watched carefully to prevent too much contact with France, mindful of the dangers of a catholic monarchy and the presence of Jacobites in exile in Rome. The separation between Britain and Europe over matters of religion and independence was extremely strong. If the effect of hieroglyphomania on Europe's aristocratic thinkers and dissident scholars was to amplify the sense of mystery surrounding the obelisk, this was of less consideration in Britain. British scholars had no hieroglyphs to compare, and though Antiquarianism was an eternal quest, it was of lesser interest when compared with the explosion of new ideas in society. This was the Age of Enlightenment, the duration of which, for British purposes, ran broadly 1660-1810, from Charles II to George III. With Charles's peaceful arrival, there followed the Fire of London. A great enthusiasm for building filled the capital and architects, beginning with Wren, became known by name. It was time again for landowners to consider the appearance of their properties.

As the the century turned in 1699, the architectural partners, Nicholas Hawksmoor and John Vanbrugh, went to Yorkshire to consult with a noble client. Whilst there, Hawksmoor met with another estate owner who wanted to have a forum in a town market place, with a tall obelisk at its centre.

II

THE EIGHTEENTH CENTURY

'If there were obelisks to bee made of what all our kings
have don of that sort the countrey would bee stuffed with
very odd things.'   Sarah, Duchess of Marlborough, 1727

John Aislabie had inherited the house and estate at Studley Royal in
Yorkshire from his elder brother. Three years later in 1702, when
mayor of nearby Ripon, he supplied half the money for a handsome
paved market, in imitation of the forum, using limestone cut from his
own quarry. At its centre, a tall obelisk made of blocks cut from the
same stone, was raised to a design Aislabie purchased from Nicholas
Hawksmoor. Hawksmoor had described his plan for Ripon in a letter
to Aislabie, as drawn 'according to the most ancient symmetry'.

Another description was that of Daniel Defoe, in his *'Tour Through
the Whole Island of Great Britain, 1724-6'*:

> Ripon is a very neat, pleasant, well built town, and has not
> only an agreeable situation on a rising ground between two
> rivers, is the finest and most beautiful square that is to be
> seen of its kind in England. In the middle of it stands a
> curious column of stone, imitating the obelisks of the
> antients, tho' not so high, but rather like the pillar in the
> middle of Covent-Garden, or that in Lincoln's Inn, with
> dials also upon it.

It was the first large obelisk in Britain. It stands eighty feet,
although at least a third of this height is taken in the tall pedestal and
base. The stone is most attractive, the colour of wheat. Originally,

four smaller obelisks were set at the four corners of the monument's base, but these were removed in 1882. The complicated copper vane at the top of the obelisk was in the form of a horn and rowel spur, symbols of the borough of Ripon and connected with an old tradition of 'the Wakeman' who sounds his horn at nine o'clock each night.

It was also the first obelisk in the country to be constructed of close-fitting blocks of stone, rather than a single slab. As such, in the eyes of 19th century Egyptologists like J.Gardner Wilkinson, it was not truly an obelisk. The same could be said of nearly every large obelisk to follow. Happily, this was not an issue in the 18th century, predating the birth of Egyptology.

There is some confusion, caused by the inscription on the Ripon monument, which implies that the obelisk was raised by John Aislabie's son, William, in 1781, although that work was confined to repairs. As it happened, Aislabie senior had risen high in politics and, as Chancellor of the Exchequer, was disgraced and imprisoned for his part in the notorious South Sea Bubble. On release, he retired to Studley, which adjoins Fountains Abbey, and commenced a program of landscaping continued by his son, who put up a pyramid in his memory. This was replaced in 1805 by an obelisk at the far end of an avenue from Ripon. A later resident, the Marchioness of Ripon, objected to the obelisk with all its overt and covert signals at the head of her drive, and contrived to hide the view by having a spired church built in front of it.

The architect's role was a major one. Nicholas Hawksmoor,1661-1736, had worked from an early age as a clerk for Christopher Wren, the architect of the restoration of London following the Great Fire. He became Wren's partner and went on to assist John Vanbrugh (1664-1726) as his 'Clerk of Works'. Hawksmoor's light is often in the shade of these two famous names, but he takes part credit for Blenheim Palace and Castle Howard and full credit for some of central London's finest churches, part of Greenwich Hospital, Oxford's All Souls and Westminster Abbey's twin towers. He extended the use of the obelisk, designing several and raising at least two. The second obelisk was about twenty-five miles from Ripon.

The Marlborough Obelisk at Castle Howard, towering at 100 feet is usually attributed to the soldier-playright-architect, Sir John Vanbrugh, but can equally be credited to Hawksmoor. Indeed, Vanbrugh had been admitted to the East India Company and had travelled in the 1680s to India. He had seen the European cemetery outside Surat, which displayed large and lavish mausolea, obelisks and other features, quite unlike anything in Britain at the time.[1]

No doubt Vanbrugh, also considered a genius, obtained the overall commission for Castle Howard from Charles Howard, 3rd Earl of Carlisle; they were members of the same elite London club.[2] Yet Vanbrugh would have been hard pressed without Hawksmoor, who was an expert, a draughtsman and someone who could talk to builders. So, while some would have it that the superlative outworks at Castle Howard can be divided neatly between the two – the mausoleum to Hawksmoor, the Temple of the Four Winds to Vanbrugh, the pyramid to Hawksmoor, and so on – there can be no doubt that in truth these divisions hardly existed. Vanbrugh took the credit wherever he could, while Hawksmoor's character was honest and not inclined to exaggerating his achievements.[3] For all this, the obelisk at Castle Howard can be assigned equally to Vanbrugh and Hawksmoor. It was Vanbrugh, however, who received a knighthood in 1714.

Significantly, the 100 feet tall Marlborough Obelisk was erected in 1714, some years before all the other outworks were completed between 1722-31. Oak and beech trees were planted on either side of the five straight miles of avenue running North-South and the obelisk was raised in the middle of this avenue, its purpose to commemorate the victories of John, Duke of Marlborough, and to fix the date of the building of the castle.

Looking South down the avenue, one sees the obelisk, like the cross-hair of a gun sight or a theodolite, cutting through the outline of the Carrmire gateway, a mile further, itself decorated by small chunky brick-built obelisks. This is almost geomancy, made possible by the length of the avenue. Up close, it is an elegant structure with a low pedestal, all of dressed blocks of light grey limestone. There are inscriptions, added later, one of which is in Latin citing the duke's victories. The one on the obelisk's West face reads as follows:

> If to perfection these plantations rise,
> If they agreeably my heirs surprise
> This faithful pillar will their age declare
> As long as time these characters shall spare
> Here then with kind remembrance read his name
> Who for posterity perform'd the same.

Following the architects' two monumental obelisks in North Yorkshire, a regional association or loyalty to them developed. Obelisks of a smaller scale were being fashioned elsewhere in the county, at Bramham Park, near Wetherby.

The owner of Bramham Park, Robert Benson, later Lord Bingley, had made the Grand Tour and seen Rome in 1697. A cultivated and capable man, he was evidently much involved in the overall design of the building of his house and gardens. Works were completed before 1710 and included a large rectangular forecourt with limestone obelisks, 8 feet tall on 3 feet high pedestals, towards each corner.

These early works are seen in an estate plan of Bramham Park made in 1725 by the architect, John Wood the Elder, and published in 1731. An earlier version of the plans, seen by a visitor in 1724, included a larger single obelisk between two cascades into the ornamental lakes. These are still known as the 'Obelisk Ponds', though that particular obelisk was not to be. However, another obelisk was some years later instated, further away from the house, in 1768, in memory of Robert Lane Fox, son of the 2nd Lord.

In later pages, the question of whether the raising of an obelisk was a covert symbol of freemasonry will be considered. One should remember though, that freemasonry was not in any way proscribed. Hawksmoor, Vanbrugh and Wren were all freemasons.

Hawksmoor was initiated at some point, probably much earlier than 1730, when his name first appeared on lodge lists. He mingled with architects and was friendly with Nathaniel Blackerby, the deputy grand master, who later became his son-in-law. When working with Christopher Wren, Hawksmoor would have known that his senior partner had been initiated in 1691. At any rate, his early use of Egyptian forms such as the Ripon obelisk of 1702, and later pyramids and mausoleums, showed his inclination and would have appealed to freemasons at the time.

However, there were also indications that, for some, the obelisk feature was a discreet link to Rome and therefore to catholicism, which had been suppressed. Catholics throughout Europe were proud of the triumphant achievements of the popes Sixtus V and Innocent X in resurrecting fallen Egyptian obelisks in Rome. The implication is that a proportion of Britain's early 18th century obelisks were, in some way, a covert signal to other catholics, who still did not have freedom of religion.

This was also the case of so many Jacobite exiles who lived in Rome in the company of obelisks, and for whom they became a reminder of the city. Add to this the intrigue that some of Britain's leading catholics and influential freemasons were one and the same people. In fact the Duke of Norfolk, England's premier catholic peer, became Grand Master Mason in 1730, though he retired early when freemasonry was condemned by the pope in 1738. After the papal decree and the exit of most catholics from masonic lodges, freemasons continued to recognise the obelisk as a symbol of freedom and independence of thought. Later in the century, for America and France, but emphatically not for Britain, freedom and independence equated political revolution.

After Castle Howard, both Vanbrugh and Hawksmoor had more obelisks to create, whether directly or not. Their architectural partnership was also involved with the Duke of Marlborough himself, at Blenheim Palace outside Oxford. This was where their third obelisk should have been, but Hawksmoor's proposals were thwarted, and his drawings and his 'Explanation of the Obelisk' survive as no more than objects of interest.

John Churchill, Duke of Marlborough, was a soldier and courtier who became supreme military commander of the English forces in 1702, during the War of the Spanish Succession. He was honoured by Queen Anne for his victories at the battle of Blenheim in 1704 and subsequent battles, and presented with land at Woodstock near Oxford and monies with which to build a grand house and estate. Much of the Duke's influence had derived from his wife, Sarah, who had a close rapport with Queen Anne. But this relationship turned very sour from about 1708 onwards and, at the same time public support for the costly European campaign dwindled.

Marlborough was dismissed in 1711 and not reinstated until the accession of George I in 1714. And thus it was that for all the honours and promises of more money, for all the efforts of the formidable Duchess Sarah, the Blenheim project became entrenched in financial dispute and recrimination.

For the two architects, appointed by the crown and hard at work to create a magnificent palace, things went bad, and then got worse. The treasury failed to pay the workmen and the wronged Duchess was spoiling for a row. She grated with Vanbrugh, who left in 1716, never to return. Hawksmoor left as well, but returned in about 1722, at which time the Duke died. Now Hawksmoor was occupied with interiors and details, and his thoughts turned to the incomplete gardens and possible locations for a Blenheim obelisk.

Almost from the beginning of Blenheim it was understood that the arrangements outside needed consideration, that a great house needed gardens, vistas, and landscape features. Vanbrugh had envisaged a great monument. The late Duke himself had agreed to plans for an obelisk somewhere in the park, and Hawksmoor had drawn plans of a variety of obelisks. The Duchess however saw embellishments to the park as an extravagance. As the writer, David Green, has noted: 'Up at Castle Howard, the Earl of Carlisle had long since shown how a hundred-foot obelisk (his modest tribute to Marlborough) could be taken in one's stride. But at Blenheim nothing could be easy; neither site, plan, materials, workmanship nor inscription'.[4]

In fact Hawksmoor had anticipated problems and presented a column as an alternative to the obelisk. His 'Explanation' of 1727 suggests that of his various obelisks, one with a star at its peak might be suitable because an obelisk had been raised at Arles, topped with an image of the sun, in honour of Louis XIV.

'But as that Parhelion or false sun was forced to Leave Shineing by the Influence of a British Starr, the brightest Europe has ever Seen....the Emblem of a Starr may not be improperly placed on the Top of this obelisk (with a motto by ye learned to make the Allusion obvious to anyOne').

Hawksmoor continued, 'I have sent two designs, one much like that set up in ye Piazza Navona by Cavalier Fontana and ye other with a Square pedestall which I like best, but your Grace may consider them and take your choice'. The Explanation ends with an estimate for building the obelisk at £1,529 and one penny.

More interesting is another letter, undated, but endorsed: 'A Letter without Signature on ye subject of ye Obelisk'[5] which was probably written by Lord Godolphin, the Marlborough's nephew. It began:

'I have now changed my mind as to the place where the obelisk is to Stand Having found two others that are better. One is, at the entrance of the avenue that leads from the bridge. The other is upon the Ground on one side of the Bridge where King Henry ye 2nds House was, That I believe would please Sr John best, because it would give an opportunity of mentioning that King whose Scenes of Love He was so much pleased with....'

At this point the Duchess has neatly crossed out what was written and added her own thoughts:

'But if there were obelisks to bee made of what all our Kings have don of that sort the countrey would bee Stuffed with very odd things'.

Where she had crossed out part of the letter, it had previously stated,

'And the Obelisk being to be very large, I don't know whether it would not be right to put some Inscription to preserve the Memory of That Building, Such a one as Mr Pope might give a pretty turn to, to Show How much...'

Beneath the Duchess's correction, the sloping hand repeated:

'I fancy Mr Pope could add something very right to This Inscription, but That His inclinations are so different from ours as to Liberty, and I don't know Him at all but if you approve of This Thought perhaps we may find some Friend of His That will persuade him to exert His Talent upon this occasion which I would acknowledge in the way that wd be most agreeable to Him'.[6]

Hawksmoor's different designs for obelisks, his letters carefully explaining the location and his alternative plan for a column were laid aside and his services dispensed with. The Trajan column which stands today at Blenheim was designed by Lord Herbert and was more acceptable to the Duchess with a romanised Duke perched on the top.

Hawksmoor moved on to great works in Oxford and London. It seems he did not get another opportunity to place an obelisk. As a younger man he had suggested to Wren that instead of a dome on St Paul's Cathedral, there should be a drum with an obelisk upon it. However, among his many London churches, one notices St Lukes, Old Street, Finsbury, co-designed by John James, also a freemason, and completed in 1733. The spire is shaped like an obelisk, an experiment never repeated. It is thought that St Luke's obeliscal spire had a solar symbolism and that its partner, St John's at Horselydown, now demolished, with its Ionic column spire, was the lunar counterpart.

Sir John Vanbrugh too, as soon as he was dismissed from Blenheim, had moved on to other things. Among numerous commissions, he worked at Stowe, of which we will hear later, at about the time 'Coucher's obelisk', also known as the 'Lesser obelisk' was in place. This was later dismantled in one of several alterations by a succession of architects and landscapists. In the 1720s he was also back at Seaton Delaval Hall, the magnificent mansion in Northumberland, which he had designed in 1707. It is most likely that Vanbrugh, who died in 1726, was responsible for one of two obelisks raised there in 1723. Only the base of one stands in the old park to the South of the house, in an avenue of trees planted according to his plan; the other is untraceable. One of them, legend has it, marked where Vanbrugh's old friend, Admiral George Delaval, had been fatally thrown from his horse. The surviving third obelisk was a later addition put up by Francis Blake Delaval in 1737 which was built in sandstone ashlar to a height of 60 feet, and could be seen from a distance.

Let us leave Hawksmoor and Vanbrugh, first in line to design and build monumental British obelisks; there is much evidence to come of other celebrated architects following this enthusiasm.

Consider instead, Mr Pope, 'whose inclination are so different from ours as to Liberty'. Why should Hawksmoor and the Marlboroughs have thought that he could exert his talent, in some way conferring good taste upon their Blenheim monument? Mr Pope already had his own obelisk.

The poet, Alexander Pope, 1688-1744, was influential, having earned enough money from translating the *Iliad* to purchase a property at Twickenham, where he created a garden 'of memory and meditation' from 1719 onwards. The Arcadian vision was already current and, as such, it would be a beautiful place, fit for reflection. After Pope's mother died in 1733, he had an obelisk built in 1735 as the visual climax and terminus of his long garden. It was roughly 15 feet tall on a stepped base with a double plinth, inscribed with clearly legible latin, translated as, 'Ah Edith, best of mothers, most beloved wife, farewell'.

The poet's garden was seen by many people and regarded by some as a proto-type in its elegaic,(rather than morbid), treatment of the memorial obelisk as a physical reminder of his mother's former presence.[7] The artists and philosophers who came to Pope's garden and saw the obelisk were very different from the usual 'green bag travellers' who toured Britain and passed comment on the great houses and estates. The Arts, especially poetry and painting, were conjuring concepts of garden as paradise, with obelisks.

If not the tomb, then a reminder, or a memorial – maybe an obelisk – entered the picturesque garden. The word mnemonic, difficult to pronounce but very apt, is preferred by J.S Curl, author of *A Celebration of Death*, meaning an aid, or trigger, to connect and improve one's memory.

An obelisk had been raised in London earlier, in 1718, by the Countess of Derwentwater, in memory of her husband, James Radcliffe, the 3rd Earl. He was a charismatic man, a legitimate grandson of Charles II, who had been brought up in Paris in the court of James II. Derwentwater returned to England in 1710, to Dilston Castle in Northumberland, and became well-known and liked by all for his kind disposition and benificence. When James III, the Stuart heir, arrived in Scotland in the brief and ineffective rebellion of 1715, the Earl was hunted as a Jacobite leader and brought to the Tower of London. His execution took place on 24th February 1716. On that night the Aurora Borealis was exceptionally bright in the North and and made Lake Derwentwater appear crimson. [8]

The Countess, who had upbraided him for not doing more, and pleaded for him to renounce after his capture, received his body from the Tower and conveyed it for burial in Northumberland. She was not popular with the Earl's friends and tenants, who attached to her a portion of blame and reacted angrily. As the balladeer, Surtees, had it in the third verse of 'Lord Derwentwater's Farewell':

> And fare thee well, George Collingwood,
> Since fate has put us down;
> If thou and I have lost our lives,
> Our King has lost his crown.
> Farewell, farewell my lady dear.
> Ill, ill thou counsell'dst me;
> I never more may see the babe
> That smiles upon thy knee.

She moved to London and rented a mansion in Horn Lane, Acton, wrongly referred to as 'Derwentwater House', and commissioned an obelisk to be raised in a dell in the grounds. Two or three years later, Lady Derwentwater moved to Europe, where she died in 1723. The Derwentwater monument was about 20 feet tall, formed of two carved blocks of Portland stone. It was moved in 1904 and stands today on the North side of Acton Park. It would seem to be London's oldest surviving obelisk.

There was once an obelisk in Dingwall, Ross and Cromarty, which was raised in the days of the first rebellion to the 1st Earl of Cromartie. He had died in 1714, just when he would have had to stand up to be counted, or not, as a Jacobite leader. This earl certainly did not trust his wife. Cromartie had arranged to be buried three and a half feet away from his supposed burial plot beside the obelisk, in order to foil his wife, Margaret, who had announced her intention of dancing on his grave. The obelisk, which was known as 'the monolith' was not a monolith at all, but a 65 ft structure built of stones. It imitated the Leaning Tower of Pisa, veering 5 ft off perpendicular. Cromartie archives maintain this was the result of an earth tremor in the 19th century. It was finally removed in about 1910, at which time the Countess of Cromartie arranged a small replica of the obelisk to be placed outside Dingwall's parish church

If, as hinted earlier, the obelisk could be a discreet signal for catholics and Jacobites, typified in the case of Lord Derwentwater's memorial, it was not an enduring perception. Several obelisks of 1788 celebrated the centenary of King Billy (William III), the protestant champion. His arrival had heralded a greater freedom of religion, though this liberty was eroded in successive years.

Another memorial, with mnemonic symbols, relates to John Aislabie, whom we remember from his commission of the Ripon forum and obelisk. When he was still in business in London in the years 1710-20, before his notorious disgrace and the return to Yorkshire, Aislabie had married a widow, Mrs Waller. Her deceased husband, the poet and Parliamentarian, Edmund Waller, had built a fine house at Hall Barn, near Beaconsfield. Aislabie lived there with Mrs Waller and had considerable effect in improving the gardens and grounds. The work was continued by his stepson, Edmund Waller, who employed the architect, Colen Campbell, from 1724. In about 1730, when Mrs Waller died, an obelisk to her memory was raised along an avenue in the grounds of Hall Barn. It was a monument to gardening, its sides carved in relief with garden tools, a relief bust portrait of Mrs Waller and the Waller emblem, the image of the oak tree.

It was by then accepted practice for some architects to consider the gardens and grounds as part of their job. Following Hawksmoor and Vanbrugh in their favour of the obelisk, were two of the finest architects of the early Georgian era, William Kent and James Gibbs.

William Kent,1685-1748, was born in Bridlington in Yorkshire, and most probably saw Hawksmoor's obelisk in Ripon as a boy. In his career he was to put up two obelisks and have an influence on at least two others. Kent was initially a painter and went to Rome to study art and architecture for a period ten years. He returned to England in the company of Lord Burlington, who had been studying the work of Andrea Palladio,(1508-80). Burlington, who had inherited Chiswick when he was a child, was to be Kent's first patron, planning with him some of the Palladian interiors of his new mansion at Chiswick House. Kent turned his hand to the gardens, outworks and surrounding landscape of the park.

An obelisk was brought to Chiswick and is shown in a painting of 1729-30, by the sculptor, Rysbrack. It shows the obelisk with a pool, previously a pond in the deerpark, its banks terraced with interspaced orange trees in tubs. About 16 feet tall in Portland stone, this is still known as the Orange Tree Obelisk. There was another, about 25 feet high, with an antique relief set into its plinth, raised in 1732, which stands near Burlington Gate Lane. There is some confusion about this obelisk, which was designed by Lord Burlington himself, as it was shown in a watercolour by the artist, Jacques Rigaud, (c1681-1754). If the scale of his draft is anything to go by, the obelisk appeared to be even taller.[9]

It cannot be said for certain that any of these obelisks at Chiswick are William Kent's work, (nor the many bland obeliscal chimneys, of dubious taste, upon the house itself), but he was certainly one of the influences. Alexander Pope of Twickenham, with his own obelisk in his famous garden, may have been another. Kent was in touch with Pope and offered him designs for garden buildings in 1730.[10] Pope managed the short journey from Twickenham a number of times and liked the place very much. In 1732, he assured, "Chiswick house has been to me the finest thing this glorious sun has shined on".

Kent was already in touch with the the Earl of Leicester at Holkham Hall in Norfolk, and was to make his mark with a large obelisk in the park in 1729, prior to other building works. It was built at the end of the very long, straight avenue, precisely where the rising ground would allow a visitor the first glimpse of the splendid house and lake beyond. With a height of 80 feet, neither slender, nor overbulked, the limestone block construction has a classical elegance, with vermiculated ashlar upon the sides of the base and an understated classical key pattern. Kent's obelisk, best seen ahead when approaching down the avenue, was entrely about landscape and bore no inscription whatsoever.

At the same time the architect was negotiating for work with Viscount Cobham at Stowe Park, near Buckingham, firstly in the house and then in the gardens. Kent's contribution to Stowe was the Elysian Fields, a wooded place of streams and pools before his 1735 Temple of Ancient Virtue and Temple of British Worthies. The wonder that is Stowe today was not only Kent's work, but the result of a train of talented architects and landscapists, from Vanbrugh, Adam, Soane, and Gibbs, to Capability Brown and Charles Bridgeman.

At Stowe, there is an older obelisk, put up in 1736 and dedicated to the memory of the playright, William Congreve. This was designed by Kent and was placed on an island in the Octagon Lakes. It has comic additions by an unknown sculptor, with an urn decorated with carved faces and upon this, a stone monkey.

However, the plans for the large obelisk were not his. At 100 feet tall, this was the 1754 work of the architectural partnership, Smith & Batchelor, and was made by deconstructing Vanbrugh's broken *guglio*, a 70 feet high water feature, and then building the obelisk in its place. It was obviously a landscape feature, although later, in 1763, it was dedicated to the memory of General Wolfe, who died in Quebec in 1759.

William Kent had a most successful career, with buildings in Whitehall and more work for Lord Burlington at his Mayfair mansion, Burlington House, now the Royal Academy. He also put up another obelisk during the time he was at Stowe. This was a day's journey away at Shotover House, Wheatley, outside Oxford. There he was commissioned to 'improve' a landscape, which he did, by adding the obelisk in the early 1730s.

He was at Badminton House ten years later, where, at the age of sixty, he built Worcester Lodge, one of his last works, on a hill at the end of a two mile avenue from the house. It had a domed roof, a dining room and two attached lodges with steep roofs imitating a pyramid. The Duke of Beaufort's estate garden consisted of deer parks radiating rides and avenues as well as more formal areas. There are two obelisks there, though it is not known if William Kent had any connection with these either.

The architect, James Gibbs,1682-1754, had been at Badminton in 1730, building two pavilions in the gardens and it would be just as easy to associate him with these obelisks. Gibbs was born in Aberdeen and went to Rome to join the priesthood. Once there, he turned to studies in art and architecture and showed great talent in his drawing. In 1709, he returned to Britain and soon became one of two surveyors for the building of 50 new churches. In 1728, Gibbs published his own *Book of Architecture* and was elected Fellow of the Royal Society in the following year. He designed the Radcliffe Library and Cambridge's Senate House and, at Stowe, the Gothic Temple and Temple of Friendship. At the same time he was working for Sir Thomas Lee at Hartwell House in Buckinghamshire from 1723 and planned and built an obelisk there in 1735.

There is something odd about the shape of the Hartwell House obelisk, though its finial distracts the eye from immediately noticing this. It transpires that the obelisk was later moved in the years around 1755, and that it became much shortened during its repositioning to the South of the house. Perhaps the finial was an addition, a device to hide the fact that whoever had rebuilt the stonework had made a mess of the peak.

Gibbs was also at Tring Park, Hertfordshire, where there is an obelisk, which Colvin states is 'presumably by Gibbs'.[11] It is hard to date this obelisk with certainty. It was dedicated to the memory of Nell Gwynn, (Gwyn, Gwynne) who died in 1687 at the age of thirty-seven. She had a meteoric career, from orange seller to comedy actress in Drury Lane, becoming the mistress of King Charles II. He was the father of her son, Charles Beauclerk, who was created Baron Hedington, Earl of Burford and, in 1684, Duke of St Albans. The obelisk dates from some time after his death in 1726, and was decided upon by the 2nd Duke, perhaps mindful of his royal grandfather's dying words, "Remember Little Nell".

Alexander Pope's obelisk in his Twickenham garden had also suggested that one did not need to be a Duke to own one. With the surname Pope, he was of course a disadvantaged catholic, only four feet and six inches tall, and in poor health. Other commoners began to raise obelisks. Two friends outside Cambridge made a pact with each other, that whosoever should die first, the other would raise up an obelisk.

This was the pleasant motive behind the obelisk monument to Gregory Wale JP, who died in 1739, raised by the survivor, James Church on St Margaret's Mount at Little Shelford, Cambridge. Designed and built by Charles Bottomly, a local mason, the slender obelisk with its 20 feet shaft was constructed of five limestone blocks and bore a globe finial. On a chalky hill surrounded by farmland, it stands on a large plinth upon a mound rendered with cement, which is itself shaped like a pyramid. The added height ensures that the obelisk, restored in 1985, can be seen from afar.[12]

Sometimes the memory was a historical reference, not an actual memory. In 1750 William Sharpe, secretary to the 2nd Duke of Chandos, raised a slender obelisk, 25 feet tall in dressed stone blocks, in the grounds of the present RNO Hospital at Brockley Hill, Stanmore, London.[13] This was the 17th centenary of the battle between the local British tribe, the Catuvellauni, and Julius Caesar's invading army in AD50. It may be the case that the dedication was an explanatory afterthought following a very reasonable wish to raise an obelisk on a hill. There was a fashion for antiquarianism of this sort, typified by the obelisk put up in 1736 at Rhuallt, near Holywell in North Wales, which celebrated the victory of Celtic Christians over Picts and Saxons in 429.

Equally odd is the Hadley Highstone at Monken Hadley, a 15 feet tall milestone obelisk of Portland stone which marked the site of the battle of Barnet. It was put up by Sir Jeremy Sambrooke in 1740, but actually marks Edward IV's victory in the mist on Easter Sunday 1471. It has been moved an eighth of a mile further North, and so its marked distances – FROM ST.ALBANS VIII MILES – are not strictly accurate. It now stands on a roadside green approaching the A1, or Great North Road. It was a vital rendezvous in mailcoaching days and a place where cattle drovers to Barnet or Smithfield met to do business. The defining toponym, 'Highstone', which became attached to it over the course of time, was perhaps carried orally from northern counties.

Less remote history was recalled by the 1759 obelisk in Upper street, Winchester, which reminds the attentive passer-by that the date signified a century since the Great Plague, which had been particularly severe in South Hampshire.

It was not long before the obelisk found its way into the churchyard. By the porch of St.John's at Layer de la Haye, near

Colchester, is a 1764 obelisk memorial to Lt General J Brown. The form of his memorial may have been influenced by the fact that he had served under the Duke of Marlborough, forever associated with the obelisk raised to him at Castle Howard.

Outside Scotland's Dryburgh Abbey, but not in the graveyard, is a memorial to James I and James II of Scotland, erected in 1794 by David Stewart Erskine, Earl of Buchan, in honour of his ancestors. It is an obelisk cut in the local red sandstone and in a most unusual way the figures of these two kings are incised-relief carved, set in recesses on opposite sides so that nothing projects or interferes with the obelisk's outline. The figures were carved in the soft stone by George Burnet of Newstead and the other two sides bear inscribed lettering and decoration.

Rare too was the building of a church with obelisk features, only tried once before with Hawksmoor's obeliscal spire on St Lukes in London's Old Street. In 1775, a private church in Charborough Park, Dorset, was transformed with a four-sided pointed bell turret and a range of pointed obeliscal pinnacles, by the owner, John Erle Drax MP, with the assistance of an unknown and subjugated architect. Also by an unknown architect, but an inspired one, was the 1714 rebuilding of Little Gidding Church, Huntingdon, which had been destroyed in the Civil War. The gable end, or main doorway front was remarkable. Narrow and upright in stone-faced brickwork, it had rising pilasters topped at roof height with short obelisks. To the centre, the classical doorway was directly beneath a stone framed bellhousing. Above this, rising steeple-like, was an obelisk outline in stone, capped with a ball. The shape had three large gaps, as if blocks of a solid obelisk were missing. The sky lit these piercings, one above two, adding to the effect.

As for church interiors, the obelisk feature, or rather its two dimensional outline was on the increase. The 1731 memorial to Hugo Chamberlen in Westminster Abbey by Peter Scheemakers and Laurent Delvaux incorporated the obelisk shape. Dramatic white marble statuary contrasted with a 2 inch-thick black marble slab, cut in the obelisk shape to provide a 'backdrop', which united the composition and enhanced the proportions of the work. This is one instance of a practice very, very common in wall mounted memorials and tableaux in English churches from about 1710 onwards, for about 150 years. There are hundreds of other examples, and among

1. Complex obelisk sundial, 1630, Castle Drummond, Crieff, Perth

The sundial topped by an obelisk was made by the royal master-mason, John Mylne III, for Lord Drummond, 2nd Earl of Perth, and sited in his garden. Complicated with masonic symbols and as many as eighty-five facets, its position in the view was central in a straight line to the horizon. It is thought that Scotland once possessed as many as seventy obeliscal stone sundials.

2. *upper left* – Garden pavilion at Montacute House, Somerset, built in 1598 and reminiscent of balustrade with obelisks brought to Nonsuch Palace about twenty years earlier.

lower left – Memorial, J Mingay, 1625, St Stephens church, Norwich. A more lavish example of the use of obelisks with church monuments would be the 1594 tomb to the Earl of Southampton in Titchfield church, Hampshire, surrounded by four 7 foot tall obelisks in black marble.

upper right – Memorial, William Foster, 1786, St Stephens church, Norwich. An instance of a practice which was very common in church wall monuments from about 1710 to 1860, in which the sculptor united the composition of features upon a backdrop outline of an obelisk, usually a 2 inch thick slab or slate or dark marble.

lower right – Little Gidding church, rebuilt 1714, Huntingdon
The gable front was narrow and upright with rising pilasters topped with short obelisks. To the centre, the doorway was directly beneath a stone framed bellhousing and above this, rising steeple-like, an obelisk outline in stone. The shape had three gaps, as if blocks of a solid obelisk were missing, and the sky lit these piercings, adding to the unusual appearance.

Nicholas Hawksmoor, painted plaster bust, c1730; All Souls,Oxford.

(*from top*)
John Vanbrugh, William Kent, John Soane.

3. Obeliscal spire, St.Lukes church,1733; architect: N.Hawksmoor.

Among Hawksmoor's many London churches, one notices St. Lukes, Old Street, Finsbury, co-designed by John James and completed in 1733. The spire is shaped like an obelisk, an experiment never repeated. It is thought that St.Luke's obeliscal spire had a solar symbolism and that its partner, St.John's at Horselydown, now demolished, with its Ionic column spire, was the lunar counterpart.

3

4.Obelisk and Forum, 1702, Ripon,Yorkshire; Architect:Nicholas Hawksmoor.

The first large obelisk in Britain was at the centre of a paved market to Hawksmoor's design, 'according to the most ancient symmetry'. It was paid for by the mayor, John Aislabie of Studley Royal, and built of limestone blocks cut from his quarry. It stands 80 feet, though a third of this is in the pedestal and it is topped by a copper vane in the form of a horn and rowel spur, symbols of the borough. Originally, four smaller obelisks were set at the corners of the base, but were removed in 1882.

5. Four Obelisks on a forecourt, Bramham Park, Wetherby, Yorkshire, c1710.

The owner of Bramham Park, Robert Benson, later Lord Bingley, had made the Grand Tour and seen Rome in 1697. A capable man, he made much of overall designs for his house and gardens. Works completed before 1710 included a large rectangular forecourt with limestone obelisks, 8 feet tall on 3 ft pedestals, towards each corner, and a gateway with a sphinx in an antique style.

6.The Marlborough Obelisk, 1714, Castle Howard; Vanbrugh & Hawksmoor.

The 100 feet tall Marlborough Obelisk was erected in 1714, before all other outworks. Oak and beech trees were planted on either side of the five straight miles of avenue and the obelisk was raised in the middle to commemorate the victories of the Duke of Marlborough, and to mark the date of the building of the Castle. Works on the great house, its temples and mausolea are divided in attribution between the two architects, though at the time only Hawksmoor had the expertise to realise a design and instruct builders.

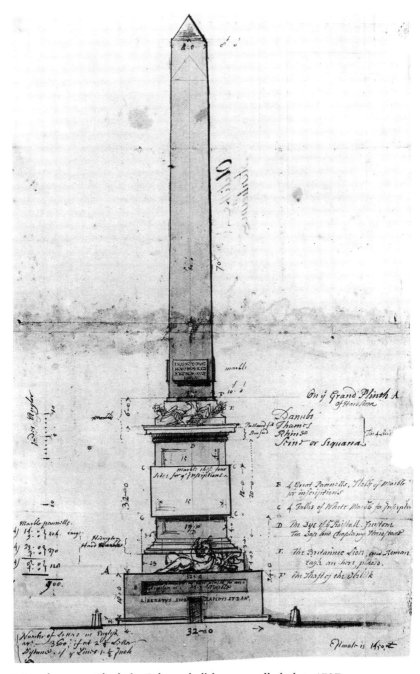

7. Hawksmoor's Blenheim Palace obelisk, a cancelled plan, 1727.

After Castle Howard, the architectural duo – Vanbrugh and Hawksmoor – went to build Blenheim Palace, near Oxford, for the Duke of Marlborough himself. Vanbrugh argued with the Duchess and left in 1716, followed by his partner. Hawksmoor returned in 1722 to complete works, including a monumental obelisk in memory of the Duke, who had since died. The Duchess was in no mood and opted for a column and statue instead. Hawksmoor's designs (this was his own preference) and a brief 'Explanation of the Obelisk', and other letters are all that remain.

8. The Orange Tree Obelisk, c1730, Chiswick Park, London.

Architectural and landscape improvements to Chiswick House were made by the young owner, Lord Burlington and his friend, the architect William Kent, on their return from Rome. An obelisk was brought to Chiswick, to be seen in a painting of 1729-30, by the sculptor, Rysbrack. This shows the 18 feet tall obelisk at the centre of a pool, its banks terraced with interspaced orange trees in tubs. A taller obelisk of 1732 with an antique classical frieze stands near Burlington Gate Lane. Neither can be attributed directly to William Kent.
photo ©Michael Cousins.

9. Obelisk, 1739, Memorial to Gregory Wale, Little Shelford, Cambridgeshire.

Two friends swore to each other that whosoever should die first, the other would raise an obelisk. The obelisk was raised by the survivor, James Church, on St.Margaret's Mount, a chalky hill surrounded by farmland. With a 20 ft shaft constructed of five limestone blocks and a globe finial, it stands on a cement-rendered mound shaped like a pyramid.

Obelisk memorial to the Earl of Derwentwater, 1718, Acton, London.

10. Hadley Highstone, 1740, Barnet, Hertfordshire.

The 15 feet tall milestone obelisk of Portland stone marking the site of the battle of Barnet in 1471 was put up by Sir Jeremy Sambrooke in 1740. It has been moved an eighth of a mile further North, and stands on a roadside green approaching the Great North Road. It was a vital rendezvous in mailcoaching days and a place where cattle drovers to Barnet or Smithfield met to do business. The defining toponym, 'Highstone', which became attached to it over the course of time, was perhaps carried orally from northern counties.

James Radcliffe, the 3rd Earl was a legitimate grandson of Charles II, who lived in Paris in the court of James II, only returning to Northumberland in 1710. When James III arrived in the 1715 rebellion, the Earl was hunted as a Jacobite leader and executed. The Countess moved to London and rented a house in Acton, where she commissioned the obelisk in the grounds. About 20 feet tall in Portland stone, it was moved in 1904 to Acton Park. It would seem to be London's oldest surviving obelisk.

11. Obelisk, 1729, Holkham Hall, Norfolk; architect: William Kent.

William Kent was in touch with the the Earl of Leicester at Holkham and made his mark with an obelisk prior to any other building work. Of limestone block construction, and a height of 80 feet, it had a classical elegance at the end of the very long, straight avenue, where the rising ground allows the first sighting of the splendid house beyond. This obelisk, best seen ahead when approaching along the avenue, was entirely about landscape and bore no inscription whatsoever.

Obelisk,1749, Umberslade Park, Warwickshire.

The attempts of builders to attain the slender outline - the true proportion of the monolithic obelisk - were difficult to achieve in stone blocks. Some of the obelisks collapsed. The one at Umberslade Park, raised to celebrate a previous Lord Archer's arrival in the peerage, appears to be supported by ivy in this photograph, taken in 2003.

photo ©Michael Cousins.

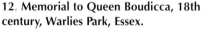

12. Memorial to Queen Boudicca, 18th century, Warlies Park, Essex.

Interesting subject, questionable history: there are two obelisks at Warlies Park: the first where the Iceni queen reputedly took poison and the second, marked by this brick and rendered structure on a hill at Obelisk Farm, where she supposedly died.

13. Obelisk, 1747, at Bicton Park Gardens, Devon.

Most obelisks have a memorial attachment, though one or two, such as the obelisk at Bicton Park, commemorated nothing. In the 1730s, the owner, Lord Henry Rolle commissioned the laying out of an Italian garden to the South of his house, with pools and fountains, terraces and ideal sculptures, all aligned upon a distant 1747 obelisk. A 70 feet high construction within an iron fence, it has no purpose where it stands other than to be seen from a distance, adding to the quality of the garden.

Obelisk in honour of Prince of Wales, 1738, Queen s Square, Bath.

Beau Nash unveiled the obelisk in Queen Square in honour of Frederick, Prince of Wales. The obelisk rose 50 feet from the ground with no plinth, in the supposed Egyptian manner, presenting the appearance of an acute-angled pyramid. Four years earlier, Nash had presided over the raising of a more conventional obelisk in memory of William III near the abbey.

14. Obelisk, 1781, Atherton, Lancashire.

Not a market cross, but the gift of a local squire, this fluted obelisk has become blackened by intense industrial activity. Fortunately it has not been cleaned and contrasts with the church wall, sandblasted in 1973. Another fluted sandstone obelisk in the vicinity was raised in 1859 at Leigh.

The Obelisk, 1771, Southwark, London. Arch: George Dance jr.

Dance designed London's best known obelisk of the period, known as 'The Obelisk', or 'The Obelisk Turnpike'. A London landmark, it stood about 65 feet tall in Portland stone blocks, including a 20 feet high pedestal inscribed with distances to London Bridge, Fleet Street and Palace Yard etc,. The site in St.George's Circus was part of an 18th century development and the obelisk was dedicated to Brass Crosby, Mayor of London.

Obelisk,1794, with figures of James I & II, Dryburgh Abbey, Scotland.

The memorial to James I and James II of Scotland was erected by David Stewart Erskine, Earl of Buchan, in honour of his ancestors. It was cut in the local red sandstone and the two figures were incised relief carved in recesses on opposites sides, so that nothing interfered with the obelisk's outline. The stone carver or sculptor was George Burnet, aided in this unique design by the softness of the sandstone. The figure shown is James II.

15. Obelisk, c1750, Chequer Square, Bury St.Edmunds, Suffolk.

This was first in the Horsemarket of the huge fairstead outside the abbey walls in the days when the October Fair was one of the greatest in the land. Within fifty years the obelisk was moved to nearby Chequer Square. About 15 feet tall, with an ornate, yet well-worn appearance in Portland stone, its plinth was carved on three sides. There are marks on the obelisk where it once carried an iron bracket, to support a lamp, or sign of the fair.

16. Obelisk, Stourhead, Wiltshire, built 1746, rebuilt 1840.

Raised when Henry Hoare commenced the great plantations about the valley, adding classical buildings and sculptures to create the famous garden, the obelisk stood to the front of the house, which was subsequently turned about, so that it is now to the rear. Constructed from inferior stone, it became unstable. It was rebuilt in 1840 by R. Colt Hoare, to a height of 105 feet, and dedicated to the memory of Henry Hoare. At its peak was placed a copper 'sun'. When rebuilt, the obelisk was struck by lightning in 1853 and needed further restoration and a stronger conductor. The view *(left)* is from the house to the obelisk.

sculptors who used the same treatment were Rysbrack, Roubilliac, Bird, Westmacott, and E.H Baily.

The practice of backing relief work, group figures and emblems was very well served by the upward pointing obelisk, which provided a clear profile to wall monuments. The shape itself varied. It is referred to by other writers as the outline of the pyramid, or 'the tapering pyramid', though it was at its best when in the shape of the top of an obelisk, with its pyramidion forming the peak. Indeed, much confusion has been made by early writers calling obelisks 'tapering pyramids'.

In two dimensions on the church wall, the precise difference between a thin pyramid and a fat obelisk is hard to define, though there are comparisons between obeliscal pyramids and pyramidal pyramids. First used with church memorials in France and Italy was the pyramid shape, which was universally recognised to signify the time-defying quality of the Great Pyramids themselves. In other contexts it proclaimed the glory, or power of the remembered one; it also implied entombment and the flight of the soul, as imagined in the time of the Pharaohs.[14] In England, however, the pyramid shape tended to be slimmer and more obeliscal, so much so, that this became the dominant shape. A practical reason for this might very well have been that inside English churches, lateral wall space was relatively limited, favouring the narrower obelisk outline over the broader pyramid shape. Obeliscal examples are to be seen in St Stephen's church in Norwich.

The obelisk was better placed in the landscape. As Georgian fashion in gardening moved away from the formal manner, with its enclosed and geometric patterns, towards a more naturalistic landscape, it passed through an Arcadian phase on its way towards the romantic or Picturesque style. This was a friendly fashion, a playful antiquarian fantasy, well mannered in those days; within a hundred years this romanticism would be transformed into the prejudice of Gothic Revival. Throughout the period, obelisks were raised in broad conjunction with all manner of strange structures in gardens and parks.

There is a parallel view in which monuments in private landscapes and enclosed parks and gardens are seen generically as Follies. Although the word implies in English a foolish whim, a costly structure without a practical use, the concept, albeit a convenient simplification, goes a long way in explaining the fervour behind building oddities in the landscape.

The inspiration was the same, the continued wish to create objects and architectural structures which would add interest to a circular walk or tour about a garden, park or great estate. William Aislabie, whom we recall as the son of the man who commissioned Hawksmoor's obelisk in Ripon, had added on to his estate at Studley Royal, by purchasing the ruins of neighbouring Fountains Abbey. His garden tour, with its genuine mediaeval ruins, was the envy of society.

Landowners were understandably competitive in their wish to make their properties more attractive and more interesting. To have one's 'folly' remarked upon with approval about the county and up in town would give great satisfaction. The era of follies ran roughly from the mid eighteenth to the late nineteenth century. It joined up several inclinations – the poet's garden, the calls to fine architects, revivalism and antiquarianism of all sorts. Among the amusing, beautiful and rarified creations in the landscape were experiments which proved to be failures or advertisements for bad taste. Throughout the period there was cheap labour and great wealth among landowners with fortunes old and new.

Hermitages, temples, grottoes and an array of anomalous structures were raised as ruins or mere outlines to be seen from a distance. Others were properly built; a favourite would have been a tall tower with a staircase which could be climbed. From the top a visitor might view an entire landscape and other features raised by the proprietor.

Frequently an obelisk might be among a collection of monuments and follies as at Stourhead, Stowe, or Shotover House and Wroxton Abbey in Oxfordshire. But it would be a mistake to call an obelisk a folly. Usually, the obelisk was there before the other 'follies' arrived. Put up by whomsoever, wherever and for whatever purpose, or lack of one, an obelisk is defined by its shape. Very often they were raised within the time-honoured definitions of Vitruvius, or Alberti, and their Books of Architecture. Leone Alberti's *Ten Books of Architecture*, written in Italy in 1452, were translated and printed in England in 1726. He stated:

> Nor should there be wanting in the prospect remains of Antiquity, on which we cannot turn our eyes without considering the various revolutions of men and things, and being filled with wonder and admiration..... There should be

columns, Pyramids, Obelisks and other memorials to remind us of great men.

The formal gardens of the 1720s and 1730s remained in situ while the extended and informal approach to landscaping prevailed for some years. In the case of Wroxton Abbey, formal gardens were designed and laid out by Tilleman Bobart in the late 1720s for the owner, the Earl of Guilford. Within ten years or so, Guilford changed his mind, and had the gardens and near landscape redrawn by Sanderson Miller, who lived nearby and was well known for his picturesque effects. Just before this change from formal to informal took place, Frederick, Prince of Wales, visited Wroxton in 1739, and a commemorative obelisk was built on a ridge a couple of years later above the water gardens, and in good view from the house. If erected in expectation of his future reign, such hopes were dashed when Frederick was killed in 1751 by a tennis ball, in those days much harder.

At Wroxton, it is still recommended that a walk in the garden should proceed in the following order: starting at the mildy-gothicised dovecote of 1745, one heads towards the classical temple, and catches sight of the obelisk on the hill for the first time. Moving on to the Great Pond and Grand Cascade, the visitor can see the pretty Drayton Arch, built by Miller. Continuing from there, over the Chinese Bridge to the Mount, where there used to be another temple, the visitor again catches sight the obelisk, before following the North bank of the Great Pond to Bobart's old terraces and the Ice House among a belt of trees.

Sanderson Miller was also a friend and neighbour of William Holbech II at Farnborough Hall, a short distance away, in South Warwickshire. Miller provided designs for North and South facades of the building and made suggestions and designs for outworks. The landscape design was such that a terraced lawn from the house front stretched away up a long ridge to the top of Markham Hill, passing a classical temple, and a little further, a domed pavilion, then terminating at the obelisk. The obelisk, for which Miller was not responsible, was of fine proportions and rose to a height of 55 feet. The date on the base was 1751, though this probably signified completion of the outworks and plantings, as the obelisk was noted by an earlier visitor to Farnborough Hall in 1746. That slender outline, the true proportion, was difficult to achieve in stone blocks and the obelisk collapsed in 1823 and was rebuilt in 1828, probably losing some height in the process.[15] The ascending terrace towards the obelisk was a fine walk, but an even better ride, as were many folly tours within parks, an aspect often forgotten by garden historians. The grassy terrace walk would not have been as smooth as it is today.

With the great amount of study that has gone into the subject of garden design and landscaping and its long history in England, one should remember that it was a valued ideal for polite folk to be conversant with art and architecture. This ideal had for long led thoughtful gentlemen to conduct their own tours of Europe, in pursuit of learning on the Grand Tour. Whenever England was at war in Europe and passage was blocked, those in search of culture would have to make it for themselves in Britain. Designers and gardeners were commissioned to improve landscapes.

Following Hawksmoor, Vanbrugh, Kent and Gibbs, were two later 18th century architects whose work was mostly in London. The first of these was George Dance the younger,1741-1825, who is seen as another pioneer of Neo-Classicism in England. Dance went to Italy for 6 years from the age of seventeen and returned as an experienced architect. He designed and raised London's best known obelisk of the period in 1771, known as 'The Obelisk', or 'The Obelisk Turnpike'.

It is a landmark in Southwark, about 65 feet tall including a 20 feet high pedestal, all of Portland stone blocks. Inscribed are the distances to London Bridge, Fleet Street and Palace Yard etc,. The site, St George's Circus, was the centre of a development, though work on an adjacent crescent of houses was hindered and not completed. Perhaps to oil the wheels of persuasion, the obelisk was dedicated to Brass Crosby,1725-93, Lord Mayor of London, who was very much alive at the time.

Dance was invited to design another obelisk in 1776, raised on Putney Heath, near Tebbit's Corner. This was to commemorate the work of David Hartley, inventor of fireproof architectural cladding. Better known for his work at Finsbury Square and additions to London's Guildhall and Mansion House, George Dance junior was elected to the Royal Academy and became Professor of Architecture in the Royal Academy Schools

John Soane,1753-1837, was his pupil, both in his practice and in the schools. A classicist, who, like the others, went to Rome, Soane is held in very high regard today. On his return from Italy he won commissions for designing country houses and additions and was retained by the Bank of England, which he rebuilt, and by Parliament and Chelsea Hospital.

Soane was always very interested in the obelisk and went to the trouble of translating into English the relevant parts of the *Discours sur les monuments publics de tous les âges* written in 1775 by Charles-Francois de Lubersac. The Frenchman's account was preoccupied with meaning, or intention, in a monument.

In the first of several Royal Academy lectures between 1806 and 1820, Soane promised to speak about obelisks, and returned to the subject in his fourth lecture. A minor extract is recorded here to give an esteemed architect's opinion, though Soane's statements and sources throughout were vulnerable regarding Egyptian uses. He was against using obelisks for decorative or mannerist effect, such as finials and roofline features, as in Elizabethan and Jacobean times. Soane also points out that the plinth was not an original support for an obelisk.

> ...the moderns, forgetting the origins of obelisks, have frequently placed them indiscriminately as decorations to buildings of various descriptions, and for other purposes. These errors show the propriety and necessity of our attending to the observation of Vitruvius, namely that the architect, by close study and unwearied attention, should be learned in history, well informed of the primitive destination and origin of things, and on all occasions be able to trace every invention up to first principles and original causes.
>
> We have already seen the column at different times twisted, rusticated, and tortured in various ways; nor has the obelisk (beautiful in its simple form and situation) been treated with more attention; for at different periods and in different countries obelisks have been placed on different substructions without any regard to their origin. Pliny speaks of an obelisk elevated on balls, and at Constantinople there is such an example. We have no instance in antiquity of an obelisk placed on an upright pedestal, except from a medal of unknown date, and from supposing that the pedestal near the fallen obelisk in Campus Martius in Rome had been used in Egypt with the obelisk itself; but this last circumstance is by no means ascertained. The moderns, however, from these precedents, have taken uncommon latitude and placed them not only on pedestals of various descriptions in form and relative dimensions, but also on pyramids and upon the backs of animals. But

notwithstanding the sanction of all these great examples, an obelisk placed on an upright pedestal can never please the judicious eye. It gives a ricketty, weak, disgusting appearance to the whole composition, and is directly contrary to every idea of propriety, and to the great principles of Egyptian architecture.

The Egyptians, to whom their origin is ascribed, placed them either on the ground, or raised upon one or more steps, or square plinths. This was consistent with the rest of their architecture,which is constantly declining from the upright. Their apertures of every kind were diminished upwards (not like modern termini broader at top than bottom). The walls of their buildings were likewise sloping in order to give the greatest idea possible of duration. This form was one of the characteristic distinctions in all their architecture; it was a part of that general and universal system which the Egyptians successfully copied from nature.[16]

A brilliant innovator of architectural interiors, Soane was a successful self-promoter through publishing his designs. In 1776 and 1778 and with a later reprint in 1797, Soane had issued his *Designs in Architecture: Consisting of Plans, ...for Temples, Baths, Casinos, Pavilions, Obelisks and other Buildings; for decorating Pleasure-Ground, Parks, Forests &c.* Looking at the 1778 issue, it can be seen in plate VII, that he does use a discreet pedestal upon a three-stepped base. Looking at Plate VIII, there is a design for an object which Soane has titled 'obelisk', consisting of a curvilinear pedestal in the shape of a bell, with a decorated and balustraded level which progressed into a short obelisk with a weather-vane on top. Frankly, the design was hideous, surprisingly so from an architect of Soane's calibre, and was not taken up.

Soane is named responsible for at least one obelisk, raised in 1790 at Beauport Park, at Baldslow near Hastings. However the 'Simeon Obelisk' is a misnomer: designed by Soane and put up in Reading Market Place a few years later, it is not an obelisk at all. Dedicated to Edward Simeon, who was still alive at the time, it is a fluted three-sided pillar with classical key-pattern on a very decorative plinth. There were other architects associated with obelisks. James Hamilton is named as the designer of the irregular obelisk memorial of 1785 in memory of members of the Frampton family at Moreton House in Dorset. Even John Nash, in 1788, when completing the mausoleum for Thomas Nash (a printer; no relation), surmounted the domed roof with a delicate 7 feet tall obelisk with a round finial at peak.

Robert Adam, 1728-92, was another classicist and an ally of the obelisk. He had studied in Rome and, back in Britain, became famous for his classical interiors. Adam drew designs for an obelisk in Edinburgh in memory of Linnaeus, the Swedish botanist whose system of classification was adopted by all. Adam's designs were adhered to by the Scottish architect, James Craig.

Craig adapted the designs in 1788 with a much larger obelisk, in memory of George Buchanan,1506-1582, scholar and tutor to James VI (I). This was 103 feet tall on a 19 x 19 ft base, and was made of blocks of local millstone grit and sited by the parish church in Killearn, Strathendrick, between Dumbarton and Stirling. Buchanan's bi-centenary was planned with great pride, and the obelisk was suggested as being 150 feet tall and to be sited in Buchanan Street in Glasgow. These proposals were made in a paper entitled, 'The propriety of Erecting an Obelisk in Honour of Buchanan'.

John Soane: Plate VII, 'Designs in Architecture: Consisting of Plans for Temples, Baths, Casinos, Pavilions, Obelisks and other Buildings; for decorating Pleasure-Ground, Parks, Forests &c'.1778 issue

39

Earlier, Robert Adam had built a strange gateway based on an obelisk. This was in 1776 at Nostell Priory in Yorkshire; the date is on the design and the entire structure was completed in the same year. Although not a 'real obelisk' in any way, this is an ingenious plan: its East-West elevations resemble a large and broad obelisk, while the North-South elevations present an even broader obelisk, more like a pylon, penetrated by a tall gateway with portico and surround. A pair of sphinxes face outwards on the walls either side of the obelisk-like gateway, inevitably named 'The Needle's Eye'.

A pair of obelisks presented a more conventional gateway at the entrance to Cotham Park in Bristol, composed of alternating bands of vermiculated and smooth blocks. Dating from the 1790s these were the remnant gate piers to Cotham Lodge, which was demolished in 1846.

Obelisks were adaptable in function. Three widely dispersed obelisks in the Great Deer Park at Richmond in Surrey were precisely sited as time-markers in a series of experiments by the esteemed Royal Society in 1778. Two remain today, their history of usefulness untold to the few hikers who stray from the paths. They are contemporary with the building of the Thames bridge at Richmond in 1777 and the 10 feet tall obelisk milestone next to it.

In 1742 a large obelisk of sandstone blocks was built on a hill by Sir Thomas Ball at Mamhead Castle, inland from Dawlish in Devon. Its function was to act as a landmark for coastal shipping, especially those boats coming in to trade in Exeter. Replacing markpoints dating from pre-mediaeval times, an obelisk known as the Crow Stone was put up in the shoreline at Chalkwell, West of Prittlewell Priory by Southend, marking the end of the jurisdiction of City of London over the Thames. In the 19th century it was considered of sufficient importance to be replaced by a new obelisk on the same spot, when in bad repair, doubtless from constant waterside traffic and having its base submerged in the estuary. A most suitable use in 1799 was as Borough Boundary marker, served by a small, plain obelisk standing in London road, Portsmouth. Other obelisks celebrated the advent of proper water supply and marked the site of the former town pumps, such as those of 1784 in Dorchester's Cornhill and in Weymouth, the latter recently moved.

A very handsome obelisk in Portland stone, surrounded by four bollards, served as a market cross in Bury St Edmunds, Suffolk. The obelisk once stood at the centre of the Horsemarket in St Mary's Square, a part of a huge fairstead, or market area, outside the abbey walls around Angel Hill. The October Fair, which was outside the jurisdiction of the abbey and lasted for two weeks, was known to have been one of the greatest in England. The obelisk dated from after 1740, though within less than fifty years it was moved the short distance to Chequer Square, at the western end of the original market area, where it stands now.[17] It is about fifteen feet in all, with an ornate, yet well-worn appearance. The plinth has carved panels on three sides, depicting swags of foliage on two faces and, barely discernible today on the third, the arms of St Edmundsbury – a wolf and head above crowns and arrows. There are marks on the shaft of the obelisk showing that it once carried a large iron bracket, perhaps to support a lamp, or sign of the fair.

To think of market crosses, of which there were very many in Britain, is to open a new and lengthy enquiry, as they comprised a multitude of forms, and served a number of essential social, civic and economic functions over several hundred years. A very few were obelisks, although, inviting research, some very old ones were distinctly obeliscal in profile.

To return, instead, to monumental obelisks, it must be said of all building works that some credit should be passed to the builders, who, in the case of 18th century obelisks, were usually estate groundsmen and farmworkers. Blame for failure, however, was generally returned to the architect. Such was the case with William Privet, a lesser-known architect responsible for building the obelisk for Henry Hoare II at Stourhead in 1746. This was when Henry Hoare commenced the great plantations about the valley and lake, adding classical buildings and sculptures to create a garden paradise which became known throughout Europe. The obelisk was to the front of the house, which was subsequently turned about, so that it is now to the rear, at the junction of a broad ride known as Fir walk, and the old approach to the house. Privet either chose or was supplied with Chilmark stone, which degraded quickly and actually became unstable.[18]

The obelisk was rebuilt nearly a century later in 1840 by Richard Colt Hoare, to a height of about 105 feet, a quarter of which was its pedestal, in sturdy grey limestone,(though described elsewhere as Bath stone). It possessed the same dimensions as the obelisk in Porta del Populo in Rome, and was dedicated *Memoriae Felici* to Henry

Hoare II, creator of the magnificent garden. At its peak was placed a copper 'sun', its face smiling in an aura of spiked radiations. Even when rebuilt, the obelisk was struck by lightning in 1853 and needed further restoration, this time with a lightning conductor.

No matter how they were constructed, obelisks attracted lightning strikes; an occurrence that may have been intended in the days of the Pharaohs. In Britain, the merits of a lightning conductor, seen on big obelisks today, was not understood until 1746, when Benjamin Franklin experimented with kite and key in a thunderstorm. Two years earlier an obelisk to Sir Robert Worsley was raised at Appuldurcombe House, on Stenbury Down in the Isle of Wight. This was struck by lightning and reduced to a stump in 1831.

The matter of lightning was a serious concern, especially for those who had experienced a strike. The 123 feet tall obelisk at Boconnoc in Cornwall was struck, though mildly, blasting off part of the peak. The owner, Thomas Pitt, 1st Lord Camelford was familiar with obelisks and their problems and, having being brought up at Stowe, he had developed a taste for architecture. Some years later, he designed a Corinthian Arch, and subsequently the South front and loggia at Stowe for his cousin, Richard Grenville, Earl Temple. A letter from one of his uncles to William Borlase, the distinguished Antiquarian, described the twenty-three year old Pitt: 'He is a true lover of both Architecture and Antiquities and surprisingly knowing in both considering his age'.

When he inherited Boconnoc, Pitt put up the obelisk in 1771 in 'gratitude and affection' for his uncle and benefactor, Sir Richard Lyttleton, who had some years earlier instated a 70 ft obelisk at Hagley Hall. After the Boconnoc obelisk was damaged by lightning, presumably in the 1780s, Pitt was concerned about the new iron conductor, which could be unsightly and was very likely to cause rust stains down his obelisk. Having decided on a course of action, he wrote from France to consult the expertise of John Soane in London, and to set him to work.

Montpellier, 5th January 1787

Mr Soane Architect
Margaret Street
Cavendish Square
London. Angleterre

I have been consulting with a French Philosopher here about a conductor for my obelisk – he advises besides the usual precautions of oil varnishes for the iron rod that the extremity should be made of ormulu – that is gold burnt in to the iron and recommend upon the tip a piece of solid gold of the value of a guinea or two to form the point which should receive the iron as the gold will never rust (sketch provided). He says likewise that the rod may be made to fit by screws or other methods of close contact in various pieces so as to be able to take down at any time the upper joint from a lower station which may be accessible on a calm day by ladder. Talk to some of our Philosophers about all this that the needful may be done in proper time. The Spring will be advancing soon. Take time by the forelock and be ready with your materials as soon as the season is fit to begin – let me know in the meantime the detail of what you are going to do with the estimate of the expense. Call on Mr Winterbottom as soon as you receive this and let him know the expense I have been at the farm at Burnham that he may judge whether in my answer in Chancery I am not to take credit it for it. I write this as it comes into my head. Ly C desires her compn.

yours faithfully,

Camelford

It is difficult not to speculate about the first ideas behind obelisk memorials in fine gardens. Was it a case of the client saying, "I want an obelisk," rather than architects putting forward the obelisk as a design feature? We will never know, but it does seem that in so many cases the obelisk and site were decided upon by the owner before talking to an architect, and that the memorial attachment was added later.

The memorial aspect threatens to obscure the view of the obelisks themselves, and yet, for many, the only identification we have is by memorial dedication. If we dispense with the memorial, there is no tag, distinguishing detail, or explanation; no more than the garden, the stone, sky and moment – quite sufficient perhaps. One or two, such as the obelisk at Bicton Park Gardens in Devon, commemorated nobody. In the 1730s, the owner, Lord Henry Rolle commissioned André Le Nôtre to lay out an Italian garden to the South of his house, with pools and fountains, terraces and ideal sculptures, all aligned upon a distant 1747 obelisk. This has no purpose but to be seen from a distance and to add to the quality of the garden and arboretum.

On the other hand, a memorial link added interest to an obelisk and explained why it was there. Of course, some memorials are more interesting than others. Looking at the reasons behind an obelisk as a means of commemoration, one sees familiar motives, some of which are far from Alexander Pope's innocent mnemonic of his mother. The desire to create an impression or court favour was surely involved in raising obelisks to royalty, such as that at Wroxton. At Thornhill House in Dorset, an obelisk of tall and slender proportions was quickly put up in 1727, in honour of the accession of George II. It was blown down in a storm and rebuilt in 1836.

Richard Nash, known to all as 'Beau Nash', presided over the raising of an obelisk to the former Prince of Orange, in Bath's Orange Square. Four years later in 1738 he unveiled another in Queen Square, in honour of Frederick, Prince of Wales. This was not inelegant, more like an extremely acute-angled pyramid, and rose 50 feet from the ground, with no plinth. For Nash, it was a perfect reminder of the Beau's great days in fashion and society, when he had publicly welcomed Queen Anne on her visit to the spa in 1703.

The Cumberland, or 'Culloden Victory' obelisk of 1746 was raised in Windsor's Great Park when George II's second son, the Duke of Cumberland was still alive. The triumphant 'butcher' had wiped out the Scottish rebellion at the battle of Culloden, finally quelling the Hanoverian fear of the return of the Stuarts. William Pitt the elder was still alive and became Prime Minister again in 1766 when his old friend, General Sir William Draper, put up an obelisk at his home in Pitt's honour. Made of limestone blocks to a height of 26 feet, it was moved to Bristol in 1883 and resited on Christchurch Green in Clifton.

An obelisk was raised in 1734 in memory of Queen Anne, twenty years after her death, near Wentworth Castle in South Yorkshire. In the castle gardens a more subtle favouring was sought by the owner, William Wentworth, 2nd Earl of Strafford, who raised an obelisk in 1747 which he dedicated to his onetime neighbour, the poet and literary belle, Lady Mary Wortley Montague. Built of dressed stone blocks to a height of over 60 feet, the obelisk was sited on a rising slope in the broad avenue where Wentworth used to meet Lady Mary when walking in the grounds. She had left the area in 1739, but was still very much alive when the obelisk was put up.

Not far away, at the rival establishment, Wentworth Woodhouse Hall, near Doncaster, Earl Fitzwilliam had a mausoleum built in 1789 to contain the tomb of his deceased uncle, Lord Rockingham, a former Prime Minister. It was a vaulted burial chamber surmounted by a 75 feet tall monument, built and probably designed as well by John Carr of York. Four years after it was finished, four identical obelisks were brought from a part of the grounds to the West of the Hall and placed at each corner.[19] It is uncertain whether the addition of these obelisks was a part of the original plan or not. About 25 feet tall and therefore not as tall as the monument, they altered the overall dynamic in the same way as the four obelisks overlooking an Elizabethan tomb, by containing and protecting it.

All the factors, of garden monument and memorial, of personal histories and heroic deeds, were involved in the choice and actual building of obelisks in the 18th century. At that time the War of Styles between new Classic and new Gothic was only a game. In the following century it was to grow in importance. In fact, as early as 1750, William Grey and Samuel Smith, Master mason and Master builder respectively, designed a folly at Belton House, near Grantham, to be used as a hunting lodge. Known as the Bellmount Tower, it completely mocked the battlelines by combining Romanesque and Gothic features with adjacent obelisks. Before long, it was modified. By the time the War of Styles was in full rage a hundred years later, a bit of fun like this would have been no laughing matter.

However, another factor was to have the greatest influence. For some reason, Napoleon decided to conquer Egypt. Nelson and the British fleet went out to meet him in Egypt, resulting in the Battle of the Nile in 1798. From this time there would be French and British artists and proto-archaeologists in the land of the pyramids.

With regard to the status of obelisks in Britain, there were three important outcomes: the birth of 'Egyptology'; the dawn of 'The Egyptian style'; and the finding of 'real' Egyptian obelisks to which they would be compared.

III

The Nineteenth century

Until Napoleonic times, when the French Emperor addressed his army before the pyramids, there was a void in understanding the remains of Ancient Egypt. Herodotus, Strabo and Plutarch, who all visited Egypt, wrote when hieroglyphic script was used and understood. Julius Caesar's burning of the library at the temple in Alexandria destroyed several hundred thousand handwritten hieroglyphic texts on papyrus. Those texts which survived were destroyed with the temple in a second fire in AD391.

Once the priests of the temple ceased to teach language and scripts, all knowledge or ability to read Egyptian hieroglyphs was lost. This was when most of Egypt's accessible obelisks were removed and shipped from Alexandria to Rome.

There were few accounts of Egypt for several hundred years. A Jesuit, Claude Sicard, travelled and charted ancient monuments in 1722. Soon after, King Louis XIV entrusted the position of Consul-General in Egypt to Benoît de Maillet. He was first in a line of consuls who handled large amounts of items removed from Egypt. His *Description of Egypt* in 1735 increased curiosity in Europe, causing more travellers to visit, writing in breathless mode of the competitive thrill of discovery.

Over in Rome, the popes had only just ceased from raising the trophy obelisks, emphasising, as always, that they been had sanctified with markings and iron crosses. Pius VI erected more obelisks, even while persecuting heretics, in particular, masonic circles in Paris, in order to assist the French Crown to defend itself against 'Liberty and Fraternity'. At the same time the pope commissioned another book about obelisks, this time from a Dr Jorgen Zöega of Copenhagen, who lived in Rome for some years in research and preparation.

Published in 1797, Zöega's *De origine et usu obeliscorum*, showed pages of exact hieroglyphs and demonstrated all that was known of their meanings, very little in fact. The 'Origins and Uses' gave little consideration to the obelisks themselves, and Zöega stated that he could see no mystery in the shape of the obelisk. He conceded it was a practical shape, strong and not without beauty. De Maillet's, if not Zöega's published accounts, were in the saddle-bags of the numerous experts who went to Egypt with Napoleon in 1798.

The Emperor of France took with his army many historians, artists and experts. Among them were mathematicians, astronomers, engineers, naturalists, excavators, draughtsmen, printers, painters, a poet and a pianist. Leading the academics was Baron Denon, who was with a detachment under General Desaix, and had the opportunity to see the monuments in Upper Egypt. Denon's book, *Travels in Upper & Lower Egypt* ran to thirty editions in France and was translated into English in 1803. The author was elevated to Director of Museums, and founded the Louvre, where he began an encyclopaedic work in many volumes, (another) *Description of Egypt*, with contributions from others in Napoleon's expedition.

The lure of treasure and the beauty of the ancient artifacts were fanning the fire, creating a market for 'antiques'. From 1803, Colonel Bernadino Drovetti, who was in the French Consulate in Egypt, amassed and sold more than one collection of items. Despite political changes in Paris, he managed to remain there until 1829. In direct competition from 1816 onwards was the British Consul General, Henry Salt, who, by paying dues to the Turkish Viceroy, built up large collections. His first was sold to the British Museum and the second to the Louvre; his third collection was sold in Britain after his death in 1827. In 1819 Salt removed the Philae Obelisk, which was destined for the young and wealthy collector, William Bankes, who had seen it while on an extended visit to Egypt four years earlier.

This obelisk, named because it was found on Philae island, was younger than most in Egypt. Inscribed with the name of the Pharaoh Ptolemy IX, ruling in 100BC, it was relatively small, a 22 feet tall, six ton granite monolith which was collected by an extraordinary agent in Salt's service. This was Giovanni Belzoni, an Italian giant with the strength of four or five men, who had appeared twenty years earlier in London's theatres as a strongman. Belzoni was also an intelligent artist and excavator, but his most useful attribute was his profession as an engineer. Belzoni's techniques were noted: he was well qualified to lift, move, pack and transport large objects.

Hieroglyphs for Cleopatra's name were also present upon the Philae obelisk. These were of vital assistance to Jean-Francois Champollion in his conclusive deciphering of the ancient Egyptian texts. From the 1820s, a fair proportion of the hieroglyphs were finally understood

The small obelisk presented by the Turkish Viceroy in Egypt to the 4th Duke of Northumberland in 1838 was inscribed on one surface. It declared itself to be one of two dedicated by the Pharaoh Amenhotep II,1427-1392BC, to his father (or the god that fathered him), Khnum-Re (another name for Ra) at the Altar of Ra.

It had been found amid ruins on Elephantine Island on the Nile. Defying general notions of size, this red granite obelisk was 7 feet and three inches from the ground, with no base, slender, with little angle on it. It was shipped with the Duke's collection to England, all of which was sold in 1950 to the Oriental Museum of Durham University.

There were not many obelisks left in Egypt and the remaining few were again regarded as worthwhile trophies. One of the obelisks at Luxor, marked with 1600 hieroglyphs, could be dated from about 1450BC, in the reign of Tuthmosis III. It was removed, a gift to France from the government of Egypt, (though suggested by Champollion) and winched onto a study craft, the 'Louxor', to be assisted by a steam-powered ship named 'Sphinx'. Together, with relatively little mishap, the cargo was transported to Paris. Any worries about erection were bravely put aside by the French who announced that the 254 ton obelisk would be put up at the centre of the Place de la Concorde in Paris, in front of a crowd on a Saturday in October, 1836. "Threats will not be needed; Patrotism combined with intelligence...will be a sufficient driving force..."

The obelisk known as 'Cleopatra's Needle' which stands in London was moved from Alexandria, a process which took seventy-seven years, all but two of which were wasted. Away back in 1801, a British patrol had come across some of Napoleon's academics and French troopers in the process of removing an upright obelisk in Alexandria. After a brief exchange, the British were unopposed. At the head of the British garrison in Alexandria, the Earl of Cavan decided it would be easier to retrieve another obelisk, which lay half-submerged nearby.

This was the 68½ feet monolith of buff-pink granite, inscribed with hieroglyphs on three of its sides. These stated that it too had originally been raised by Tuthmosis III of the 18th dynasty of the New Kingdom. The very fact that it lay in Alexander's city indicated that it had been taken from further up the Nile, from Heliopolis, it is thought. The weight of the Needle was calculated precisely at 186 tons.

Cavan engaged a military engineer, Major Bryce, to make a plan and organise a 'whip-round' by which the garrison made a subscription to pay for the undertaking. However, they could not move the object and anyway the politicals at the Foreign Office ordered them to drop the project, lest it offend the Khedive, or representative, of the overruling Turkish Ottoman court. The subscribers were re-imbursed. The plan was put aside and forgotten until the Khedive's successor, Mohammed Ali, conspired to oppose his Turkish masters and acquire a small navy, with which to defend Alexandria. In 1819, to persuade the British government to provide ships, the Khedive offered to load the obelisk for transport to London. The government did not consider this seriously, though Ali's offer remained.

Several decades passed and little serious attention was paid to the uncollected trophy. The original officers of the garrison at Alexandria grew old and their pleas to the Admiralty and Whitehall came to nothing. Even when the French had retrieved 'theirs', and it became a matter of national honour that British ingenuity should impress the world, the obelisk remained where it was. Somehow, the story was resurrected in London newspapers, by articles claiming that the Khedive was proposing to donate the Needle elsewhere, or that the great stone was being chipped away by English souvenir hunters. This was probably true, as more and more Europeans visited the Nile.

Finally, in 1875, General Alexander resolved to do something. His great-uncle had been Bryce, the engineer who had tried to shift the stone in 1801. The general went to Egypt to see the prone obelisk for himself. He met the new Khedive, Ismail Pasha, and discovered that the object of his quest had been surrounded by a fence by a Mr Demetrios, owner of the land upon which it lay. Agreements were reached and the formal donation made by the Khedive. Through contacts, General Alexander was introduced to an engineer,

Waynman Dixon, who was confident that he could transport the stone to London. As for money, he turned to a very wealthy friend, Dr Wilson, who agreed to underwrite the cost of the venture.

The story of what followed is well known as a result of the great interest paid by London's newspapers, who reported the story in full. Dixon's proposal was to make a long cylinder from sections of boiler plating, and to lay the obelisk in this. To turn this into a ship, a deck, cabin and rudder could be added and the whole thing towed to England. Dixon had employed an experienced mariner, Captain Carter, to master the iron cylinder ship. The captain went to Alexandria to watch the boiler sections arrive from England, which were soon bolted together. Dixon's theory was that when the obelisk was packed inside, providing its centre of gravity was a little lower than the axis of the iron tube around it, the whole thing would always right itself in the sea.

Dynamite was used to make a shallow in the little port, through which the obelisk ship could be pulled. This was regretted in the 1990s as international archaeologists discovered that the waters covered an extended area of palaces, statues and ancient port facilities, possibly connected with the colossal Pharos, a skyscraper of a lighthouse and Wonder of the Ancient World.

Work progressed on the obelisk ship, which was to be called 'Cleopatra'. In late August 1877, it was rolled down the beach in front of many onlookers. Somehow, it got punctured by a stone and had to be repaired. Back in order, it was towed off to a floating dock to be fitted out. The captain hired a crew of Maltese sailors and after ceremonies, 'Cleopatra' was towed away on 21st September, by 'Olga', an English steamer out of Liverpool. The whole process had been carefully reported by English newspapers, especially *The Illustrated London News* which had an artist compose drawings of the events, which were engraved for weekly editions. The London populace were being primed for any news of Cleopatra's Needle, and the account of what happened next became well-known in England.

'Cleopatra' was an uncomfortable craft which was awkward to tow and subject to flooding. Carter had to crawl about the separate compartments, checking the stability of the steel ballast and the bilge pumps. Reaching Gibraltar, Dixon came ashore from 'Olga' to hire two or three more crew. He was cautioned about possible storms, but proceeded slowly up the Iberian coast. Passing the northern cape, both craft were faced with heavy weather and Carter on the 'Cleopatra' and the Captain of 'Olga' were tested to the extreme. Lashed together on a long hawser, the ships could hardly communicate. 'Cleopatra's ballast shifted and Carter and his crew struggled inside the iron tube of a hull, thrown about in the high sea. Seeing Carter's plight, the tow-ship's captain ordered a lifeboat to collect the men from 'Cleopatra'. Six of 'Olga's' crew volunteered to row over to 'Cleopatra'. They were never seen again.

'Olga' came along side early the following morning and removed Captain Carter and his men from 'Cleopatra' and cut loose the tow. A few hours later, as the storm subsided, 'Olga' returned to recommence towing, but the iron cylinder and its ancient cargo had disappeared. 'Olga' turned for home and a signal was sent to England, announcing the loss of the skiff and its oarsmen, and the disappearance of the obelisk.

Dixon's hopes lifted within a day, when, by fortune, 'Fitzmaurice', a small steam-ship out of Middlesborough, came across 'Cleopatra' 90 miles off the North-West tip of Spain. The news of the loss of the obelisk was still breaking in England, while 'Fitzmaurice' put into port in Spain, towing its salvage.

Back in England, once the situation was established, deals were negotiated and the salvage demand was lowered to £2,000. Another steamship was sent out, 'Cleopatra' refitted, and the obelisk's journey continued in January, 1878. The new tow, 'Anglia', was more powerful and although there were more gales and heavy seas, the remaining passage was less eventful, reaching the Thames within a couple of days. A telegram was sent by the Queen, congratulating Dixon. 'Cleopatra' was towed to the East India Docks, while various institutions argued about where the obelisk was to be placed. The British Museum was considered, as was Parliament Square and St Paul's. However, the chosen site on the Embankment meant that the process of unloading,

transporting and suspending the 186 ton monolith, could all be done more-or-less in one motion. 'Cleopatra' was able to carry her load to within a few feet of its resting place. To make this possible, Dixon had made a wooden frame. This would suspend the obelisk horizontally, allowing it to be carefully rotated and then lifted into position. This was captioned 'The English Method of erecting the London Obelisk'.

The base had been prepared together with a pedestal which incorporated stylized wings in iron; these clasped and held the worn lower end of the obelisk. The base was flanked by two bronze sphinxes, each 19 feet long, which had been cast by Vulliamy & Co. Their moulds were expanded forms of Egyptian sphinxes at Alnwick Castle, thought to be contemporary with the little obelisk

Cleopatra's Needle on the Embankment, *The Illustrated London News.*

from Elephantine, which the Duke of Northumberland had received in 1838. The plan for the two sphinxes was an echo of depictions of twin lions or lionesses guarding the 'double horizon' on either side of obelisks in Ancient Egypt.

'Cleopatra' was moored at St Thomas's, opposite Parliament, where she attracted much attention. She was then moved to the Embankment where, for four months, workmen prepared the site. 'Cleopatra's' iron plating was partly removed to reveal the obelisk and

Dixon's wooden derrick was moved into position. On the appointed day, the 12th of September 1878, before a large crowd, the lifting and positioning began and was completed within thirty minutes without mishap.

Famously, a time capsule had been placed in the pedestal, which included specimens of the hawsers used, a set of coins, a photograph of Queen Victoria and twelve more photographs showing beautiful British women, along with cigars, bibles, hairpins, newspapers and standard imperial measurements for feet and pints. The imagination of the London crowd, already full of muddled Egyptology and myth, was drawn to the notion of a future civilisation inspecting these artifacts of 1878. Even if they did not understand the exotic hieroglyphs, the antiquity of the great stone held them in awe.

In a publisher's tie in with the great event, a small book had been published while the thing had been at sea, entitled, *The Obelisk – Notices of the origin, purpose and History of Obelisks*. It was a little premature as the obelisk's location had not been chosen. The writer was none other than Hargrave Jennings, author of *The Rosicrucians*. He was not beset with doubts about repeating well-worn theories with certainty and he began in a grand manner.

> 'The Alexandrian Obelisk is the property of the British Nation. It is the noblest gift of which the English people have been ever put in possession. It is the rarest example of antiquity of which our metropolis can boast'.

He included descriptions of the obelisk, its rounded lower end, its measurements, and repeats the etymology and generally understood origins of the word 'obelisk', from ὀβελός. Jennings was troubled by the translated lack of grandeur in the word 'spit'. He suggested an older origin, which is difficult to dispute.

> 'But the truth is it is not truly a Greek word, but an eastern term of sacred import and vast antiquity. The Greeks in their excessive vanity, disdained to acknowledge a foreign origin for any word they adopted into their language; neither would they trouble themselves to enquire into its ultimate meaning. Hence they fell into innumerable errors, and, in adorning them to posterity. Nay, they proceeded still further, and did not hesitate to canonise falsehoods… ὀβελός is compounded of the ancient sacred titles Ob (serpent) and El (the sun) with the customary Greek termination signifying together – Pythosol'.

53

Their use was well known, Jennings claimed, immediately repeating the often made generalisation that they (by implication all) were set up in pairs before the great temples. He had copied all relevant texts and credited the sculptor, John Bell, and his lecture for a number of topics drawn up. The book recorded the corroborating Latin texts of Pliny and Polydore Vergil, and Jennings put in the idea that the obelisk may have been 'the parent, progenitor, the leader-off to the important family, the long succession of "columns" succeeding in natural production afterwards'.

With regard to the London location of the obelisk, Jennings did not have time to adapt his text. He had assumed an earlier plan to have Cleopatras's Needle placed before St Paul's Cathedral, though this would have involved removing the old statue of Queen Anne. A keen promoter, Jennings called for attention to the great stone on its way

> 'We – Londoners – are now about to receive His Imperial Majesty Obelisk the First of an unknown number of thousands of years of age (spent in Egypt), where his head is in the clouds (of antiquity), while his feet are touching England in anticipation (in reality). Let his Emperorship, the "First of the Obelisks" then arrive. Not only to assume his state, but to remain the first of our monuments, and the boast of the country'.

Of the monuments of Thebes, he wrote, 'There is no doubt that these obelisks are the *ne plus ultra* of what design and execution – or art generally – can offer for the admiration of the world'. Capable of epic description and ready with the last word, Jennings imagined a walk to be taken by a time-traveller who arrives at Luxor.

> '... and around these stupendous templar-masses, to receive first impressions; staying his foot occasionally and listening to the echoes, which seem to roll away in prolonged subterranean thunder. It is thus – and thus only – that he begins to comprehend the supernatural sublimity of these vast remains. Also the mightiness of the silence in which everything stands'.

There was deep Rosicrucian enchantment here, though a little later, on page sixty, it seems there was a printers error: 'You seem to see the possibility of the immorality of the soul'. (A little 't' makes a difference). One doubts if Jennings' readers comprehended his lines of thought, though some have entered lore. There was more to come, for it was Jennings who also produced *Phallicism*, a book five times longer than *The Obelisk* of 1877. It was the former title which was to be responsible for a new misunderstanding surrounding obelisks, to be discussed in a later chapter.

As stated, there had been two 'Cleopatra's Needles' at Alexandria, one standing and the other fallen. They were not identical twins and may not have been made together. The British were given the standing stone, but had decided, in the event, to remove the fallen one. The standing obelisk, which might be called, 'Cleopatra's Other Needle', was removed to the USA soon after 1878. The American methods of transportation and erection were equally ingenious, but different to those of the French, or British. In order to place their ancient but newly acquired purchase in Central Park in New York, the Americans were obliged to drag the obelisk for two miles, which in itself took nearly four months. Its arrival in the USA was a surprising adjunct to the long prepared Washington Monument, the largest obelisk monument in the world. The image of the latter is most often seen in Britain on televised dispatches from the White House.

The story of the journey of 'Cleopatra's Needle' had spanned three-quarters of the century. From the 1870s we must return to the early 1800s to examine the effect of all the discoveries in Egypt. How did they affect obelisks made in Britain?

Two immediately noticeable changes were an increase in the number of monoliths built and the widescale use of granite. This was the composition of the ancient obelisks of Egypt. When polished, however, British granite was effectively a new material. From 1833 onwards, it became first choice for obelisks.

The first granite obelisk in London caused a minor commotion as crowds formed about a new obelisk in Ludgate Circus. 'Within days of its completion, the "wanton curiosity" of a public determined to discover whether the granite was real, had caused damage to finer detail'. *The Times* reported that it would be a disgrace if a beautiful work of art would have to be enclosed by railings. Moreover, above an angled plinth with a broad ledge, the 18 feet tall Devon granite shaft was in one piece; the people had never seen such a thing before. This was the 1833 obelisk memorial to Robert Waithman, sometime Mayor, Sherriff and MP for the City. Raised by subscription, the memorial was designed by the architect, James Elmes. It was later moved to its present location in Salisbury Square, near Fleet Street. The granite surface was smooth rather than actually polished, and it is encrusted today with a harmless lichen. Its previous companion in

Ludgate Circus, the Wilkes Obelisk, an 18th century lamp holder converted into a monument, broke up as it was being moved.[1]

Another sign of the impact of discoveries in Egypt was that both France and England immediately experienced an Egyptianising style in architecture, furniture, decoration and painting. The style was popular in Britain, and yet, as early as 1808, an English architect, Charles Busby, claimed, 'Of all the vanities which a sickly fashion has produced, the Egyptian style in modern architecture appears the most absurd: a style which, for domestic buildings, borders on the monstrous. Its massy members and barbarous ornaments are a reproach to the taste of its admirers; and the travels of Denon have produced more evil than the elegance of the engravings and splendour of his publication can be allowed to have compensated'.

The Egyptian Hall, since destroyed, was built in London's Piccadilly in 1811 and was lated used by Belzoni for his first display of Ancient Egyptian artifacts. Other surviving buildings of an early 19th century Egyptian style include a library in Plymouth, a house in Penzance, a flax mill in Leeds and the Clifton Suspension Bridge built by Brunel in 1836. The new cemeteries, to be entered in the next chapter, exhibited much Egyptian style, notably at Highgate, with its two cement rendered brick obelisks before the gate to 'Little Egypt'.

There were Egyptian additions to Freemason's halls and lodges, which were respectable places in Britain's cities. In the imaginative interiors could be found two large pillars and all manner of antique emblems, but no especial role for the obelisk. Masonic connections have proved something of a blind alley. The closeness of the association of the obelisk with freemasonry has been exaggerated by contemporary American writers. Writing in America in 1980, Peter Tompkins produced *The Magic of Obelisks*, a fascinating text, in which he drew together all possible links between generations of European societies and the masonic fraternity in Britain and her colony in America, asserting that the obelisk was a symbol of Liberty to all freemasons.

There is a danger in connecting everything, every strand of belief, myth and scandal in one mighty web of conspiracy and disinformation. That way, as the contemporary writer, Umberto Eco, tells us in *Foucault's Pendulum*, lies brilliant madness. Freemasonry had certainly been one of the ideologies in Revolutionary France and America, and it had been on Napoleon's mind when he ventured his army and scholars to the Nile. Regarding Britain's outlook, however, the links were tenuous. No matter how strong the ties of secret societies in the late 18th century, those had been the days of Revolution, and in the case of both France and the USA, Britain had been for the status quo. During the American War of Independence, there was no question of rebel and British freemasons sharing the same hopes for the outcome. As for France, there had not been a shred of amity between the two countries for very many years, and Britain was deeply suspicious of the French Revolution. The obelisk had not been a symbol of Liberty (and brotherhood) in this country because Britain believed it already was free.

Freemasonry originated in Britain, and while it must have taken up ideas and symbols from European sources, its roots and branches were in Britain, with more in the colonies. There were 12th and 13th century links with the Knights Templars, through Templars who had gone to Scotland, out of reach of the pope's agents. It is quite likely that Templar rituals and symbolism, cloaked in secrecy, became a part of the proto-masonic movement which surfaced in the 16th century.

One abiding emotion identified with the Templar movement was the sense of loss. After their banishment in 1312 under Pope Clement V and having had their own law, wealth and military power, their own arts, rituals and temples – especially the Temple of Solomon in Jerusalem – they were reduced to an enigmatic footnote in history. This feeling of loss would later tie in with obelisks in Rome, inscribed with a lost language

It has been suggested that the masonic movement also drew influence from the wandering ex-priest, Giordano Bruno, who visited England and was subsequently tortured and executed for heresy by Pope Clement VII in 1600. Like Queen Elizabeth's Doctor Dee, Bruno drew voices from the air. He was a freethinker in an age of dogma and he practised techniques of recalling memories and information through visual associations, in order to connect with divine states. Followers of Bruno's revelatory techniques were part of the masonic movement in Scotland at the end of the 16th century. They instructed initiates in the Art of Memory and it became regular practice for masons to test each other on the finer points of the craft. The significance of these techniques is that they relied on symbols and signs to activate the memory, which was precisely the intention behind all memorials.

Whatever their origins, ever since the opening of the first Grand Lodge in London in 1717, British masons have been part of the establishment, led by the Royal family and an array of Dukes, and manned by tens of thousands of doctors, lawyers, judges, soldiers, policemen and secret-service men. Winston Churchill was an initiate. Women have always been disallowed but the reigning monarch, Queen Elizabeth II, is the current patroness. With the reputation of being a behind-the-scenes force affecting public office in this country, the inference is that freemasonry was hardly a revolutionary force.

How easy it would be to extrapolate from freemasonry in the United States and France the idea that obelisks were exclusively a freemasons' favourite on this side of the seas. As for those who erected obelisks in Britain, might one compile a whole list of names and find out, if one could, which individuals were freemasons? Doubtless, the research would provide intriguing tales, many coincidences and more contradictions. Overall, it would not be a profitable exercise in research.

It is well-known that British masons increased in number and followed an interest in Ancient Egypt, its gods, rituals and beliefs. It is true that this was a factor in the raising of obelisks listed in these pages, but it would be incautious to make any generalisations. Whatever the connections, appreciation of the obelisk was by no means confined or exclusive to masons.

As the 19th century progressed, matters of style and fashion became part of an altogether noisier debate. For London's Egyptomania in general, there was criticism, as Leigh Hunt famously ranted, 'Egyptian architecture will do nowhere but in Egypt. There, its cold and gloomy ponderosity ('weight' is too pretty a word') defits the hot, burning atmosphere and shifting sands. But in such a climate as this, it is worth nothing but an uncouth assembly. The absurdity, however, renders it a good advertisement. There is no missing its great lumpish face as you go along. It gives a blow to the mind, like a heavy practical joke'.

By the 1830s any style was inevitably and quickly enmeshed in the greater War of Styles, which had moved into an aggressive phase. As John Gloag, author of *Victorian Taste*, put it: 'Gothic for Romance, Classic for Reason: that was the civilised, tolerant Georgian view. The Victorians, less gracious but far more serious, would have none of it: Gothic for Christianity, Classic for Paganism was the war cry of the Gothic revivalists in the battle of the Styles'.[2]

The interminable struggle between classic and gothic affected nearly everybody and everything in Britain throughout most of the 19th century. Somehow obelisks avoided the main fury of the gothicists attack, which was spent against the greater classical items, the temples, columns and statues of Greco-Roman gods; all were non-christian.

The most outspoken of the gothicists was Augustus Pugin, who said, "The moderns, in their pretended imitation of the classic system, are constantly producing the greatest anomalies; and we are called upon to admire their thrice-cooked hashes of pagan fragments (in which the ingredients are amalgamated in utter confusion) as fine national monuments of the present age"[3]. Writing today, it is difficult to discuss the minefield of good and bad taste without accumulating prejudice. We may laugh now, especially at those bearded Gothics of the 1860s, but they had considerable power. Nobody dared laugh at Pugin with his all-important pretty Gothic Revival folly, the new building of Parliament.

So attitudes to the obelisk were mixed. From the gothicists point of view they were to be seriously resisted. Allied to the classical, they were still slightly infra-dig to classicists as non-Grecian. The new Egyptologists did not take British obelisks seriously. New evangelicals saw all monuments as marks of pride or arrogance. Some opposition, in practice rather than principle, came from certain sculptors who were weary of a well-worn, or formulaic route to making memorials. Their livelihood depended on commissions which utilised their skills with marble statues, rather than obelisks, which were monumental, complete in themselves and could be purchased 'off the peg'.

An 1839 drawing by the artist, John Buckler, is all that remains of an obelisk erected in 1836 on a nine-stepped circular base on Banwell Hill in Somerset. Within four years the obelisk was removed and replaced by a gothic tower at the order of the Bishop of Bath and Wells. This change of heart could have been for religious reasons, or the result of similar forces at work in the War of Styles. How many obelisks were cancelled, as the gothicists spread their disinformation, will never be known. Equally, how many other obelisks were raised in order to keep the bearded ones at bay?

Despite these interesting questions of good and bad taste and the shift in perceptions, the popularity of the obelisk increased throughout the century. Raised in their thousands in the new cemeteries, they also continued to hold their place in fine gardens and open landscapes.

In fact the Egyptian obelisk from Philae was placed in the garden at William Bankes's family home at Kingston Lacy, near Wimborne in Dorset. The foundation stone of the new base had been laid by the Duke of Wellington in 1827, but the arrangement was not complete until 1839. The duke was well acquainted with obelisks, in fact he had as many of them inscribed with his name as any Pharaoh. As the most famous man in England, Wellington had every honour, with numerous statues and monuments.

At the time, a huge three-sided obeliscal monument was being built in his name on the Blackdown Hills above Wellington in Somerset. After a public subscription had been opened locally in 1815, the architect, the younger Thomas Lea, apparently experimented by designing the structure three-sided in order to economise on labour and materials. In fact it proved rather more complicated, as it was to have a central staircase to the top, and was not completed until 1892. Another suggestion had been for three dwellings on the hill for Waterloo veterans to live in and act as caretakers. Moreover, the original idea had been to have a statue of the duke at the top. When this plan was discontinued, another five feet had to be added to height of the obeliscal monument which has the appearance of a gigantic bayonet. It is 175 feet tall and stands on a line of hills, a very prominent West country landmark. If it had been four-sided, it would have been the largest obelisk in Britain.

It had to be larger than Stoodley Pike, the 120 feet tall Obelisk monument to the Peace of 1814, raised by public subscription near Todmorden in West Yorkshire. Built of stone blocks, with a gallery, this became unsafe and collapsed in 1854. It was rebuilt two years later, with a bit of a bend in the profile of the obelisk, and much more strength from eight buttresses, like rocket fins, at its base. Built of blocks, the tallest obelisk in Europe was the 'Wellington Testimonial' at 197 feet, raised in Dublin's Phoenix Park in 1817 and designed by the architect, Robert Smirke.

The Peace of 1814 had only lasted a few months as Napoleon escaped from his first exile and raised the army which Wellington met at Waterloo in 1815; the conclusive result and ensuing peace, ending trade blockades and income tax, was justly celebrated. At Chicksands

Priory in Bedfordshire, where Sir George Osborn had added to the ancient building, a 60 feet tall obelisk was raised to commemorate the end of the Napoleonic wars. The owner of Bispham Hall, nr Wigan, had an obelisk raised in Wellington's honour in 1816, featuring a cannon ball at its peak. In the following year, an obeliscal tower commemorating victory at Waterloo was built overlooking the river in Torrington, Devon. There were more obelisks to the Duke: a tall one at Wynyard Park in Durham; in Pontefract (a badly built 40 footer known as the 'Cranky Pin', since demolished); and at Woodhall Spa, Radway Grange and Bremhill Court. The same feature, non-partisan as ever, was chosen at Lydford in Devon in memory of French soldiers imprisoned for the war's duration.

Lord Nelson died in 1805 and was fully honoured, while the Iron Duke lived for many years until his death promoted a second wave of grand memorials and statues in the 1850s. The important development of the area of central London around what we now know as Trafalgar Square was in progress before Nelson's death at Trafalgar. It took another sixty years before it was completed and the biggest hold-up was in the planning for a sculptural monument to Nelson at its centre. There was an Egyptian association with the sea hero's victory at the Battle of the Nile and the statue of the admiral on a tall column, the final choice for the commission, had been in the early stages in competition with a pyramid, a naked Nelson and at least three proposed obelisks.

In less central areas, a number of commemorative obelisks sprung up, at Acton in Northumberland in 1805, and at Springfield Park, Liverpool in 1810. More personal was the obelisk built in 1808 before Old Swarland Hall in Northumberland, commemorating a private friendship with Nelson. The largest was 144 feet tall, built on Glasgow Green in 1806, while the nation was still in mourning. Designed by the architect, D.Hamilton, it was one of the first memorial monuments to Nelson. The hero's battles, Aboukir, Copenhagen, etc., were inscribed in large letters on the sides of the obelisk, which was lightning-struck in its early years and needed rebuilding in 1810, with the addition of a strong conductor. This is evident in the inevitably mismatched colour and finish of the stone blocks towards the top.

These heroes were more consistent than the crown, which went through another crisis of succession as the aged George III half-recovered from his well-known madness and remained on the throne until the end of the wars with France. In 1810, his Golden Jubilee was marked with an obelisk in the small town of Broughton-in-Furness, Cumbria.

During the decade of George IV's reign, the king had passed through Ramsgate on his way to France. John Shaw, an architect who had recently built a Clock-house by the harbour, was quickly put to work to commemorate the royal visit. He designed a hefty obelisk in pale brown granite blocks, with a latin inscription recording George's departure in 1821. George IV, so long in waiting, was ageing too and had for many years been married to Princess Caroline of Brunswick, whom he later attempted to divorce. They had one daughter, Charlotte, Princess of Wales and Saxe Cobourg, and future heiress to the throne. She married Prince Leopold in 1816, but died tragically in the following year, at the age of Twenty-one.

A wealthy Bristol tobacconist and brewer, Jacob Ricketts, at the age of 64, was apparently so affected by this, that he had an obelisk raised to Princess Charlotte in a personal memorial in 1818. About 15 feet tall in Bath stone blocks, it was sited in the back garden of his home at Redland Hill, Bristol. The bronze plaque, which survives, was properly engraved with Georgian flourishes and lettering. The inscription finishes by explaining, 'Thus were the Vine and Branch of true Whiggism, and Britannia's most blooming expectation, by one irresistible stroke, together cut off'.[4]

Another grandaughter of George III was more fortunate. When George IV died, the crown passed to his brother, William IV, and, upon his death in 1837, to the Duke of Kent's young daughter, Victoria. The 1838 obelisk monument, known as the 'Jubilee obelisk' in Royal Avenue in Bath is a misnomer, since it celebrates Victoria's coronation in the previous year. It bears a relief portrait of the young Victoria on the East face, and plaques, added later, with Royal Coats of Arms.

Compared to the numerous statues of Queen Victoria there are relatively few obelisks dedicated to her. Notably, an obelisk was raised to her at Kingston Lacy in Dorset, home of the Pharaonic 'Philae Needle'. When Belzoni was removing that six ton object from Egypt, he had difficulty loading it into a boat and the obelisk had slipped into the Nile; retrieval had tested his strength and engineering skills. The same thing happened with another 'Victoria' obelisk, raised in 1846 at Fowey in Cornwall, in honour of Victoria and Albert's visit to the town. Sited on the quay, it somehow toppled into the harbour and remained underwater for many years until retrieved and replaced in 1977.

Concerns over the matter of the succession went back further and, as in the previous century, were linked to commemoration of the events from the Civil War. Two of the war's most illustrious leaders were remembered with obelisks marking the battlefields where they had fallen. Firstly, John Hampden, Parliamentarian and military commander, was remembered at the bi-centenary of the minor battle in which he died, with the placing of an obelisk at the site in Chalgrove, Oxfordshire, in 1843. Lucius Carey, Lord Falkland was a more romantic figure, often portrayed in elegant statues. A cultivated man, he had not wished to join either side of the war; initially with Parliament, he turned, in a crisis of conscience, to the Royalist cause. An obelisk was sited on the Andover road at Newbury in 1878, marking the battlefield where he died.

As Belzoni was removing the Philae obelisk, it slipped into the Nile.

Doubtless, to have a battlefield on one's land was an asset, a fact not missed by the squire at Naseby, Northamptonshire, who had built a twenty feet tall obelisk in 1823 to commemorate the conflict of 1645. Reminiscent of cannon balls, a pile of stone spheres sits at the base of the obelisk, which is enclosed within iron railing. This actually marks the place where Naseby windmill once stood, and the battlefield is about a mile away, marked by another monument.

A less well-known event was commemorated by a remarkable and virtually unknown artist, who, in 1851, made an obelisk in stone and placed it on a remote moor at Black Dub, near Reagill and Maulds Meaburn in Cumbria. Either as a local commission, or more probably for his own reasons, Thomas Bland, a self-taught sculptor, chose to recall the place where Charles II rested with his troops while marching from Scotland to Worcester in 1651.[5]

Regional pride was a motivation for raising monuments, and a purpose for which obelisks were well suited in open country, as mark stones. Apart from anything else, they cost less than a sculptural monument, and the building of them provided work for local labourers, who had to endure poverty throughout most of the 19th century.

A regional pride in the navigator, Captain James Cook, who had been born in 1728 beneath the North Yorkshire moors near Great Ayton, prompted Robert Campion of Hartlepool to raise a subscription for a public monument. He approached Mr Emmerson of the Easby Estate, near Great Ayton, where Cook's father had once worked as bailiff. The squire was persuaded to allow his moorland to be used, and his workforce to be hired for the building of a big obelisk. In 1827, the monument was erected, and dedicated to the explorer.

The Cook Monument brings more questions of viewpoint, and reminds me of a personal experience. I can remember myself, twenty-seven summers, or half my life ago, riding my brown cob from Hexham to Whitby, a distance of 150 miles. It was a return stage of a ride around Britain. I had begun early on the roadside, North of Bishopton, blowing on the embers of the night's fire to make tea. Saddling up, we went through Whinny Hill and crossed the Middlesborough road, and a railway leading to chemical factories. I had to go through Egglescliffe and Yarm, over the Tees and then we were in Yorkshire. For the next three or for hours I rode with the line of the moors ahead, standing like a lost kingdom, a sudden rise of a thousand feet, pointed by a distant obelisk bathed in sunlight and the volcano-like cone of Roseberry Topping.

I climbed the hill onto the moors this year and found that the Cook Monument was very unlike a pin, as I had seen it from below. It was more obtuse, blunt, or shortened in appearance, only about 70 feet in height, and built of rough-dressed stone blocks and mortar. A depression in the cliff and signs of quarrying indicated the possibility that the freestone was cut on the hill-top, rather than hauled up. Standing by the obelisk structure and looking down onto the plain below, to the route I had once followed on horse, I understood that what mattered here was the view from afar, seen by many. For little cost, the region dignified its hero, and the rough obelisk on the crest of the moors provided a view for everybody for several miles around, a view which calls to mind specifically Ancient British ways with upright stones and cairns in the hills.

Digressing to long distance riding, my thoughts turn to John Wesley because of his ceaseless ride. His horses must have covered a vast distance between the 50,000 outdoor sermons he was said to have

17. Lansdowne Monument, 1845, Cherhill, Wilts; architect: Sir Charles Barry.

One of the most outstanding obelisks in the British landscape, seen on the Downs from as far as thirty miles away, the 125 feet tall monument stands on Oldbury Castle, an iron age hill fort. It was built by the 3rd Marquis of Lansdowne and dedicated to his ancestor, Sir William Petty,1623-1687, though it was more than a memorial, marking the eastern limit of his estate, centred on Bowood. The soaring obelisk on the fortified hill, the highest point in the area, suited the unique landscape around Avebury, which hums with antiquity, mounds and megaliths.

18. Obelisk,1804, memorial to 4th Earl of Bristol, Ickworth park, Suffolk.

Early in the century in 1804, the Herveys of Ickworth Park in Suffolk received an obelisk paid for by the people of Derry, where Frederick Hervey, 4th Earl of Bristol, had also been the bishop. Over 40 feet tall, it was sited in a quiet part of an immense deer park, to be viewed from garden terraces in front of the house.
photo © Michael Cousins.

Captain Skinner s Obelisk, inscribed 1832, Holyhead, Anglesey, Wales.

The man in charge of the Irish mail, by paddle steamer out of Holyhead, was Captain J. Skinner. A valiant one-armed and one-eyed veteran who owned a raven which flew out to meet him, the Captain was drowned at sea in a storm in 1832. He was honoured by a 30 ft tall obelisk monument overlooking Holyhead Bay. About the base were carved details of inverted torches and amphorae pouring onto an eternal flame. Above this, bulging from the lower part of the obelisk, were two halves of a funerary urn, and the prow and stern of a boat. Still higher on the East face was the carved winged disc of Horus. This was one of only very few instances in which British obelisks bear the mark of the early 19C Egyptianising style. photo; Don Matthew.

19. Cook Monument, 1827, near Great Ayton, North York Moors.

Seldom seen this close, the misshaped bulky landmark provides a perfectly good pinpoint for viewers 20 miles away. Set in a dramatic landscape near Roseberry Topping, it was built in proud memory of the local-born explorer, Captain James Cook,1728-1779. Mr R Campion of Hartlepool raised a subscription and approached the squire of Easby Estate for permission to use his moorland. Another obelisk stands in Hawaii, where Cook was knifed by an islander.

The Mail Coach Monument near Llandovery on the road between Brecon & Carmarthen

Mail Coaching Monument, 1841 Brecon to Llandovery road, Wales.

Refreshments at coaching inns amounted to a great deal of alcohol, leading to mishap and another obelisk. Just before Christmas 1835, Edward Jenkins, the coachee, had left Brecon with his team at speed, covering 6 miles in 20 minutes. Meeting another wagon he overtook on the wrong side and coach, passengers and horses went over a precipice. The inspector of Mail Coaches and subscribers raised a 6 feet tall obelisk outside Llandovery with an inscribed tablet, an early admonition against the perils of drinking and driving. There were no fatalities. Watercolour, G. Harrison 1884.

20. Obelisk, 1805, Studley Royal, Ripon, Yorkshire.

The landscaping and gardens of Studley Royal were increased in the 18th century by John and William Aislabie to incorporate the ruins of Fountains Abbey and a series of lakes and follies. Away from these and in view of the house, an obelisk was raised many years later in memory of John Aislabie, in replacement for a pyramidal monument. Subsequently, when the house was occupied by the Marquis of Ripon in the 1870s, the Marchioness had objected to the obelisk at the head of her drive. To hide it from her view, a church with a substantial spire was built in front of it. photo © Michael Cousins.

Obelisk, 1812, Melville monument, Comrie, Perth.

The obelisk memorial to Henry Dundas, Lord Melville, on Dunmore Hill above Comrie can be reached after a steep climb. It is mostly seen from a distance, a white prominence emerging from surrounding forestry. Highland monuments from the days before forestry are gradually being hidden from view.

Rosary Road Cemetery, Norwich.

The Rosary was the first cemetery to open in 1821. In the same year, in the preface of 'Adonais', Shelley had written, *'The cemetery is an open space among the ruins... It might make one in love with death, to think that one should be buried in so sweet a place'*.

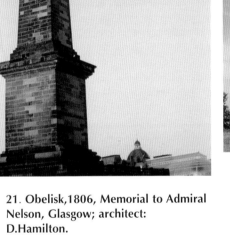

21. Obelisk,1806, Memorial to Admiral Nelson, Glasgow; architect: D.Hamilton.

Britain's hero was honoured with many monuments and some obelisks. London's Trafalgar Square monument took six decades to decide upon and complete while this monumental obelisk on Glasgow Green was unveiled in the year following Nelson's death. With a height of 144 feet it was taller than anything else at the time. The names of battles, Aboukir, Copenhagen, etc., were inscribed in large letters on the obelisk, which was lightning-struck in its early years, and needed rebuilding in 1810. This is evident in the inevitably mismatched colour and finish of the stone blocks towards the top.

Wellington Monument, completed 1892, Blackdown Hills, Somerset.

Many people have seen this from afar, a 175 ft tall landmark on a line of hills. A public subscription for a monument had been opened in 1815 after the Duke of Wellington's victory. The architect, the younger Thomas Lea, experimented by designing the structure three-sided in order to economise on materials. This proved more complicated, as it was to have a staircase, and work was not finished until 1892. The monument's appearance has been likened to a bayonet. If it had been four-sided, it would have been the largest obelisk in Britain.
photo © Michael Cousins

22. Model of obelisk for The Great Exhibition Memorial; John Bell, Sc, 1858.

John Bell,1811-1895, was a leading sculptor and very active in the Great Exhibition, not only with sculptures inside and outside, but as a committee member of the Society of Arts, which, with Prince Albert as its President, promoted the Exhibition. Afterwards, Bell wanted to celebrate the achievements with the first truly great obelisk, all in one piece of granite, on the Exhibition site in Hyde Park. Bell's lectures on the obelisk form a part of this book, but the great monolith was not to be, as the prince died unexpectedly in 1861. The plan was replaced by a national shrine, the Albert Memorial in Kensington Gardens, for which Bell sculpted the West corner symbolising 'America'.

Photo © 1858 in copy, The Conway Library, The Courtauld Institute.

23. John Bell,1811-1895.

John Bell had success with commissions for city monuments, marble figures and casts in iron, terracotta and Parian ware. As well as proposing a huge obelisk for Hyde Park, Bell designed obelisks and lectured about them to the RSA and RIBA, advancing the concept of entasis and 'The Definite proportions of the Obelisk'. Significantly, he saw the obelisk as a feature of art.

Obelisk,1865, memorial to John Speke, Kensington Gdns, London.

The explorer, John Speke,1827-1864 found Lake Tanganyika and went on to discover and name Lake Victoria, but back in London, his claims to have discovered the source of the Nile were refuted. He travelled to Africa again and on his return encountered more scepticism from geographers. Hours before he could defend his reputation at an important gathering, he was killed in an accident. Speke was honoured with an obelisk raised in Kensington Gardens with a 24 ft shaft composed of three polished granite blocks. It was a very choice spot in the metropolis and no distance from the Royal Geographical Society' s headquarters in Kensington Gore.

24. Obelisk, c1450BC, Cleopatra s Needle , The Embankment, London.

"It is the noblest gift of which the English people have been ever put in possession".

(H. Jennings, The Obelisk,1877)

The 68½ feet granite monolith is inscribed with hieroglyphs of the Pharaoh, Tuthmosis III. The French, British and Americans followed the example of Rome in removing large obelisks from Egypt. The British one, found in Alexandria and popularly known as 'Cleopatra's Needle', took 77 years to get here and its perilous passage in an iron cylinder is legendary. The riverside location was a relatively easy option. The science of hoisting the 186 ton object onto its new base was achieved in one motion by W.Dixon's machinery, before a large crowd on 12th September 1878. Other sites, discussed heatedly, had included Parliament and St.Pauls.

photo © Bob Partridge, Ancient Egypt Picture Library.

25. The Philae Obelisk, c100BC, Kingston Lacy, Dorset.

The obelisk was seen in 1815 on Philae island in the Nile by a wealthy Englishman, William Bankes. It was relatively small, a 22 feet tall, six ton granite monolith which was carried away by the engineer, Giovanni Belzoni, to the Consul, Henry Salt, who shipped it to England. Here it was placed in a garden at Bankes' new home at Kingston Lacy in 1839. The first Ancient Egyptian obelisk to reach Britain, it was younger than most, inscribed with the name of Pharaoh Ptolemy IX, ruling in 100BC. Hieroglyphs for Cleopatra's name were also present which were of assistance to Champollion in his revelatory deciphering of the ancient script.

photo © National Trust Photo Library.

26. **Cemetery views**

upper left – Kensal Green, London.

upper right – The Rosary, Rosary Road, Norwich, the first cemetery, opened 1821.

lower left – Highgate Cemetery, cement-rendered obelisk and Egyptianised entrance to columbarium.

lower centre – Dumbarton Cemetery, opened 1854.

lower right - Kensal Green, London.

**27. Obelisk, 1858, memorial to J. Richardson, Kensal Green;
Design & Manufacture: A MacDonald.**

A superb 24 foot monolith of red polished granite in the main avenue towers over a
classically fronted mausoleum on one side and a gothic one on the other. With its pedestal
and base, it reaches a height of 35 feet, and may be equal to the biggest British obelisk in a
single piece (see next page). It was an apt memorial to Joseph Richardson, who died in 1855,
and members of his family. A Cumberland mason, he discovered that strange music could be
made by striking slices of certain rocks. He had created an instrument called the 'Rock
Harmonicon', which his family played in public. Apparently, some of the audience fell into
trances.

28. Obelisk, 1875, memorial in Jehpson Gardens, Leamington Spa, Warwicks.

Opposite the famous Pump Rooms are the finest municipal gardens for a very long way. Here are river-fed lakes, temples, statues, several ornamental fountains, and an obelisk of 1875 which commemorates the benefactor, E. Willes. This is a Victorian beauty, with a complex stone plinth emblazoned with a crest, and rising 15 feet from it, a white, polished granite monolith.

29. Monolithic Obelisk,1872, memorial to Henry Bell, Helensburgh, Glasgow.

Henry Bell,1766-1830, was the pioneer of iron steamship construction and first to use steam power for the purposes of navigation. In 1812 he built a paddle-steamer, 'The Comet', which crossed the water from Helensburgh, where he settled, to Gourock and Port Glasgow. The superb obelisk on the waterfront was a 24 foot tall, red polished granite monolith on a stepped base. This was the work of Alexander MacDonald and the Aberdeen Granite Works and it is either the biggest, or equal to the biggest monolithic obelisk made in Britain.

30. Gurney Drinking Fountain Obelisk, 1861, Stratford, London; J. Bell, Sc.

Humanitarianism was at the heart of the Metroplitan Free Drinking Fountain Association, founded by the philanthropist, Samuel Gurney. It was responsible for the installation of a number of handsome drinking fountains in different styles. When Gurney died in 1856, his friends wanted to put up a public memorial in his home borough, in Stratford Broadway, London. The sculptor, John Bell, took on the commission and, for his own reasons, combined the drinking fountain with a large obelisk, 42 feet high. Constructed of nine blocks of pale granite, the obelisk sits on a plinth and inclined pedestal with rounded basins and cast-iron floral plaques on either side.

Gurney Drinking Fountain, 1861, Tombland, Norwich.

Echoing the London monument, the Gurney family in Norwich put up an obelisk combined with a Drinking-fountain and trough, all in polished red granite. It stands in Tombland outside the cathedral and marks the spot where there was once a well and machinery for gathering water.

Obelisk Drinking Fountain, 1871, Brighton; architect: Robert Keirle.

31. Obelisk Drinking Fountain, 1880 Leamington Spa, Warwickshire.

The big obelisk and drinking fountain in memory of Henry Bright could be seen from the length of The Parade and was inaugurated with a ceremony. Its 32 ft shaft was built of four vast blocks of polished red granite and stood on a 10 feet tall base. It is still described as a Drinking-fountain today, though long since dry.

About 18 feet tall in speckled-white granite, this was raised in Grand Parade by the mayor and the Metropolitan Free Drinking Fountain Association. The obelisk was built in two pieces and had a mysterious piercing high in the shaft, perhaps to receive a gas lamp. It stood on an elaborate plinth and stepped base, with double drinking fountains and a surround of curved water troughs for horses. Attached plaques display civic emblems and inscribed lettering confirms its design by Robert Keirle, consultant architect for the Association at the height of the Drinking Fountain movement. The temporary ring on the obelisk in the photograph is a bicycle tyre.

The way the granite went: Peterhead.

All larger obelisks of polished granite, whether monolithic, or made of blocks, seem to have been cut from red Peterhead. Unlike some of the other granite quarries of Aberdeen, which had started as small plots rented from farmers, and which went deep, the quarry at Peterhead was broad and near to the port. Overlooking the harbour where the granite was taken away, was the old graveyard, and inside it, a single obelisk of polished Peterhead granite. This would have been drilled from the adjacent quarry and shipped to Aberdeen to be cut and polished, before return by sea. Also in view, the obeliscal war memorial of the 1920s, made of the town's rock, though unpolished.

32. Obelisk, memorial to J. McGrigor,1858, Duthie Park, Aberdeen.

James McGrigor,1771-1858, had progressed to Director General of the Army Medical Department and had been on many campaigns, including those in Egypt, where he had visited Thebes. He was an Aberdeen man and the commission for the £2,000 memorial went to Alexander MacDonald's firm in the city, the world's premier granite finishers. It was an impressive obelisk in polished red Peterhead blocks, with one third of its 72 ft height in the base. It was first sited at Marischal College in the city, but moved in the 1890s to Duthie Park. With more confidence about techniques to suspend and raise an obelisk in Britain in the 1850s, Alexander MacDonald might have made this in one piece.

delivered. In 1858, a Methodist group in London had an obelisk raised to him in Marylebone High Street. On Newcastle's Quayside, a 15 feet obelisk and drinking fountain of 1891 marks the place where Wesley first preached, his horse resting awhile. Another saddlebag traveller was Daniel Defoe when researching his *Tour Through the Whole Island of Great Britain,1724-6*. He seemed in favour of the obelisk he described at Ripon, and might have approved the choice of one raised in his memory many years later in 1870. This was in white marble,10 feet tall on a 4 feet high plinth and base, at the place of his burial in Bunhill Fields in the City of London.

If names impress, there was an obelisk memorial to the Lincolnshire genius, Isaac Newton, raised in 1847, more than a century after his death. It was sited at Stoke Rochford Hall, primarily as a garden feature in front of the house. Constructed of well-cut limestone blocks, it was 60 feet tall, though the plinth and base accounted for a third of this height. Commemorating the polymath and intellectual star, local pride was the primary motive. The inscription declared: 'May the inhabitants of the surrounding district recollect with pride that so great a philosopher drew his first breath in the neighbourhood of this spot'.

New to the 19th century, especially in North Britain, were municipal or public memorials to industrialists and inventors. These were nearly always statues, with a few exceptions, some of which were obelisks. The place, rather than the look of the man, was the issue for the commemorations to Henry Bell,1766-1830, pioneer of iron steamship construction. One memorial obelisk of 1836 is high on Dunglass Castle, by Dumbarton, overlooking the river and the great ships which passed. Henry Bell had also been the first to use steam power for the purposes of navigation, having built a paddle-steamer, 'The Comet', which crossed the water from Helensburgh to Gourock and Port Glasgow in 1812. His idea of steamships had been proposed to the Navy in the 1790s, though dismissed by the Admiralty, in spite of Nelson's recommendations.

Five miles down the Clyde at Helensburgh, where Henry Bell settled and died, there was a second and more public obelisk raised in 1872 on the waterfront. A superb red polished granite monolith, it was 24 feet tall in one piece, raised on a straightforward base and steps. It was another work of Alexander Macdonald and the Aberdeen Granite Works, to be encountered in later pages. As far as the author knows, it is either the biggest, or equal to the biggest monolithic obelisk made in Britain.[6]

Another man of iron was John Wilkinson, 1728-1808, who worked as a boy in his father's Barrow-in-Furness ironworks before venturing southwards. He earned a fortune in the Midlands, helping with Watt's first steam engine, the famous iron bridge at Ironbridge and the making of the world's first iron boat. He returned to Cumbria and built a castellated residence at Castlehead. When he died, it was decided that if his memorial was to be an obelisk; it had to be of iron. This was the first iron obelisk, one of only two or three in Britain. Installed in about 1810 and weighing 20 tons, it was a 15 feet tall black-painted shape which features a relief portrait of Wilkinson and an inscription, picked out in white. Once in a while a restorative coat of anti-rust, or blacking, brings these details back to life. Erected at Castlehead, it was later moved to Lindale, in Cumbria's High Furness district.

Public subscription, an extremely good idea not much followed these days, became common in the 19th century, and many statues and monuments were financed in this way. Somebody would propose a commission to commemorate a worthy subject and friends and associates would start a subscription fund, to which all were invited to contribute money. This resulted in more public monuments.

Moreover, public subscription in the 19th century meant that monuments could be put up by different groups of people, quite unlike earlier times. Among these were new humanitarian, missionary and charitable societies. The plight of chimney sweeps was one of the charitable causes, drawn to society's attention by Charles Kingsley's book, and made worse by the complexity of flues in the new town houses. When a chimney sweep in the Isle of Wight, a ten year old girl named Valentine Gray, was found dead in an outbuilding in 1822, a public subscription was gathered, affording a small obelisk memorial in Newport's Church Litten Park. In Wales, little Mari Jones had crossed mountains in a long walk to town to buy a bible. When she died in 1866, the Merioneth Sunday School Association subscribed to her memorial, a polished granite obelisk, at Llanfihangel-y-Pennant, near Abergynolwen. [7]

Humanitarianism was at the heart of The Metroplitan Free Drinking-Fountain Association. It was founded by the philanthropist, Samuel Gurney, MP for Falmouth, who was the nephew of the campaigning reformer, Elizabeth Fry. The Association was responsible for the installation of a number of very handsome drinking fountains in different styles. When Samuel Gurney died in

1856, the Drinking-fountain movement showed no signs of halting, later extending care to providing granite water troughs for the city's horses.

Gurney's friends and admirers wanted to put up a public memorial in his home borough of Stratford, East London. At some point, one of the subscription committee came in contact with a sculptor of high repute. This was John Bell, an influential figure who will be introduced in the following chapter. Bell had obelisks on his mind in the late 1850s. Of course the Gurney memorial was to be a Drinking-fountain, but now, with John Bell, it was to be an obelisk too. The sculptor was on the committee at the Society of Arts and lectured on practical aspects of public sculpture, including 'Art connected with Drinking Fountains'. However, the involvement of Quakers, who would not have wanted an ornamental treatment, ruled out decorations, and for his part, Bell, for reasons which will later become clear, was keen to make the obelisk bigger than expected.

Finally raised in the middle of Stratford Broadway in 1861, the Samuel Gurney Drinking-Fountain was a 42 feet tall obelisk monument. It is prominent today in this very busy location, surrounded by traffic and the nearby railway. All of pale grey granite, the obelisk was constructed of nine cleanly dressed blocks seated on a plinth and inclined pedestal. The plinth was boldly inscribed with Gurney's name on the West face, with drinking-fountains, rounded basins and cast-iron floral plaques on the North and South sides.

Also in 1861 and echoing the Stratford monument, the Gurney family in Norwich put up another obelisk combined with a drinking-fountain and a trough. The whole thing is built of polished granite and the obelisk is a 12 feet monolith. It stands in Tombland outside Norwich cathedral and also marks the spot where there was once a well and machinery for gathering water. The granite geometry of the obelisk contrasts, in a thought-provoking manner, with the cathedral spire in the background.

A decade later in 1871, a very handsome obelisk and drinking-fountain was put up at the North end of Brighton's Grand Parade. About 18 feet tall in speckled granite, the obelisk is built in two pieces and has a mysterious piercing high in the shaft, perhaps to receive a gas lamp. It stands upon an elaborate plinth and stepped base, with double drinking-fountains and a surround of curved water troughs. Attached plaques display Brighton's civic emblems and inscribed lettering, barely legible, declares that it was presented by Fredrick Chatfield and designed by Robert Keirle. Keirle was consultant architect for the Metropolitan Free Drinking Fountain Association from 1858-1895, during the height of the Drinking Fountain movement.

Other obelisks combined with drinking-fountains were built and plumbed in, mostly in polished granite, the preferred material for water basins and street furniture. In South London there are examples in Woolwich and Bexleyheath, and another, in limestone, dating from 1866, at the junction of Lewisham Hill and Lewisham Road. It is 15 feet tall and unusually graceful. It should be noted that none of these drinking-fountains actually flow with water today.

Some of the drinking-fountains also served as memorials in public places, such as the 16 feet high obelisk in Park Road North, Birkenhead, which assuaged thirst and marked the memory of a Mr Jackson. The big obelisk and drinking-fountain in memory of Henry Bright, put up in Leamington Spa in 1880, could be seen from the length of The Parade and was inaugurated with a ceremony. The 32 feet shaft was built of four vast blocks of polished red Peterhead granite, and stood on a 10 feet tall plinth and base.

It is an impressive monument and still described as a Drinking-fountain today, though it has long been dry. Water is no more than a few yards away at the spa's famous Pump Rooms. Opposite these are the Jehpson Gardens, the finest municipal gardens for a very long way and comparable to anything on a Duke's estate. Here are river-fed lakes, temples, statues, several ornamental fountains, and an obelisk of 1875 which commemorates the benefactor, E Willes. This is a Victorian beauty, with a complex stone plinth emblazoned with a crest, and rising 15 feet from it, a well-shaped, grey-white, polished granite monolith.

Another Drinking-fountain obelisk was the 1858 memorial to Richard Vaughan Yates, in Prince's Park, Liverpool.[8] In polished red granite, it stands 15 feet tall in two pieces, above a pedestal and base. It is clearly signed, A.MACDONALD, ABERDEEN. Mr MacDonald is another influential figure to be met in subsequent chapters, someone who was to make more obelisks than anyone else in the world.

It seems so sensible of the British people to have applied the obelisk to good functional use. The advances in sciences of timekeeping, surveying, astronomy and cartography required a reference standard. In 1824 a series of Greenwich Meridian markers, which were obeliscal, but flat-topped for attaching instruments, were sited at various points. The one at Pole Hill Park near Chingford in Essex, was later found to be 19 feet off the Meridian. It is 10 feet tall, and made of white painted concrete. With no architectural quality at all, it was a fore-runner of the much later Ordinance Survey trig-point markers, which were shaped like truncated obelisks, about 3 feet high, set in concrete, to be found on prominent British hills.

Observant commuters into London will have noticed the short squared posts which appear by railway embankments, waterways and roads leading into the city. These are coal tax posts, mostly dating from the Coal & Wine Duties Continuation Act of 1861. At these points, twenty miles from the centre of London, coal carters and wine carriers were obliged to pay freight duty to the City of London. There are over two hundred still in place, most of which show only three feet above ground. They are square section pillars with little pyramidions and feature the city's crest, picked out in red paint. However, there are a few, reserved to railways and canals, which are actually obelisks and are a little taller than the regular posts. These too are of cast-iron, and occasionally of stone, cut in one block. A coal tax obelisk stands on the embankment about thirty yards from Whalebone Bridge at Chadwell Heath, near Barking in Essex.[9]

A Meridian marker of a different sort, a large obelisk 100 feet tall, was built in 1850 near Obelisk Lane in Durham City's Framwellgate. This was for the use of Durham University's newly built Astronomical Observatory, and once had an interior staircase. Students looking through the telescope from the observatory could refer to the obelisk marker looming over the rooftops, in accord with the oldest astronomical uses of the obelisk in Ancient Egypt. The structure in Durham, which is of sandstone and not in good repair, bears a latin inscription clearly stating co-ordinates and altitude above sea level.

Out at sea, landmarks on the coast served as fixed navigational points for saiors. The Earl of Yarborough, first commodore of the Royal Yacht Club, who died in 1846, was remembered by a large, blunt obelisk, built of stone blocks, at Bembridge, Isle of Wight, and well known to East Solent yachtsmen.

A few years earlier, in 1840, another obelisk landmark had been raised on Walhampton Hill, overlooking the harbour at Lymington, Hampshire. This was the monument to Admiral Sir Harry Burrard

Neale,1766-1840. The eulogy inscribed at the base states that the Dowager Queen Adelaide, William IV's widow, was responsible for raising the subscription. The obelisk is about 80 feet tall, constructed of pale limestone blocks. The architect, George Draper of Chichester, added an Egyptian motif. Carved in relief near the top of the obelisk is a large winged disc, an incarnation of the god, Horus.

A few obelisks remind the passing motorist that the 19th century was the age of Coaching, before, during and even after the coming of the railways. Twenty-two Mail coaches left London every evening except Sundays in 1825. For coachees and passengers, the obelisk had qualities which made them ideal for roadside use. They were tall and sufficiently sturdy to act as sign and mile posts, with exact distances marked.

This was the case at Craven Arms, a place which was nothing apart from the eponymous coaching inn, where passengers were refreshed and teams of horses were changed. On the road from Cheltenham to Holyhead, or Liverpool, it was one change South of Shrewsbury for numerous coaches, such as the 'Hibernia' and 'L'Hirondelle' – nicknamed 'the del'. The obelisk which was put up in 1810, was formed from limestone blocks and is quite elegant in shape; it advertised the place and therefore the inn. The distances were deeply inscribed at a suitable height to be seen from a coach.

Telford's new road to Holyhead took the Irish mail to Telford's bridge over the Menai Straits. The man in charge of the mail from then on, by paddle steamer out of Holyhead to Ireland, was Captain Skinner. A valiant one-armed and one-eyed veteran of the American War of Independence, he impressed all with his dedication to the Post Office and his character 'of unvarying friendship and disinterested kindness'. Skinner was drowned at sea in a terrible storm in 1832, whilst safeguarding the mail. He was honoured by an obelisk monument, 30 feet in total height, raised by public subscription and sited on land at Morawelon overlooking Holyhead Bay.

Built of smooth, grey stone blocks, the 20 feet tall shaft of the obelisk is somewhat compressed and should have been taller. About the base and lower part of the shaft are a series of carved details of inverted torches and two Egyptian amphorae, which pour onto an eternal flame. Above this, bulging from the lower part of the shaft are two halves of a funerary urn, and at right angles to these, the prow and stern of a small carved ship. Still higher on the East face is a carved winged disc of Horus. This and the forementioned 1840 obelisk to Admiral Neale at Lymington are two of only a very few instances in which monumental British obelisks bear the mark of the early 19th century Egyptianising style.

Quite soon, with the coming of rail, there was need for a new bridge over the Menai Straits. The Britannia Bridge was built in 1849, incorporating pseudo-Egyptian features, with heavy pylons and sphinxes resembling 'British' lions. Navvies and engineers killed in accidents during the bridge's construction were honoured by a 25 feet tall obelisk at Llanfair Pwllgwyngyll, on the Anglesey side,

At a crossroads in the centre of England and just off Telford's road was another milestone obelisk of the coaching era, put up in 1813. It stood 16 feet high on a stepped base in front of the Dun Cow Inn at Dunchurch, near Rugby. It was not a true obelisk as the four side edges were chamfered to make the shaft eight-sided, or octagonal in section. Distances to London, Oxford, Holyhead and Leicester were inscribed on a sandstone block in the middle of the shaft.

Refreshments at coaching inns involved a great deal of alcohol, leading to mishap in this dangerous mode of transport, and another obelisk. The 1841 'Mail Coaching Monument', a five or six feet tall obelisk on the roadside outside Llandovery, was erected by J Bull, Inspector of Mail Coaches, and forty-one subscribers, in memory of the passengers on board the Gloucester Mail, driven over a precipice by a drunk coachee. In fact nobody was killed and so this is an unusual memorial. The inscribed tablet remains a unique and early admonition against the perils of drinking and driving.

> 'Six days before Christmas, 1835, the London & Milford Haven mail Coach met at this place a wagon on the wrong side of the road; the mail Coachman, Edward Jenkins, (being at the time intoxicated) tried to pass it on his wrongside, his leaders got on the low bank by the roadside, then coach and horses all went over the bank. The horses were caught by a tree, but the coach rolled over and over down a steep slope into a brook some 80-100 feet below the road. As the coach left the road, the driver, guard and Col. Gwynne of Glanbrane Park (who was the only outside and on the box seat) were thrown off, but one inside went with the coach and was taken out of the foreboot into which he had been forced in the fall, unhurt'.

Apparently, when Jenkins had left the Castle Hotel in Brecon he had his team at speed, covering the first six miles in 20 minutes. People who had seen the coach said that they thought there would be an accident. The driver was fined £5 by Carmarthen magistrates and was apparently tormented with guilt, heightened, no doubt, by the raising of the Mail Coach Obelisk.[10]

Whatever we think of Queen Victoria's long reign, none can deny that those were days of adventure, not only clattering four in hand through the shires, but in the humid jungles and wide deserts of India and Africa, wherever Britons roamed. The acquisition of an Empire was an occupational hazard of this roaming, though some would say it was the purpose. Unsurprisingly, there were casualties, mostly in the military, and those who fell in far corners of the world were honoured with memorials at home.

A 20 feet tall obelisk on the Greenwich riverside forms the monument commemorating officers and men lost in New Zealand's Maori War of 1863. A large granite obelisk, the Afghan Campaigns War Memorial, was put up below Nottingham Castle in about 1880 to a design by W Jackson. A much smaller one in pink granite, recalling the Egypt and Sudan Campaign of 1884, was placed prominently in the Victoria Fountain Gardens at Brighton. The tall obelisk raised at the Royal Hospital, off Chelsea's Kings Road, was designed by S.Cockerell. Made of granite blocks and topped with a gilded globe, it honoured the memory of 255 officers and men of the 24th Regiment, lost at the battle of Chillianwallah, at end of 2nd Anglo-Sikh War. Within closed grounds, it is not a public memorial.

Some of these monuments were technically not war memorials *per se*, as they tended to commemorate named individuals. The very tall landmark obelisk on Beacon Hill on Bodmin Moor in Cornwall, was built in 1856 as the memorial to Lt General Walter Raleigh Gilbert, who served in India at the time of the Mutiny. At a height of 144 feet this is among the tallest in the country.

The 28 feet tall obelisk which was put up in 1860 on a ridge above Hatherleigh Down in Devon is a memorial specific to Lieutenant Colonel William Morris, although it commemorates an action in which many had died. Morris had died in India in 1858, but had been an officer of the 17th Lancers, who were at Balaklava with the doomed Light Brigade. The bronze relief panel on the base illustrates the aftermath of the battle, as stretcher bearers remove the wounded or dead.

By way of contrast, another Crimean war memorial was a large obelisk of millstone grit blocks raised by public subscription in Lancaster Cemetery in 1858. There were other obelisk memorials to the Crimean War put up in Bath and in Portsmouth, where the sea front and Clarence Gardens became home to a whole range of smaller obelisks. These were memorials to ships and crews lost in service in distant seas: HMS Active, Powerful, Victoria, Shah, and Royal Sovereign, the last of which was sunk in a collision.

The 56 feet tall obelisk in Birmingham's St Philip's Square was the memorial of an army officer and imperial adventurer, Frank Burnaby,1842-1885, who was fatally wounded during the Sudan campaign. Ten years earlier he had written and published *A Ride to Khiva*, describing his mountainous trek from British India into Russian Asia, a foray in the 'Great Game'. Back in London, Burnaby had cut a dash in society and co-founded the magazine, *Vanity Fair*.

More concerned with exploration than empire, or so he thought, was John Speke,1827-64. He found Lake Tanganyika in 1858 and went on to discover and name Lake Victoria, but back in London, his claims to have discovered the source of the Nile were refuted. He travelled to Africa again and on his return encountered more scepticism from geographers. Just hours before he could defend his name at an important gathering, Speke was killed in an accident when rough shooting with friends in the country. Speke was honoured with an obelisk monument raised in London's Kensington Gardens. This is a graceful monument, with a 24 feet shaft composed of three polished granite blocks, and a stepped base. Moreover, it is in an attractive setting, a very choice spot in the metropolis, to the South of the park's Italian gardens and no distance from the Royal Geographical Society's headquarters in Kensington Gore.

At least Speke got home from his travels. Hauntingly poignant was the story behind the 35 feet tall, red granite obelisk designed by Philip Hardwick and sited near Greenwich Pier in 1855, especially as it was raised to a Frenchman. This was Joseph Bellot,1826-53, an officer of the French navy who joined two separate expeditions searching for Captain Franklin, whose ship and ill-fated crew had disappeared in searching for the North-West Passage. Bellot was last seen on an iceberg carried out to sea in a storm.

The obelisk is an oddly appropriate marker of memories. Could anything have been more suitable for someone who met such an end? It was the selected memorial for the 1862 Hartley Disaster in which coalminers died in Hartley New Pit, near Whitley Bay on the Northumbrian coast. The huge beam pump at the pit head had broken and fallen down the shaft, blocking it with debris, imprisoning the men and sealing off the air intake. It was a treated as a national disaster and a very large crowd came and witnessed the unsuccessful attempts at rescue. When the dead miners were finally reached, some days later, they were found lying in rows, or sitting on benches, sons with their hands on their fathers' shoulders. Was an obelisk the chosen memorial because Seaton Delaval Hall was only half-a-mile away and the pit stood on Delaval lands, or because it was a symbol which could be invested with memories, but was not in itself an object of gloom?

A less famous incident was the drowning of Timothy Trow, a tram-conductor who could not swim but entered a canal to save a child. His 1894 memorial was a small obelisk, paid for by subscription and sited in Stoke-on-Trent's London Road. This story contrasts with the tale of Mark Addy, a publican who was a very good swimmer, plucking fifty individuals on different occasions from the Manchester Ship Canal. The lifesaver was honoured in 1891 with a 24 feet tall obelisk in Salford.

Other reflections of changes in 19th century society are demonstrated by obelisks which have been displaced while remaining in the same spot as London expanded. A Mrs Martin, or Marvin, was buried in 1751 among orchards and meadows to the West of London and her grave marked by an slender limestone obelisk. Urban growth in the early 1800s engulfed the area, and the obelisk and grave are now in Chelsea Square, amid elegant town housing. Miles out in Lewisham, a new street called Monument Gardens contains a graceful 14 feet tall limestone obelisk. It dates from 1721 and stands upon four stone globes on a patch of grass surrounded by 20th century housing. Nobody seems to know anything about this stray from some great house or long-gone park, yet it is London's second oldest surviving obelisk.

As London grew and traffic in the 20th century began to dominate, countless monuments of all sorts were moved. Some were never seen again, so it is gratifying to hear the account of a handsome obelisk which was sold many decades ago by an owner of Hurst House, in East London's Woodford Green. Later, in the 1970s, the then owner of the house saw the same obelisk in pieces in an antique dealer's premises. It was 10 feet tall with four large globes around its base. He purchased it and put it back in its original location on the green in front of the house.[11]

Allthough there was an exodus from the countryside throughout the 19th century, high farming and great estates continued to dictate the social order. One of the biggest landowners in Britain, the 1st Duke of Sutherland was honoured in 1833 with an impressive 70 feet tall obelisk at Lilleshall, paid for by tenants of his Shropshire estates. In the same way, a lesser Shropshire landlord, Sir Andrew Corbet was presented with a 15 feet obelisk in 1842 by his tenantry at Lee Brockhurst, near Wem. In 1885, tenant farmers of Mr Lloyd of Llangurig in Powys put up in his name a 20 feet tall granite obelisk and stepped plinth.

It is typical of the associations of Brititish obelisks that, by comparing one to another, so many differences are revealed in inscription details, yet somehow united in the singular stone shape. Illustrative of differences of property and power in the land, there was a 16 feet tall granite obelisk erected in the village of Llanarmon-yn-Ial, near Ruthin, which recalls thoughts of land reform. It was the memorial to John Parry, 1835-97, a tenant farmer evicted, it is believed, for suggesting that parish tithes should be paid by landowners rather than tenants.

Despite every change in society in the 19th century, and unaffected by the discoveries in Egypt, obelisks continued to be erected in British gardens and landscapes, just as they had been in Georgian times, though in fewer numbers.

The Lansdowne Monument in Wiltshire is one of the most outstanding obelisks in the British landscape, seen on the Downs from as far as thirty miles away. It stands on Oldbury Castle, an iron age hill fort, at Cherhill Down. It was erected in 1845 by Henry Petty-Fitzmaurice, 3rd Marquis of Lansdowne, who was a Cabinet Minister, Lord Lieutenant of the County and one time President of the Royal Academy. It would have been easy for him to summon the eminent architect, Sir Charles Barry, for the design. The obelisk was built to a total height of 125 feet, though the pedestal and base account for a third of this. The carting of stone up to the site would have been hard labour for estate workers, and their wages were surely not included in the £1,395 final cost of the obelisk. It was restored in the 1980s by the present custodians, The National Trust, for £220,000.

Lord Lansdowne had dedicated the monument to an ancestor of his, Sir William Petty, 1623-1687, though it is much more than a memorial. The soaring obelisk on the fortified hill, the highest point in the area, suited the unique landscape, which positively hums with antiquity. The whole area is peppered with tumuli, megaliths, barrows and earthworks, in conjunction with Avebury stone circle and Silbury Hill. It was a statement of power, located at the eastern extremity of the vast estate centred upon Lord Lansdowne's home at Bowood House, nearly five miles distant.

The Ten Books of Architecture declared that the Romans had set up statues and terms to mark victories and 'distinguish the limits of their conquests'. This was taken, in an English context, to confer tradition upon the positioning of obelisks at the limits of country estates. On a smaller scale, a landowner, George Messiter, had workmen build four rough structures, one of which was an attempt at an obelisk, at each corner of his estate around Barwick House, near Yeovil in Somerset. The obelisk of sorts was about 25 feet tall, in rough freestone, its shape twisting in contortion. The others were follies and were larger: a tower, a cone and an arch called 'Jack the Treacle Eater', all in the same jumbled finish. Their building provided work for a group of unemployed glovemakers from Yeovil, no doubt doing the best they could. Such work, hauling stones and so on, was appreciated and not resented. Up in Scotland, the 1856 obelisk to the 6th Earl of Haddington, at Tyningham House in Lothian, bears an inscription commending his example of planting (forests) extensively at a period 'of the greatest national depression'.

Up in the Highlands, inland monuments were either on hilltops or in valleys. It was perfectly natural in such landscapes to place the obelisk on a hill, though this was unorthodox in Egyptological lore. However, now that early plantations have reached maturity, views are affected, presenting vistas of forested hill with only the head and shoulders of an obelisk emerging. This was the distant view I saw of the 1812 monument to Henry Dundas, Lord Melville, a large obelisk on Dunmore Hill outside Comrie in Perthshire. After a steep climb, I reached the summit. Sheep bolted and stared among the sweet-smelling gorse around the obelisk, which was stone block built to a height of 72 feet and contained within iron railing. The views were far reaching: I spied another obelisk on a lesser hilltop at Trowan, just East of Comrie, where a less large obelisk, the 19th century monument to Sir David Baird, was also half-hidden by trees.

Regarding prices of monumental obelisks, Pevsner makes particular note of the cost of the Welcombe obelisk, a large monument in open country just outside Stratford-on-Avon. It was erected in 1876 'in token of the deepest esteem and affection' for Mark Philips, by his brother, Robert, heir to the Welcombe estate. Both men were Lancashire MPs with philanthropic leanings and the monument co-commemorated their father, 'A friend to liberty in evil days'. The 120 feet tall obelisk was constructed of rough-cut Welsh granite blocks in the Welcombe Hills. It bears three large panels containing very lengthy inscriptions and a coat of arms. The carving of this lettering and complex heraldry into granite would have accounted for a surprisingly high proportion of the overall cost of £4,000.[12]

In established gardens and grounds, the feature was as desirable as ever. Early in the century in 1804, the Herveys of Ickworth Park in Suffolk received an obelisk paid for by the people of Derry, where Frederick Hervey, 4th Earl of Bristol, had been the bishop. About twenty feet tall, it was sited in a quiet part of an immense deer park, to be viewed from garden terraces in front of the exquisite house. The beautiful grounds at Stowe received another obelisk in 1864, making three in all. Sited in the park to the North of the house, this was a memorial to the 2nd Duke of Buckingham.

At the end of the century came two of the most remarkable gardens, which were planned with care to use the obelisk as a repeated upright feature. One was small and round and survived: the other large, rectangular and soon destroyed. The 'Corona' at Athelhampton House, near Dorchester was part of the overall garden design by Francis Inigo Thomas. He was assistant to the architect, Sir Reginald Blomfield, author of *The Formal Garden in England*. The work at Athelhampton was done by Alfred Cart de Lafontaine between 1891 and 1899, and amounted to a new garden in an old and formal style, to stand aside the 15th century hall. To the South of the house, beneath a cedar tree, the Corona, a circular enclosure between two gardens, was ringed by a wall with a series of stone obelisks acting as finials. The walled circle has entrances from the four quarters, and at the centre a fountain makes water music. Like sentinels around a place of privacy and peace, the obelisks are outlined to the West by several large pyramids of clipped yew in the adjacent garden enclosure.

The garden designed at Copped Hall, near Epping in Essex, was much larger. It was begun in 1883 when young Edward Wythes,1868-1949, succeeded his grandfather and immediately set about making additions to an older house and completely reconstructing the garden.

For the design of the garden, Wythes approached an artist, Charles Eamer Kempe, 1834-1907. To understand what sort of artist he was, readers can reach for Pevsner's 'Buildings of England' series: pick any county and open any page and there will be Kempe, credited for stained glass in the local church. He must have done thousands of windows.

In fact Kempe had begun his studies and training as an architect, working under George Bedley, known as the 'Tractarian Architect', He progressed from furniture and church screens to stained glass, setting up his own studios in London in 1866. He soon became an authority on mediaeval stained glass and an exponent of the techniques of its production.

Doubtless, Kempe had picked up a lot of architectural ideas on his travels. The design he made for Wythes was without compromise and expensive. A square area of ground was levelled, then a surrounding wide terrace built on all sides, retained by a balustraded wall. Capping this wall at regular intervals were obelisks which functioned as finials and, as the total length of the four terraces was considerable, there were a lot of them, perhaps forty or more. Each was 6 feet tall, cut in a single piece of Portland stone and stood on four small spheres on pedestals as high as the balustrade; above this the line of obelisks stood proudly and jabbed the sky. Down on the garden level, amid formal bedding and lawn, were two large marble fountains with associated figurative statues. Two taller obelisks stood at the end of the central raised walk.

At the two corners of the garden closest to the hall, Kempe designed identical pavilions, or summerhouses. To my eye these were as fine as anything similar, even the lodge designed by William Kent at Badminton House in the previous century. Kempe's pavilions were on three levels, with gracefully canopied window openings on the upper floors. At the top storey of the summerhouses were eight obelisk finials, two at each corner and all identical to those on the garden wall.

What a sight it must have been! It was not finished until 1905 and Kempe died a couple of years after that. The garden at Copped Hall was visited by *Country Life*, and the magazine's photographer took some photographs, one of which is shown in this book. A few years later, in 1917, a raging fire destroyed the hall. The gardens were maintained, after a fashion, until the bereft owner's death in 1949.

Within a year or so, everything was sold – all the obelisks, fountains, and stonework went away, leaving Kempe's summerhouses to the elements, while the former garden became a forest of sycamore seedlings.[13]

To restore the house and grounds, great efforts have been made of late by Alan Cox, an architect and the energetic founder of the Copped Hall Trust. In years to come, the great house and summerhouses will eventually be restored, though to return the garden to its Edwardian condition would be to triumph against the odds.

Many English gardens have been lost to neglect and upheaval, but that array of over forty obelisks will probably never be seen again. Their use as garden or terrace ornament went back three hundred years earlier to Nonsuch Palace and Montacute House.

IV

JOHN BELL'S LECTURE: THE DEFINITE
PROPORTIONS OF THE OBELISK AND ENTASIS,
OR THE COMPENSATORY CURVE.

A part of this book consists of lectures about the obelisk by John
Bell,1811-1895. One of the top sculptor's of the mid 19th century,
John Bell was my great-grandfather's uncle. Some of his papers came
to me, causing me to examine his life and write about him. In doing so
I introduced myself to the subject of sculpture and then, by tracing the
man's life, into the subject of obelisks. A friend of mine has said that
Bell has been my guiding light, though for me the perspective is not
only on sculpture and monuments, but on landscape and history as
well. I hope it will cause a wry chuckle in readers who have
experienced monomania when I state that obelisks are linked to all
these subjects, and a few more besides.

As a sixteen year old boy in the late 1820s, John Bell came up from
Norfolk to London to attend the Royal Academy Schools, where he
was awarded the highest prize. Working for himself and exhibiting at
the Royal Academy, it was not long before he attracted much
attention with 'The Eagle Slayer' in the year of Queen Victoria's
coronation. In 1846 he met Henry Cole – 'The coal who raised the
steam for the Great Exhibition' – and it was he who introduced the
sculptor to Herbert Minton, the Pottery magnate, and Francis Darby,
Ironmaster of Coalbrookdale. Bell began to provide art works for
manufacturers to reproduce.

Thus he was extremely active in the promotion of The Great
Exhibition, with numerous works, inside and in the grounds of the
Crystal Palace in Hyde Park (and again when Paxton's building was

moved to Sydenham in South London). He was a friend of Prince Albert and a close friend of Henry Cole, the two men most responsible for the Great Exhibition, through the auspices of the Royal Society of Arts, of which the prince was the president.

As the whole world knew, The Great Exhibition was hugely successful and, when it was all over, Bell wished to honour Prince Albert and celebrate this success with a large monument on the site in Hyde Park. He proposed 'The Great Exhibition Memorial' in the prince's honour. Prince Albert, naturally reticent, did not relish a personal treatment, remarking that it should not be a thing which might frighten horses in Rotten Row.

Bell decided it was to be an obelisk. Moreover, Prince Albert liked the idea. In February, 1858, he and the Queen had viewed proposed designs in the architectural gallery of the South Kensington Museum, now known as the Victoria and Albert Museum. The sculptor had designed and worked up a plaster model of the obelisk to scale, showing bronze figures and drinking fountains at its base and extensive inscriptions on all four faces.

Bell had conducted his research and obtained information from people who had spent years out in Egypt. Regarding obelisks in Ancient Egypt, it had become clear that a granite monolith, that is to say, of one single stone, was 'the real thing'. Bell decided the obelisk was to be of granite and monolithic and he wanted to prove the Greatness of Britain by making this a big one. He talked of a shaft of either 80, or 100 feet of solid granite, far greater than anything other than the tallest obelisks in Egypt or Rome. This was at the time of the first railways and innovation in the cutting and polishing of granite using steam power. It was extremely ambitious, but not unviable, to be paid for by the government, the Royal Society of Arts and numerous others very keen to subscribe.

In his research, Bell began to break new ground. Being an artist and a classicist he realised that as one looked at an extremely tall obelisk, there would be incurvation, apparent to the eye, unless a very slight compensatory convex curve was added to its outline.

This principle was well known to the Greeks, who added minute and delicate curves to their pillars. For reasons which I do not know, the ancient Greeks did not adopt, let alone adapt the obelisk. So Bell had to experiment, to try and find the proportions of the ideal obelisk and the entasis, as it is called, of the compensatory curve.

It is to be stressed that readers should not lose sleep over Bell's concern for fullness of outline. It is not an everyday problem, because as far as I can tell, questions of entasis only affect obelisks over 40 or 50 feet. However, it was most important to Bell, who claimed, 'This insuffiency, or apparent concavity, is painfully noticeable to the educated eye'.

So one thing had led to another: from the prince and The Great Exhibition Memorial to the plan for The Great Obelisk. Bell's lectures to the Society are of great benefit: they are comprehensible, recorded, down to earth and, above all, imbued with art and the artist's striving for beauty.

The obelisk that was to be? The greatest monolith in Britain and a memorial to the Great Exhibition – what happened? Who was to know then that within a matter of months Prince Albert would be dead? Within days of the shocking news, Bell went round to Henry Cole's house on 30th December 1861, seven days after Albert's funeral. Cole's diary records, 'Bell wanted his obelisk taken up by the department'.[1]

The obelisk became the first and only proposal for Prince Albert's memorial. From that point on, that is to say, after the lectures, hopes of a great obelisk were gradually dimmed and finally extinguished. A public meeting was held at the Mansion House which resolved that the design and mode of the memorial should be approved by the Queen and an initial subscription was opened. The Queen requested the Earl of Derby, Earl of Clarendon, the Lord Mayor and Sir Charles Eastlake, who was President of the Royal Academy, to assist in selecting and executing a suitable design. Most of these men did not live long enough to see the work completed. Eastlake, in particular, would be chief adviser on the artistic realisation of the memorial. Since it was hoped that the memorial would be accompanied by some sort of cultural institution (The Albert Hall), the idea of using Hyde Park and the Great Exhibition site was rejected.

The obelisk issue did not last long either, once Victoria and her select advisers took over the planning of the memorial, although the Queen herself is believed to have favoured John Bell's scheme, which, before all, had been known to the late Prince. As the official handbook of the Albert Memorial put it later, 'The first plan for the consideration of the committee was that of a lofty obelisk surrounded by sculptural decoration. This suggestion was carefully examined, but after much investigation it did not appear that this form of memorial would prove satisfactory'. [2]

However, when Bell delivered his lecture on 25th May 1859, the prince was alive and so was the obelisk plan. Bell was still in a state of high enthusiasm and keen to enlist support from all quarters. He began with a brief history of the obelisk:

'In the primitive state of the world nothing was more ready as a record of an event than to set up a stone in the place in which it occurred. Thus, as the bible informs us, did Jacob set up in Bethel the stone which had been his pillow, in record of his dream and the promise made to him, and the vision on that spot.

Subsequently, such consecrated stones were often called baituloi, or beitile, from Bethel. Another word which appears in the Hebrew in the bible, Matsebah, which is in some instances translated as 'pillar', and in others as 'image' when it is apt to be thought to indicate a human figure. It appears, however, rather to be used to indicate a high stone or obelisk. Selden[3], in his 'De Jure Gentium', says, "...nor while the word 'Matsebah' is translated 'statue' does it signify what statue ordinarily does, that is to say, the human figure". Spencer also agrees that it indicated a column or huge stone, rather than a human figure.

Sanchoniathon[4] states that the Phoenicians and the Egyptians, consecrated columns to those who benefitted mankind, and to the elements. Clement of Alexandria, quoting an old author, says that the Delphic Apollo was originally a column, and on the old coins of Apollonia that deity is recognised by the representation of an obelisk.

In fact, reverence for the sun, one of the purest forms of early worship, was connected with the erection of the obelisk, which from its being pointed at the top and increasing at the base, bears the general form of a ray of light (coming towards us), of which, according to some old authors, the obelisk was intended to be expressly a representation.

Mr Bonomi[5] considers that the image of gold set up by Nebuchadnezzar, on the plain of Dura, to have been by no means the statue of a man, but a gilt obelisk. It was at the beginning of the third chapter of the book of Daniel that the words occur: 'Nebuchadnezzar, the king made an image of gold. The height of it was three score cubits, and the breadth thereof six cubits. He set it up on the plain of Dura in the province of Babylon'.

Thus, as regards the proportions of this image, the height was ten times that of the breadth, which, it is evident, is wholly inconsistent with any proportions of the human frame. On the other hand, it agrees closely with those of the more graceful Egyptian obelisks, of which the whole height is usually about ten times that of the side of the base. This view may also suggest that the worshipping commanded by the king was in some way connected with the worship of the sun, of which fire was the worshipped type, as it was also 'a fiery furnace,' to which those were condemned who would not fall down before this great 'ray of light'.

The obelisk of the most extraordinary proportions of which ancient writings give us any record, was that of Queen Semiramis – which is thus described by Diodorus Siculus:- 'Semiramis likewise caused a great stone to be cut out of the mountains of Armenia 125 feet in length and five in breadth and thickness'. So it was twenty-five times as long as it was broad and thick. 'This,' Diodorus continues, 'she had conveyed to the river by the help of many yokes of oxen and asses, and there put in on board ship and brought it safe by water to Babylon, and set it up in the main highway of the city. From its shape it is called an obelisk (obelos in Greek signifying a spit, or projection), and it is accounted one the seven wonders of the world'. If this account of its proportions is correct, it would have been unusually tall with the appearance of a spike. It would have to have been secured in its erect position by being sunk in a socket, the treatment applied to Egyptian obelisks, solely to prevent their shifting on their bases.

Obelisks have been widely adopted as they are a simple feature in architecture. Indeed, they seem a form which is the common heritage of man, closely suggested by nature, as for instance, by the Needles off the Isle of Wight.

As the pyramid is a kind of scarped mountain, so is an obelisk a splinter of rock fashioned on four sides, and from its monolithic nature, more lasting than even the pyramid itself. Mr Bonomi, speaking generally about obelisks describes them thus: "These monuments of Egypt may be described as long quadrilateral stones, diminishing from the base upwards, till within about a tenth of the whole height".

In the British Museum there is an Assyrian obelisk,

truncated, from Nimrod, in black marble, used by means of relief carvings, as a record of events. As a feature of Art, the growth of the obelisk is evidently after this fashion. It first appears as a rude, solitary stone, set up on end, of a long form. As the arts advanced, features were fashioned and inscribed so as to become what Strabo, 64BC-AD23, emphatically called them, 'Books of History', the legitimate use of the obelisk's surface being for inscription. Their use as such enduring and dignified records appears by no means, however, to have been confined to Egypt as Sanchoniathon expressly tells us they were erected on Phoenicia prior to their adaption in Egypt. Yet it appears that it was in Egypt that they were most developed, the granite on the banks of the Nile lending itself so aptly to this purpose.

Looking at remaining individual obelisks from antiquity, we will proceed to some consideration of the best examples, and first to those of Egypt, which were transported to Rome by the Caesars.

I preface what is to be said of the Egyptian obelisks in Rome, with a list of those contained in Europe. There are four in Britain, *(other than Cleopatra's Needle, finally brought to London in 1878, ed)*, and they are all small. The largest is at Corfe Castle, no more than 22 feet in height, *(now at Kingston Lacy, Dorset, ed)*. There is one at Alnwick *(now at Durham University, ed)* and two smaller ones, truncated in the British Museum of black basalt. In France, there is one at Arles and another in Paris, an unbroken monolith, 76 feet and 6 inches above ground, brought from Luxor which forms the central decoration of the Place de la Concorde. In Florence there are two, in Istanbul two, and in Rome twelve.

Those in Rome are, for the most part, important in size as well as number. Also, they were the first removed from Egypt, the Emperors of Rome appearing to have a perfect passion for Egyptian obelisks. However, one must remember that there were originally forty-eight obelisks in the city. The catalogue or inventory of obelisks was compiled by Publius Victor, in the time of Valentinian and Valens, in AD364. The places of some of the missing obelisks are suspected, but at least thirty others are still to be accounted for.

The largest ancient obelisk now existing in the world is that called the 'Lateran', from its situation in front of the

Lateran Basilica in Rome. *(This is not the case, as the Obelisk of Hathsharpad at Karnak in Egypt is 129 ft and 9 inches, ed)*. This splendid obelisk, originally, as it appears, 105 feet high, in one block, was, in the first instance, erected at Thebes, in Upper Egypt, in the propyloeum of the Temple of Ammon Ra.

Pliny, in his encyclopaedia, 'Historia Naturalis', relates its first being set up in Thebes, writing: 'When it was on the point of being elevated, the king, being apprehensive that the machinery employed might not prove strong enough for the weight, with the view of increasing that might be entailed by due want of precaution on the part of the workmen, had his own son fastened to the summit, in order that the safety of the prince might, at the same time, ensure that of the mass of stone'. Pliny says this took place during the reign of Ramesses, king of Egypt during the Trojan war around about 1200BC. But obelisk readers discovered on it also the name of Tuthmosis III or IV, the 5th king of the 18th dynasty. Ungarelli assigned it an antiquity of 1740BC.

After remaining 2,000 years on its original site, the obelisk was floated down the Nile to Alexandria by the Emperor, Constantine, and conveyed by his son, Constantius, to Rome. The sea crossing was made in a vessel with 300 oars, and thence up the Tiber, to be taken on low-wheeled waggons, to the Circus Maximus, on the spina of which it was set up in AD357. Subsequently, at some time, it fell off its base and was discovered in 1588, interred to a depth of nearly twenty feet and broken into three pieces. It was re-erected in its present site by the architect Fontana at the orders of the energetic Pope, Sextus V.

Mr. Joseph Bonomi's notes about this are useful and he is extremely well-informed on the subject of Egyptian obelisks. He says:- "Having the opportunity of mounting on top of the pedestal in the winter of 1838, I found, by taking the dimensions of the lower part in a horizontal line, that it measured 12 palms 6 onei on two sides and on the other two sides 12 palms 10 onei".

The sides were dissimilar in breadth. When it was re-erected, from the necessity of cutting the base, so as to make it secure, and in the joining of the broken pieces, it seemed to have lost some of its length. It also received alterations to the pyramidions and apices and the addition of a cross and pedestal. With these additions it now measured 145 feet from the ground. It is supposed to weigh 450 tons. It is covered on all four sides with hieroglyphic characters, in which the various titles of the pharaoh (Tuthmosis) are recorded. Thus he was 'Lord of the upper and lower regions, and pleasant in his kingdom as the sun in heaven'. The same king is represented at the top of the obelisk as kneeling before Ammon, and presenting him with two cups, while the god in return holds out to him the symbol of life. Above him, cut in hieroglyphics, was this inscription: 'The bestower of perfect life, fortitude and all goodness, Ammon Ra, Lord of thrones'. Elsewhere on the obelisk, Horus is mentioned as 'Horus resplendent, the distributor of dominions and guardian of the double watch'.

Next in size and probably the best known, is the obelisk which stands in the centre of the piazza in front of St Peter's in Rome. Mr Bonomi measured this at a height of 83 feet and two inches, without the base, which was added at its re-erection in 1586. It has no hieroglyphs and was probably commissioned, rather than removed, from Heliopolis during the reign of Caligula to ornament a central development in Rome, which then became known as 'Nero's Circus'.

Significantly, this was the first large-scale fallen obelisk to be set up again in relatively modern times, and weighed 331 tons in one unbroken mass. Whilst workmen struggled to re-raise the stone, Pope Sixtus gave orders that no one should speak above a whisper, especially during the last moments of its attaining an upright position. Apparently, there was a fault of some kind and the machinery was 'chock and block' before it was quite vertical. The workmen could haul no more, and there it hung. There is a story which tells of this breathless crisis, and of a sailor, who, in defiance of the pope's order for silence, shouted out that they should wet the ropes. This done, the ropes contracted enough to draw up the huge monolith to its correct place. With the additions of base and ornaments to it, the obelisk reaches to 127 feet and 6 inches, and with the markings on the piazza paving, enacted by Pietro Maccarini, it serves as a gnomon of a vast dial.

A third notable obelisk is the Flaminian obelisk in the Piazza del Populo, a genuine Pharaohonic example. The Campensis obelisk on the Monte Citorio has beautiful hieroglyphics and the Pamphilian obelisk, in the Piazza Navona is associated with a fountain. There are also the Trinita del Monte and Aurelian obelisks, and five others, none of which are large.

Of the notable obelisks remaining in Egypt, the principal of these is the one standing at Karnak, which, at 93 feet and 6 inches from base to apex, is second only to the biggest in Rome. The Karnak obelisk comes from the time of Tuthmosis I. Its proportions are slender, and yet is has stood for nearly 4,000 years, which is proof of permanence. This contrasts, for example, with 'Cleopatra's Needle', which is only 69 feet tall, but has much wider proportions. These two well-known examples may be taken to represent the opposite limits between the massive and the taper of graceful proportions in obelisks, the ideal being somewhere between the two. Besides this, there are six other obelisks of large size still erect in Egypt, though not undamaged. In addition there are prostrate twelve more, all Pharaohonic; and, in the quarries at Asswan, at the first cateract, there is one partly cut'.

There was much that Sir John Gardner Wilkinson enjoyed and agreed with in this brief history, the first part of Bell's exposition of the obelisk, and yet he felt uneasy about where it was all leading. In seeing the obelisk as something of Egypt, he could hardly share the lecturing sculptor's view that the obelisk was a feature of art, and that it could be improved and improvised.

Then Bell continued, altering the course of his lecture to mention Definite Proportions and to introduce Entasis and the idea of the compensatory curve.

'Up to this, what I have put before you is greatly composed of the words of others, chiefly Mr Legrew, The Rev Richard Burgess and Mr Bonomi. I am unavoidably obliged to recount my own doings in regard to the additions of definite proportions and entasis to the obelisk. To begin with I will explain entasis and how it applies to Greek architecture.

Those few people who are in the habit of looking with interest upon features of architecture, have surely noticed the apparent concavity of long perfectly straight and flat forms. In regarding these, an appearance of concavity arises, insomuch that those who are not aware of this delusion of the eye, are apt to pronounce the sides actualy concave. No precise point or points can be specially indicated for this appearance of insufficiency, which seems to wander up and down tall forms, eating into their outline. This insuffiency, or apparent concavity, is painfully noticeable to the educated eye.

The adding of a compensatory fullness to lines of this character was not an occasional thing with the Greeks, but was one of their constant architectural principles, as is well exemplified in their columns. It is true that formerly this fact was not sufficiently regarded; nevertheless actual and most precise measurements on the spot have fully proved that this curvilinear and compensatory treatment was universally adapted in Athenian times.

What is extraordinary is that this compensatory treatment should ever have been lost sight of. Vitruvius, in his well known treatise on architecture, a text book of ancient art, described explicitly this treatment of both upright and transverse lines in architecture and registered this as a received principle in his time. Writing of columns, (in Book 3, Chapter 2), he says, 'The eye is constantly seeking after beauty, and if we do not endeavour to gratify it by proper proportions and increase of size, when necessary, and thus remedy the defect of vision, a work will look clumsy and disagreeable'.

Investigations in Athens have been made in our time by Messrs Pennethorne, Cockerell, Donaldson and Penrose; the elaborate work by the latter gentleman having now become the text book on the subject. Penrose resided in Greece for a considerable period and was indefatigable in measuring by the most delicate and accurate means the remains of Athenian edifices. In his investigation into the principles of Greek architecture, he stated, 'One of the principal objects of this work is the investigation of the delicate curves which form the principal architechtural lines of certain of the Greek buildings of the best period, which in ordinary architecture, are, or are intended to be, straight'.

I will try to lay before you some results of this gentleman's observations in as condensed form as possible. Firstly, regarding the column, and for brevity I will confine this to those of the Parthenon, although his research includes others with analoguous results. The sides of the columns of the Parthenon are not straight lines, but are somewhat curved and convex, or to use the express term, have an entasis on their sides.

The term entasis is derived from the Greek verb εντεινειν meaning to stretch a line or bend a bow. Thus the greatest amount of bend has come to be called the arrow or sagitta of that bend, and thus when we speak of the amount of entasis – we say an entasis of such and such a sagitta.

Now the 'sagitta' of the entasis of the columns of the Parthenon, that its greatest divergence from a straight line, is very slight, for it only amounts to $\frac{1}{552}$ part of the whole height (or 0.0019) of the shaft of the column. This, one might say, is so small that it could not be appreciated, but in practice, it fully does its duty and the shafts of the columns do not look hollow on the sides or weak in their intermediate portions, which they would have done had their contours been absolutely straight. The compensatory curve 'to remedy the defect in vision' has in this case, been so admirably adjusted as to offer a standard example, not to be surpassed, of this delicate architectural refinement.

Naturally, it next occurred to Penrose to find out what exact line of curve this was. He soon discovered it was not to be produced by a circle, however long the radius might be. It could not be a segment of any circle, for in that case the sagitta, or greatest deflection, would be at a point half-way up the column, which is not the case as the sagitta is rather between one third and one fourth up the column from the base.

As you look at the column, you will keep all this distinct from the general tapering of these columns. All columns of this character taper, which is seen from first sight. What these remarks on entasis apply to, is that they do not taper in straight lines, but in curved ones. Although the agreeable result and effect is perceptible to all eyes, they are so delicate in their degree of bending, that their curvature is not recognised at first, except by an eye expressly educated to the fact.

These curved lines of the Parthenaic columns, although they nearly approach to some portions of the conchoid of Nicomedes, and also of the catenary curve, are solely capable of being made by one geometric line – that of one of the simple conic sections – the hyperbola. Thus, Penrose pronounced the entasis of the Parthenon's columns to be a portion of a hyperbolic line, of which the more bent part is at the base and the straighter portion to the top of the shaft. Now, whether this line was in fact obtained by the Athenians from a strict conic section, or by a minute correction of the conchoid, adopted since by Vignola, or by use of the catenary curve, it is not necessary for us here to enter into.

With the horizontal, or transverse lines of Greek architecture, the same principles of delicate curves apply. Vitruvius said that these lines should rise somewhat towards the centre, or else they would appear to 'sink in the centre'. Again there is need of the compensatory curve, found on all principal Athenian structures, not only on the basement and stylobata, but also in the range of capitals of the columns and in the entablature. In these cases, Penrose pronounced this curve not to be that of the segment of a circle, but that of another of the simple conic sections, the parabola. The line of the front of the Parthenon is little more than 101 feet, and the rise in the centre is not more than between 2 and 3 inches. With respect to the whole setting out and structure of the Parthenon, Penrose held that even in the body of the building this slight rise in the centre takes place and even the tops of the columns are inclined somewhat inward towards the body of the temple

I will go no further into the adjustments of smaller details, as I am about to compare the elevation of the obelisk with the front of a Greek temple. Although of different proportions, the two general features possess similar elements – these are the upper and lower transverse lines, the sides and the roof lines. The shaft of the obelisk answers to the colonnade and entablature, and the pyramidions to the tympanum. In this way we may accept in a general point of view that the front of the temple is very wide, short obelisk, and the obelisk is a very tall temple.

We have seen that the sides of the columns of the parthenon taper and slope; so do the sides of the obelisk. We have also seen that these columns do so, not with straight sides, but with sides of very delicate entasis. I conceive that an obelisk should also have a lateral entasis and further, that the flat faces of my obelisk should have elliptical entasis on plan of very delicate sagitta all the way up. As therefore this treatment runs from the base of the shaft to the apex it adds a slightly upward arch to the base of the pyramidion.

THE OBELISK OF DEFINITE
PROPORTIONS AND ENTASIS

My attention was called to the subject of obelisks some years ago, by my having selected this feature for a memorial to The Great Exhibition of 1851.

In consequence of this, and in looking at two or three other obelisks, especially those models of Egyptian obelisks presented to the British Museum by Mr.Bonomi, it appeared to me that there was an appparent weakness and insufficiency in their form, and that their sides looked concave.

I at first attempted to remedy this defect, by contracting the shaft at the top, by sloping the sides more, still however, keeping those sides straight. This did not work and moreover, it marred the proportions of the obelisk and had little effect on the apparent concavity.

I determined to put in practice an idea which had been floating in my mind for some time; that was to add entasis to the sides, analogous to what the Greeks did with their columns. For this purpose I had a cast of my little obelisk split down the centre of the four sides, and opened out at the top somewhat more than the due proportion, so to allow for rounding the sides upwardly a little, the divisions being filled up level with plaster. I then rounded the sides with a gradual but almost imperceptible entasis upwardly, until I had done away with the look of concavity. I did this with rasp and sandpaper until I had satisfied my eye, and I confess the result pleased me. This was the first step .

However, when I had done this, I conceived that the surfaces looked somewhat concave horizontally on plan, and that I might obviate this, I decided to make these slightly convex horizontally, by a segment of a circle bowing outwards. For this line , eventually, I substituted a segment of the flat side of an ellipse, as more suitable for an obelisk. I then curved the top transverse lines and surfaces of the pyramidion and so on until not a straight was left on base. These were all, however of a very delicate entasis, only compensatory, and considering the small scale and material of my model, necessarily incomplete.

At about the same time I had taken the opportunity of setting forth somewhat prominently a proposal that the principal feature of the memorial of the Great Exhibition of 1851, should be a polished monolith obelisk of British granite, with all the names of the participating countries inscribed on it, combined with a public drinkingfountain, to be placed in the centre of the site of the Great Exhibition in Hyde Park, and that it should be an obelisk of entasis.

Consequently, I was invited by the Royal Institute of British Architects to lay my views before them of the principle of entasis as applied to the obelisk. This I had the honour of doing last May (1858). At the commencement of the evening a most interesting paper was read by the Rev. Mr Burgess, entitled, 'On the Egyptian obelisks in Rome, and Monoliths as Monuments in Great Cities', in which he recommended their adoption here in Britain. This introduced my paper, from which I will provide an extract.

I said that had the Greeks adopted the obelisk, as they did other component parts of Egyptian architecture, then in all probability they would have modified it in some degree, as with the column. The tomb of Beni Hassan, in Egypt, presented pillars, which, on account of the remarkable similarity between them and those of the Greek Doric order, had received the name of 'Proto-doric'. These Egyptian pillars, however, are destitute of entasis, which the Greek Doric examples possess on scientific principles. In certain other Egyptian columns the shafts contract boldly at base, but this was not a scientific compensatory entasis analogous to the Greek in principle.

I detailed the making of my sketch model, and how in its case the mission of entasis did not appear to end while there was a single straight line remained on the obelisk, nor the eye be satisfied until every portion was clothed with these delicate curves. I remarked on the yearning which a straight-sided obelisk seems to express for compensatory adjustments. Desiring also to test before such authorities whether I had been anticipated in my views and experiments, I invited information on that point. In the discussion which followed, Mr Bonomi said that when he and Mr Angell had been in Rome together, Angell had suggested the erection of scaffolding to measure the obelisks, with a view to ascertain whether they had any entasis. But this idea was not carried out. Both Bonomi and Mr Poole, both residents for a considerable time in Egypt, told me that they had never detected any entasis on obelisks there, nor does any other authority allude to it. And if, it was remarked, these features of art were in early times symbols of the sun's rays, this does not favour entasis, as assuredly a ray of the sun has no entasis.

Now, as regards my own attempt at a solution of this problem of applying curvilinear treatment to the obelisk, I have brought you up to date with last year's meeting at the Institute, at which time I had made no more than a little sketch model, the scale of which was not suitable for refinements of detail. I have now built a larger model, not far short of 20 feet, which has afforded me the opportunity of carrying the whole problem considerably beyond the point at which it then rested.

In my first little model, I had adjusted its proportions and lines solely by eye, and executed them by what in homely phrase is called, 'the rule of thumb'. Now that I had to have an enlarged one executed by workmen, I had, of course, to furnish them with definite proportions to work by. I went to work, therefore, for the first time with my compasses, to seek out in the first little model what definite proportions it really contained. I had told my assistants that I thought the pyramidion a hair's breadth too short, and so I added a slight increase to the working drawing. It was a very small correction and the only variation between the original model and the drawing, which showed the ground plan of each member.

As for my method, I now began to measure my little model to find out which definite proportions it contained, when the following coincidences came out quite unexpectedly, between what I had done by eye and a consistent code of definite geometric proportions.

In the first place I found, with my compasses, that the diagonal of the base of the pyramidion was exactly equal to the side of the base of the obelisk. In searching further I found that this also gave the exact vertical height of the pyramidion. So here was a treble coincidence, of the most simple and definite nature.

Firstly – that the diagonal of the base of the pyramidion; *secondly* – the side of the base of the obelisk; and *thirdly* – the height of the pyramidion, should all be one and the same measure.

Encouraged by this, I hoped that applying this fortunate unit of measurement to the whole height of the obelisk, I might be favoured again as to find that it formed some quotient part of this. But no, it would not fit any: the measurement broke down and I felt I was at fault. Having, however, already found that the diagonal of the pyramidion gave the side of the base of the obelisk, it occurred to me to try the diagonal of that base, that of the obelisk itself, and having taken this, I began with my compasses walking up the vertical height of my obelisk, 1, 2, 3, 4, 5, 6, 7, when to my surprise, and, perhaps you will smile when I add, to my great satisfaction, I found that I landed with the seventh stride of the diagonal of the base exactly at the apex!

Thus, seven times the diagonal of the base of the obelisk was the exact measurement of the vertical height of the obelisk.

So here were all the general proportions of my obelisk defined by one simple code of exact geometric proportions, of which the pyramidion was the key and pivot. There were others in my studio, who witnessed the progress of this obelisk and they know that I have not 'cooked' my account in the least.

As regards the number 7, as it is an element of so many things of great import, and characterised, as it is, as 'the perfect number'. In the same way that in the Parthenon, Penrose declared, all proportions bear relations, one to another, and there is a pivot measure, the difference between the diameters at the top and base of the shaft of one of the columns. In like manner, all proportions of my obelisk possess a direct geometric relation. Taking a base of a cone of which the vertical height is equal to the diameter, the inscribed square is the base of the pyramidion, and the circumscribed square the base of the obelisk and so on.

This application of the cone to the pyramidion will serve to introduce the second portion of my treatment, that of applying the conic sections to clothe it with its various entases.

As you know, the simple conic sections are of five different characters:

      1.-Rectilinear section through the apex, of which the side of the pyramidion is an example.

      2.-Circular section, cutting the cone in a plane at right angles with the axis.

      3.-Elliptical section, cutting the cone across, but not at a right angle, slanting as it were.

      4.-Parabolic section, which is a section parallel to the sides of the cone and which would never cut the cone, however much it was extended.

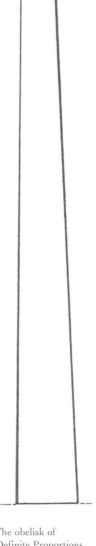

The obelisk of Definite Proportions drawn by Richard Barnes, after Bell's formula.

5.-Hyperbolic section, which from its direction further approaching that of the axis still wider, avoids cutting the cone across.

Lines derived from each and all of these qualities of section come in to complete the obelisk and base and endue with a compensatory fullness the cone produced by the definite proportions. The hyperbolic line which would indicate the lateral entases should be at a point on level with two diagonals of the base below the base, as in the case of the Parthenon. This also indicates the depth of the base, and entasis is struck from the ground line of this base. There appears a principle in this, and the entasis thus obtained for the obelisk came out quite satisfactory, being just compensatory and no more. The sagitta of this curve is little more than one inch on the elevation in an obelisk 77 feet and 9 inches tall. This entasis is less than that of the columns of the Parthenon, but more than that on those of the Erectheum. Guidance throughout has been through conjoined working of all the five simple conic sections, together with the perfect number 7 and a code of definite geometric proportions, of which each bears a direct relation to every other.

I would be sorry to be thought presuming that the code I have adopted is the only one to be applied to the obelisk. I am very far from thinking this, although I might hope that some general points of value may be indicated by the adventures of my solution. Also, in regard to the conic sections, although I myself think these marvellous curves which regulate the paths of heavenly bodies are also those which chiefly form the curves of the leaf, the petals of the flower and the graceful contours of the female form – I am delighted to acknowledge the charm of other natural curves such as the conchoid, the cardioid and the catenary etc., as applicable to art.

The view which I take of the obelisk is that it is a feature of art yet undeveloped, one which, as far I can discover, is in the same state in which it was left by the Pharaohs. Also, that it is a feature highly suited to monumental record; and therefore for these two causes, offering a fine fresh field for invention, both in regard to general proportion and minor details. My own I have introduced as a humble illustration of the working together of the eye in accordance with geometric proportions. My illustration may be inadequate, but the general principle is one which few people these days will be found to ignore, viz., that Science and Art should work together. The Greeks have amply proved their adherence to this maxim, which I offer as the moral of my remarks here.

This is not to suggest that a work of art is to be built up by the Rule of Three. To hold that would, in my idea, be pedantry. We have been endowed with direct perceptions of beauty, which we should be absurd to lay aside to take up, instead, logarithms or algebra, but as in sort geometry is the essence of reason, so, rightly applied, it comes in to give definition and satisfaction to all forms of art.

'Nature' has been said 'to work by geometry'. In the achievment of forms of beauty, I hold that definite geometric proportions may be of the greatest practical use in aiding the eye, when you are so fortunate as to discover that ratio of their code which is in harmony with the subject at hand. In undertakings of this kind, the square and the circle, mutually inscribed and circumscribed, appear to afford a code of great value, not only as applied to the Parthenon, and to the obelisk, but also to the proportions of the human frame and a good many other things.

In the progress of the special problem of the obelisk, I have only the pleasant duty of acknowledging the liberality of feeling extended to me by the architectural profession. Mr Angell, Mr Bellamy, Mr Bonomi, Mr Tite, Mr Donaldson and others have given me special encouragement and I have had much assistance from Mr Penrose in Athens. I have especially to acknowledge the direct assistance of Mr Joseph Jopling, a gentleman who is well known as having made definite proportions and scientific curves his special study. Perhaps also, in conclusion, the best excuse that I, as a sculptor, can offer for my having taken up this subject at all, is to be found in the remark made by that gentleman (himself an architect) one day in my studio, when he said to me, "You sculptors have your minds and eyes so constantly directed to form that your training is especially adapted to educate your perception of proportions and curves".

V

OBELISKS IN CEMETERIES AND THE RISE OF POLISHED GRANITE

The largest number of obelisks in Britain, let us say somewhere between one thousand and one and a half thousand, dating from about 1820 to 1890, stand in cemeteries.

The first non-denominational public cemetery, The Rosary, was begun in Rosary Road, in Norwich in 1819, opening for business in 1821. It was about twelve acres of hill and vale and within eighty years it was full. Among the memorials it has sixteen obelisks dotted about, some in groups; these include two fifteen feet tall monoliths, though most are 7 footers of red, black, or grey-white polished granite. There are others of limestone and sandstone. Some are ivy-clad, others slightly askew as the roots of those trees, planted nearly two hundred years ago, lift and buckle the pathways.

In London, cholera in 1832 and again in 1848 as well as a general rise of infectious diseases in the growing city populations, brought about the Parliamentary legislation leading to the rise of new cemeteries and necropoleis. There had been other problems, including widespread grave-robbing for corpses. London's old grave yards were full and overflowing, a fearsome sight, where dogs and rats roamed among broken tombs. Cremation, of course, was still illegal. The considered response was to move the dead out of the urban centres to a safe distance, where land could be bought cheaply and sometimes by compulsory purchase, where memorials could safely be placed along sylvan paths near a pretty Chapel of Rest.

All over Britain, cemetery companies were set up and new land acquired for this business. In 1825 the Low Hill General Cemetery, also known as the Liverpool Necropolis opened, as did the neighbouring St James's Cemetery. Within five years the latter was returning a dividend of 8% to its shareholders. A return dividend of 12% was sometimes achieved, considerably more than the railways or other investments could offer. From 1851 onwards most new cemeteries were governed by Burial Boards and from 1890 controlled by municipal authorities.[1]

Kensal Green Cemetery, a 'Victorian Valhalla' consisting of 80 acres in West London, purchased in 1831 and consecrated in 1833, was noted for its grandness, not only of the overall design, but in the quality of memorials. Cemeteries such as this, where death had been made beautiful, were a civic amenity proudly shown to foreign visitors. Polite society might stroll among Grecian temples, or Neo-gothic chapels, beneath cypress trees. In the case of Kensal Green, the selection for trees was changed from Loudon's recommendations; instead of cypresses, the avenue plantings were of sweet chestnut and oriental plane, which were to cause problems for obelisks long after.

At Kensal Green, there are about seventy obelisks, which appear positively minimalist among the mausolea and commemorative extravaganza. They seem to cluster: a group of three are a memorial to the family of Henry Wheeler,1790-1860. Elsewhere, two or three minor obelisks in Carrara or Sicilian marble have had their outline and surface badly degraded. These materials are not suitable for British winters, the problems exacerbated, Pevsner suggests, by pollution from the adjacent gasworks, not to mention acid rain from modern times. The cemetery is also bordered by a canal and a railway line, essential for transporting heavy masonry. The coming of railways caused stone from faraway regions to be transported easily and granite, the true composition of the obelisk, had become available.

Polished granite memorials are unaffected and their surfaces are still in very good order. A grey granite 1892 obelisk, the memorial to Helen Mackenzie, has delicate decoration with patterns and lines cut by light grit blasting. The 1878 memorial obelisk to Arthur Litchfield stands over grave 26537, its base surrounded by six miniature granite obelisks, only two feet tall. The biggest obelisk, with a 24 ft monolith and a 10 ft pedestal, all of Peterhead red granite, was raised in 1868 to Sir Richard Mayne, the first Commissioner of the Metropolitan Police and paid for by his officers and constables. It is currently caught in the branches of the mature chestnuts of the avenue and cannot be seen properly.

There is another obelisk of the same red polished granite in the main avenue, towering over a classically fronted mausoleum; this too has a 24 ft monolith supported by a pedestal and base, reaching a total height of 35 feet. It is perhaps a suitable commemoration of Joseph Richardson, who died in 1855, and subsequent members of his family. Richardson was a Cumberland mason, who had discovered that strange music could be made by striking slices of certain rocks. He had created an instrument called the 'Rock Harmonicon', which his family played in public. Apparently, some of the Richardson's audiences would fall into trances, later claiming that the strange sounds had affected them, vibrating their bones and brains to the core.

These two magnificent monoliths of gleaming red granite in Kensal Green share the title of the largest monoliths in Britain. The other contender, made by the same firm in the same granite works, was the memorial to Henry Bell on the esplanade at Helensburgh near Dumbarton. If anything, the obelisk at Helensburgh may be a fraction bigger, though it has a stepped base rather than a plinth.

Questions of taste are extremely interesting and will be discussed at length. It is worth mentioning the personal choice of John Claudius Loudon,1783-1843, the one armed Scottish gardener and architect. Loudon was also a busy publisher and founder-editor of *The Gardener's Magazine*. In the year of his death he issued a book, *On the Laying out, Planting, and Managing of Cemeteries and On the Improvements of Churchyards*. He observed that, 'All burial grounds... when once filled... should be shut up as burying grounds and a few years afterwards opened as public walks or gardens...'

Loudon was the very arbiter of good taste and the unparalleled authority on cemetery landscaping. For his own Kensal Green memorial, Loudon chose an urn on a plain pedestal. He had previously put up in 1831 an extraordinary memorial to his parents in Pinner churchyard, which featured either ends of a sarcophagus emerging from a clumsy obelisk. This surreal concept was designed to part-appease his father's request to be buried above ground[2]. However, the choice of memorial was seldom made by the deceased, but by their family, very often with the guidance of suppliers and agents.

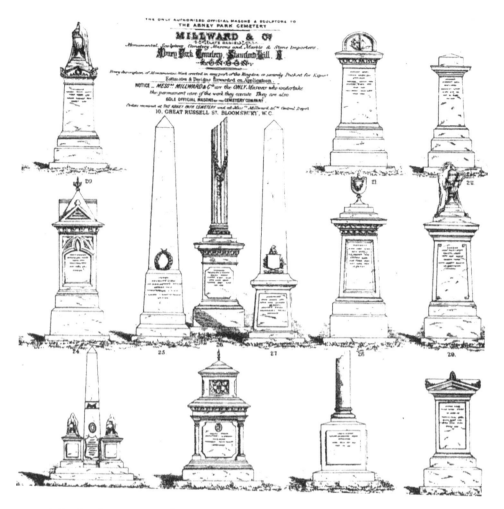

While the finest mausoleum, as seen in Kensal Green or Nunhead cemeteries, might have cost cost five or six thousand pounds in 1860, about a quarter of a million today, obelisks came much cheaper. There were a number of obelisk 'designs' in stock. Looking at the catalogue of memorials from Milward & Co, formerly Daniels, 'The only authorised and official Masons and Sculptors to Abney Park Cemetery', one sees several memorials on a single page. Three of these are obelisks and the rest are broken columns, shrouded vases and neo-gothic roofed miniature structures.

Of the obelisks, there are two with pedestals, one smooth in outline, the other with a sort of moulded balustrade between pedestal and shaft. One is inscribed, the other has a bronze plaque with an inscription. These would use less ground area than the third, which does not have a plinth, but rises straight from a wide stepped base,

Considering prices for obelisks, it can be seen from copy orders at Farley's Monumental Masons, situated opposite the gates of Kensal Green, that polished granite was referred to as 'highly polished'. Further details inform us that all inscriptions were drilled and then blacked or filled with white lead and then perhaps painted gold. The following copy order entry supplies a scaled diagram of an obelisk with a three stepped base. The height of the shaft was 9 feet, 9 inches; the overall height of the memorial was 15 feet, 6 inches. The sum quoted did not include the price of the plot at Ilford.

> Friday Feb'u 5th 1875
>
> A highly polished red granite Obelisk with York Landing to be fixed at Ilford Cemetery on grave No 450X, and the following cut and blacked-
>
> In Memory of Joseph Edward Fisher, who died Jan'y 4th 1875, Aged 54.
>
> "Not lost but gone before".
>
> Obelisk & Landing £34
>
> letters -at 7d each

This is a useful gauge, providing a price for the obelisk, the 'landing' or stone paved area around it and the letter-cutting price of 7 pence per letter – or 34 letters to the pound.

Difficult though it is to understand these old prices in a modern equivalent, it is known that a week's wages for an ordinary stonemason in Manchester in 1887 was close to £1-10-0, or £1.50 a week. All in all, this suggests that this obelisk memorial at £34 in 1875 represents at least £6,000 today.

There are many obelisks in cemeteries which are difficult to identify individually by inscriptions on granite surfaces. In the case of granite, the hardness posed a problem for some workmen. They might have done the best they could and finished there, or added paint, to mask the fact that the lettering was not cut deep enough to be lastingly legible. Where bronze plaques were used to overcome the difficulty of inscribing granite, they were liable to become detached.

Obelisks stand, in their hundreds, among other memorials in London's suburban cemeteries in Highgate, Kensal Rise, Brompton, Norwood, Hanwell, Nunhead near Peckham, Little Ilford, Willesden and others places. At Brookwood near Woking, The London Necropolis and National Mausoleum Company, opened in 1854 having made arrangements with several London parishes. In all there are 103 cemeteries within a nine mile radius of central London, comprising a total of 3,000 acres. The list of provincial cemeteries is very long: Barnstaple, Bath, Bradford, Arno's Grove in Bristol, Exeter, Liverpool, Mansfield, Hull, Leicester, Norwich, Manchester, Sheffield, York – to name a few. Scottish cemeteries are very fine indeed, especially those at Arbroath, Dumfries, Edinburgh, Dumbarton and Glasgow's Necropolis.

Dumbarton Cemetery, opened in 1854, became the place for wealthy shipbuilers to be buried. I made a visit and saw about forty obelisks among mausolea, crosses and shrines. The biggest obelisk, a 20 feet monolith of millstone on a 10 feet high base, was the 1854 obelisk to William Denny, shipbuilder. Three or four others are memorials to other family members. Elswhere in the cemetery, obelisks line the path; two of them resemble tree trunks because they have their upper parts firmly stuck in an ornamental evergreen, quite typical in old cemeteries.

Within a few years of their opening, most cemeteries were practically full. Where obelisks were juxtaposed with the whole panoply of British memorials – the tombs, mausolea, urns, sarcophogi, crosses, angels and so on – they suffered a loss of impact. Sometimes they were allowed the space to pierce the clouds, as in the cemetery at Undercliffe in Bradford, where Joseph Smith, the surveyor of the cemetery, pre-selected a hilltop site for his own 1858 memorial, a tall grey granite obelisk.

And, while the Quaker Movement considered all memoralia as vanity and arrogance, the Society of Friends decided to raise an impressive large obelisk, about twenty feet tall, in an unconsecrated part of the 60 acre Great Northern Cemetery. This was supposed to serve as communal memorial for numerous Quakers who would be buried around it in the 1890s, though nowadays its identifying plaques have gone. Occasionally, an obelisk was put up in a cemetery without an associated grave. The 1851 Martyr's Memorial in Nunhead Cemetery, raised by subscription by J Hume MP, was an obelisk in memory of a group of Scottish Nationalist reformists who were exiled in Australia in 1793. In Kensal Green there is a granite obelisk raised to Robert Owen, one of the fathers of Socialism, who died in 1858 and was buried elsewhere.

The presence of obelisks, which are basically not funereal, in direct association with burial in cemeteries, affects the way people perceive them. It has also led this enquiry towards a narrow view of the history of cemeteries. The whole subject is truly fascinating, especially since it directly altered attitudes to death in Britain, and indirectly elsewhere. A recommendation to all readers is *The Victorian Celebration of Death*, in which James Stevens Curl's enthusiasm, architectural knowledge and pleasing writing enhance a very interesting history.

Today, many of Britain's memorial obelisks inside these cemeteries, and indeed the cemeteries themselves, are under threat. Ground can be easily cleared and structures moved or demolished. Land hungry local authorities and property developers lurk by the perimeter, eyeing crumbling memorials and planning what they would like to do with the place once the site is cleared. Needless to say, there are other modern threats: theft of marble details, typically the decapitation of angels, and vandalism – usually in the drunken form of pushing down an upright memorial. The undergrowth does more than threaten. Those shrubs and trees of the original plantings, with bulging, sinuous ivy the chief culprit, have completely hidden parts of cemeteries which were accessible thirty years ago.

As the decay through neglect proceeds in a cemetery, the obelisks among the memorials present a strong resistance to final destruction. Nearly all of them are monoliths on plinths, secured by alloy pins, and they can be pushed over. Their granite solidness will endure and some will sink into the ground just as they did in Rome.

Anybody who as ever been to a cemetery and seen the contrast between memorials of polished granite and those of any other commonly used stone, will bear witness to a very obvious fact. When it comes to endurance against corrosion from pollution, lichen, frost and ice, there is no comparison. The granite monuments, aged about 150 years, appear as if they were raised a few days ago. All other materials are in a degraded state, their surfaces pitted and maybe blackened.

All ancient Egyptian obelisks are granite. In the mind of John Bell, there was no question that obelisks should be anything other than this stone. Still in full spate to promote his proposal for a Great Exhibition

Memorial obelisk, he offered another lecture. After looking into his books and questioning great men of the day, he appeared at the Royal Society of Arts, where he was on the committee, on 14th March 1860. He arrived with some sacks containing different samples of granite and a jumping iron. This lecture about granite is notable and very much in keeping with the pre-occupation with the obelisk, and Bell's earlier lectures upon 'that feature of art'.

"The subject on which I am about to make a few remarks is The Art Treatment of Granite surfaces. This is an occasion to speak of the ancient Egyptians as our masters of this art, but also to give some practical reference to this country and the present day.

Although granite has occasionally been worked in this country locally, it did not come largely into use in our national and large structures until the late 18th century, with Old Westminster, and Southwark, and London Bridges, by the Rennies being practically the earliest in which it was the main material. The style of workmanship adopted in these cases has been in blocks, large, simple and massive. The Egyptians treated it in the same mannner, but with this difference, they also added to the broad surfaces thus attained a variety of decorative and illustrative encised ornament.

Various of the world's oldest structures are in granite. Some of the simpler features surviving in Egypt, nearly perfect, date back between 3,000 and 4,000 years. The value and interest that attaches to this material for architectural purposes, spreads over a great extent of human time.

This, however, is of course but yesterday to the remote period when the granite was itself formed. It is an igneous or volcanic rock, though not irruptive, formed when the solution of its contents in water reached high temperatures. It is liable to divisions of a bubble form, like the layers of an onion, known to quarrymen as 'the bedway' and the scale of things is such that it does not prevent the obtaining straight blocks of 100 feet and more.

The well known constituent parts of granite are quartz, mica and felspar, but these questions are not in my specialty. Enough has been said to show that these are compounded into one mass of great compactness and also, as we know, in different cases, of various colours. In the few examples I have before you, however, you see that red and grey form the two great varieties in granite, yet that there are many intermediate gradations in which nature appears to have ranged her tints to suit all tastes. Most of these are vastly improved by polishing, then also affording examples of completeness combined with endurance of surface not be reached by any other material except gems. In thus speaking of this quality of stone, I of course include the syenites, basalts, and porphyries, which are of the same family. Black basalt was used occasionally, both in Egypt and in Assyria, for art purposes, as also porphyry, both stones of great beauty and hardness.

I dare say many of those present must have seen the porphyry sarcophagus of Napoleon I, in the noble cenotaph in the chapel of the Hotel des invalides in Paris, rising from the centre of the vault in so grand a manner, and which is destined to hold the ashes of the great warrior. The block of porphyry out of which this was formed, was of such hardness that no one person or set of men could be obtained to go through with the execution of it. Nearly every workman in Paris had a touch at it, but necessarily gave it up in weariness. It broke their hearts as well as their tools. Not that each did not do something, for each did, and thus eventually it became completed and polished, and a magnificent sarcophagus it is; but it was too intractable to suit the vivacity of our French neighbours. All this was told to me by a young French carver when I was in Paris in 1855, who added that he himself had three days of it, which was quite enough.

Indeed the hardness of this class of material is one of the considerations that renders the vast architectural and sculptural works achieved by the ancient Egyptians, so great a marvel. Although recent research has told us so much about ancient Egypt, and, lit greatly by the lamp of that invaluable obelisk, the Rosetta stone in the British Museum, has so well deciphered the hieroglyphic writing that we know much about the history and manners and even domestic customs of ancient Egyptians, but we still do not know how they worked their granite.

It is true that for other purposes they had tools of steel, as knives, represented blue in their paintings, as well as copper or bronze ones, represented red, yet in the paintings the chisels for stone work are usually painted of the latter colour. Thus it is considered that they used bronze chisels. If so, they must have had a very superior mode of hardening that alloy to any we possess.

Even as regards steel, our own tools of modern times soon get abashed before the surfaces of the harder granites. Difficulty was experienced with the well-known fragment of Memnon, in the British Museum, more properly Tuthmosis III. This great bust has a fracture on the shoulders. In fact the head was first obtained, and the other portion was sent over to us by the French. To attach this to the other portion, it was thought fit to have a hole made to receive a bar to connect them. Our workmen were six weeks making this hole and broke a great number of tools in the operation.

The use of emery powder and of the drill and wheel has been suggested as having aided in cutting the encised work on granite, and anyone who has witnessed the rapid manner in which this process cuts our hardest glass, hardly to be scratched, even by anything other than a diamond, will acknowledge the unexpected power of this process. It has also been conjectured that emery powder was used in sawing Egyptian granite. No doubt it was in polishing it, of which we have many representations. This however does not help us much as to the more general fashioning of the great granite structures of Egypt.

One element of workmanship, the ancient Egyptians possessed in profusion, under their system, namely that of labour and time. Undoubtedly the marvels of Egyptian granite workmanship were mainly produced by the unpitying use of these. Water dropping will, in the end, wear a hole in the hardest stone, but we do not now like to see human hands and energies lavished in drudgery of that description. We desire the utmost economy of these now. They had no such ideas. Year after year, for instance, no doubt passed in fashioning an obelisk, and completing its decorations.

I have no doubt that our modern steam power and machinery, if properly used, would easily accomplish within weeks what the Egyptians took years to achieve. In modern days the great columns of St Isaac's church in St Petersburg, which are cach of one block of red granite, 50 feet high, and 10 feet across the base, took a long time in executing. These magnificent shafts are also polished. The shaft of the column of Alexander in the same city, is yet higher than these, being 80 feet in one block. The block out of which it was fashioned was originally 93 feet, the same height as the great obelisk at Karnak, but the proportions of the column having been decided upon, they cut off 13 feet, which seems a pity!

In Britain machinery has been applied to turning granite pillars, to working mouldings and to polishing, but not as yet to cutting decorations. As things stand, our modern times have never reached to the achievements of ancient Egypt, either in the works of granite or in the decorations of its surface.

The most favoured decorations encised in relief in granite were connected to the Nile, being encised reliefs of floral designs from stems of Papyrus and petals of the Lotus or Water Lily. Most will be aware of the usual treatment of relievo, or relief, as in the Greek and Roman relievi, in the British Museum, and as usually practised in the present day. This consists of a flat surface, or background from which the sculptured figures project, more or less. This was not the practice of the Egyptians. Their figures in relievo did not project, but were rather impressed, being tacked in, as it were, round the edges into the surface – the highest part of the figures being only level with the surrounding plain face into which they were cut, and this is called incised relievo, in contradistinction to projecting relievo.

One remarkable art quality which must not be overlooked in this encised method of relievo , viz., that while it finely decorates a surface it does not disturb its breadth, enough of the true original surface always remaining to assert that. Nor does it take away from the impression of solidity, nor does it injure the profile. You would recognise at once the effect of an obelisk would be destroyed by any projecting relievo on its faces, how its grace and character would be lost at once. Another advantage of this style of work is its enduring character, especially in granite as with Egyptian works, in which encised relievo has stood exposed to the atmosphere for more than 3,000 years, without being materially injured.

Before we go into the subject of decorations and further uses of granite, it may be interesting to glance over our chief localities of native British granite. Scottish granite of Aberdeen and its neighbourhood is much and justly celebrated, that from the quarries of Darncing-Cairn-Rubislaw and Tyrebagger is grey; around Peterhead the red granite chiefly prevails, of a fine deep colour. The West of Scotland also yields fine granite, some of the best being from Mull. Ireland also has granite of various qualities, from Wicklow, Down, Newry,&c.

Various parts of England yield granite. Leicestershire provides, among others, the brownish-red kind, known as the Mount Sorel, which is very hard and has come much into use of late for paving. Of the southern part of our Isles, however, no portions are in this respect more celebrated than Devon and Cornwall. On the extended plains of Dartmoor, there are on the surface, or only partially embedded, boulders of granite, sufficiently large, apparently, to furnish blocks as big as those used in Egypt. Heytor granite is notable, and so is the nearly white granite from near Okehampton.

Cornwall is a most prolific county for granite. Various granites of this county were used in the new Westminster Bridge, from the quarries of Lamorna, Penryn, &c. Granite from the quarries near the Cheesering on Bodmin Moor was much used in the bridge, and gives much satisfaction. It is of a fine even texture, of which the crystals, while large enough to be seen as granite, are yet not so large as to interfere with the appearance of decorative work put on it. From its delicate grey tint, especially when polished, it forms a most pleasant combination with gold, as in letters and devices cut into the surface and gilt.

The modes of working the granite are, I believe, much alike in all British quarries. Holes are drilled or 'jumped', into the rock; these are supplied with gunpowder and fired, and thus the great masses are blasted out, which are afterwards split into blocks with gear consisting of steel wedges and 'feathers' as they are called. These are inserted into a partial split, once a crack has been started. After that a block may be fashioned with a large hammer, called a muckle and pitching tool, and various picks, points and chisels. If a fine surface is required, it is axed.

When holes are to be made, they are frequently jumped. The jumping iron is a long bar, thick in the centre to hold it by, with a chisel edge at both ends. It is used by being raised and let fall with a jumping motion, whence its name, and by being partially turned after each blow, thus wins its way through the hardest block. Polishing, when required, is now done greatly by steam. This process much enhances the appearance of most granite, but it is, from the hardness of the material, necessarily costly. In a general way the cost of polishing may be set down as an addition of one-half the previous cost. Thus if a column costs £20 fine axed, it will cost £30, or something more, polished.

Perhaps it will be interesting to you to hear of three different ways in which long blocks of granite, adapted to columns and obelisks, have, in different countries, been safely detached from their native bed. In Egypt the blocks are said to have been greatly wrought on three sides in their native bed; the stone in front, above, below, and at each end, having been worked away, so as to leave them projecting, and attached only by one side to the rock. Then the process was also to cut, between it and the rock, holes at intervals. Into these holes were driven, quite tight, very dry small billets of wood, exactly fitting them, which, afterwards beng amply and continuously supplied with water, swelled by absorbtion, and burst off the block. This mode was formerly used in some of our own quarries.

In India, a long block was in a similar way fashioned horizontally on its native bed, at last in like manner hanging to the side of it. But this was detached by a different process, the aid of fire being called in as well as water. On the top surface, between the obelisk and the rock, a long deep groove was chiselled extending the whole length. This was kept full of fire, of live embers, at a great heat for some days, when all at once these were swept out and cold water poured in the whole length of the groove, when the sudden contraction split off the mass neatly from end to end.

In Russia a still different method was applied – that of frost. When the huge columns of St Isaac's church had been similarly wrought in their native bed, holes were made all along their attachments, and filled with water, which, expanding in freezing, burst off the block. So, as can be seen, there are several ways in which this apparently difficult process may be simply effected. Practically, however, in the British quarries, when a large block is pretty near separation, and is left for a night, it frequently detaches itself, owing, also, as is supposed, to some effect of change of temperature".

Bell's lecture continued with much reference to suitable forms of encised relief decoration. At the end of the evening, members of the audience spoke from the floor. At least three of them, including Sir John Rennie, whose father had built London Bridge and Waterloo Bridge, related experiences with granite. All agreed that it was expensive to buy, transport and work. Polishing added at least another half to the final cost.

Though there were granite works in other regions, none could compete with Alexander MacDonald & Co, Limited, Aberdeen Granite Works, Constitution Street, Aberdeen – Quarry Masters and Workers in Polished Granite to The Queen. The firm manufactured a large proportion of Britain's obelisks.

Alexander MacDonald,1794-1860, was a crofter's son from Perthshire who had completed an apprenticeship as a stone mason before arriving in Aberdeen in 1820. He opened a stonecutting yard in the city's Denburn district and soon acquired larger premises in West North Street. Initially making hearth and headstones and minor marble pieces, he made no attempt with the local granite. For a number of reasons, the region's granite industry was already beginning its rise to pre-eminence. Thomas Telford's improvements to the dockyards gave access to all sea routes, and Scottish stone received preferential shipping as ballast. Turnpikes paved with granite setts to accommodate heavier loads, the construction of the Inverurie canal and the coming of railway lines connecting the inland quarries to the port – all helped.

Significantly, in 1829, Alexander MacDonald heard of an exhibition of polished granite works from Ancient Egypt which was to be held in London[3]. The Egyptologist-showman, the mighty Giovanni Belzoni, had returned from Egypt, and presented samples and finds from the Nile, including pieces of polished granite, to the British Museum. MacDonald made the sea journey to London and, after seeing the exhibits, returned home and began to experiment with Scottish granite and different hand polishing techniques, which were more akin to the jeweller's art with gemstones. He was soon able to take advantage of available steam power from his neighbours, Stewart's comb factory, and quickly set about inventing belt-driven polishers.

These were the Lathe, the Pendulum, and the Carriage or Waggon polisher, the last for use on flat surfaces. The Pendulum was a frame attached to the roof of the workshop with iron rods and a series of iron rings through which the stone was passed back and forth. Other innovations of the period came from elsewhere, such as vertical polishers and the hand-held Bush hammer, a multi-bladed adze or axe for cutting stone. Much later came the 'Jenny Lind', a polisher which sang as it emery-polished.

The quarries provided MacDonald with polishing stone, which was granite of sufficient quality to be worthwhile polishing, and which cost more than the average stone. Initially, the surface was flattened by rubbing, or 'shotting', with sea sand. Water was sluiced over the stone throughout. Then the process was repeated using emery sand, which provided a slightly polished finish. Finally, the granite was rubbed, or 'rouged' with iron-oxide until a satisfactory polished effect was attained.

By 1832, Alexander MacDonald was sufficiently confident with early results to send down a sample work of polished granite to London's Kensal Green Cemetery in the same year of its inception. Orders were to follow in colossal numbers, his firm eventually accounting for half Britain's obelisks, for which polished granite was the authentic material, as in Ancient Egypt.

It was a new material and the beginning of a great industry, one in which Scotland was to lead the world. MacDonald's Aberdeen Granite Works exhibited and won prize medals at The Great Exhibition, The Paris Exhibition of 1855, and The International Exhibition of 1862. In time, his polished granite would form the Trafalgar Square fountains, parts of the Imperial Opera House in Paris, and the sarcophagus in the Royal Mausoleum at Frogmore. MacDonald moved the firm to much larger premises in Constitution Street, where it was known for many years as the Aberdeen Granite Works. Several hundred men were employed and there were many other projects, some of them overseas, such as Brisbane Town Hall and a bank in Buenos Aires. MacDonald himself even made statues of granite (previously thought impossible except in Ancient Egypt), notably that of the 5th and last Duke of Gordon in Aberdeen's Golden Square.

Because of the size of his operation, the unlimited supply of granite and the immense new market in the first cemeteries, MacDonald was able to manufacture obelisks and other memorials with different pedestals and bases. The range of obelisks which were made of a single piece went from 6 ft to 12,15,18 and 24 ft, in a variety of colours, red Peterhead being the most common and easiest to identify. Having seen many polished granite obelisks in 19th century cemeteries, it is gratifying to know where so many of them came from. MacDonald was responsible for far more obelisks than any Pharaoh, pope, or duke in history.

Size was not a constraint for Alexander MacDonald as regards the manufacture and delivery of an obelisk. However, in the case of obelisks with shafts of over 25 feet, it was obviously much cheaper and easier for the purchaser to have the obelisk supplied as a quantity of cut and dressed granite blocks for onsite assembly.

This would have been the principal consideration for Alexander MacDonald when he priced the 1858 memorial to James McGrigor,1771-1858. This was an impressive obelisk monument of polished Peterhead granite blocks, one third of its 72 feet height being in the base. It was first sited at Marischal College at Aberdeen's university, but moved in the 1890s to Duthie Park. McGrigor had finished up as Director General of the Army Medical Department and had been on many campaigns, including those in Egypt, where he had visited Thebes. The price of the commission for the obelisk was £2,000, but if it had been of a single piece the price would have been much higher. (It also would have made the authorities think twice about moving it). Had there been more confidence in the machinery to suspend and raise an obelisk in Britain in the 1850s, MacDonald might easily have made this in one piece.

All the larger obelisks of polished granite, whether monolithic, or made from blocks, seem to have been cut from red Peterhead. Unlike some of the other granite quarries of Aberdeen, which had started as small plots rented from farmers, and which went deep, the quarry at Peterhead was broad and near to the port. Overlooking the harbour from where the the granite was shipped, was the old graveyard, and among the old graves a single obelisk of polished Peterhead granite.This would have been drilled from the adjacent quarry and shipped down the coast to Aberdeen, where MacDonald's cut and polished it, and then sent it back to Peterhead.

Alexander Macdonald died in 1860, having amassed a fortune. The business was taken up by his son, Alexander Macdonald the younger. Although an invalid, the younger Macdonald was a cultivated man with an eye for business, taking as his partner Sidney Field, an artist and architect, who further raised the firm's reputation with his designs. Macdonald, Field & Company moved from strength to strength. By this time, they had an establishment in London at 369-375 Euston Road, where a variety of their products were on view, and a staff of men were based. They erected memorials all over Britain.

The seven firms manufacturing granite in Aberdeen in 1850 increased to seventy by 1890. Steam power had mechanised the quarrying of granite as well, most importantly with steam cranes, first installed at Rubislaw in the 1850s, and later, in 1868, the Scottish Steam Derrick with a movable jib. Finally, in 1872, there was the 'Blondin' a suspension cableway crane named after the famous tightrope walker. These cranes enabled large stones to be lifted from the quarry floor, and were indispensable, as the quarries went deeper and deeper.

The main railway line to Glasgow was influential, enabling the shipping of considerable quantities of manufactured granite to America. Interestingly, Scottish granite workers went to America to labour in granite quarrying and construction, thereby earning enough to start their own quarries and yards back in Scotland. Their stories of superior British granites and the quality of polishing in Aberdeen ensured the sale of some hundreds of thousands of small gravestones to the USA. Known as 'Yankee dies', these, together with quality memorials for the Boston and New York markets, were put on the train and shipped from the Clyde.

The younger MacDonald was an art collector and some of the granite fortune was spent on paintings by Millais, GF Watts, Tenniel and others. When he died in 1884, the collection was added to by his wife and then given to Aberdeen Town Council, along with one third of his estate, the interest from the fund to be used in buying more paintings. 'Thus it is that the MacDonald Collection has become the pride of the Art Gallery and one of the treasured possessions of the Granite City'.[4]

The Aberdeen Granite Works continued, now a limited company, under different directors. In 1912, it was acquired by Henry Hutcheon, whose father had worked for the elder MacDonald, and who carried on running the business in the same way. Within a few years the workforce rose to the occasion and satisfied the huge demand for making memorials in 1919 and the years to follow. Most poignantly, the granite manufacturers used their stone for memorials to their own friends and family. Peterhead's War Memorial is relatively large, a 40 feet tall ornate obeliscal pillar of unpolished red Peterhead granite.

VI

THE TWENTIETH CENTURY

Another thousand or so British obelisks were raised in the 20th century, and in connection with war. It transpired that the 'early' war memorial obelisks of the late 1800s would be few compared with what was to follow. As the century turned and the Victorian age faded with its queen, Britain became embroiled in South Africa. A surprising amount of fatalities in the British forces, volunteers rather than professionals, precipitated the flow of war memorials in town squares and on village greens throughout Britain. Some of these were obelisks. There were larger ones put up in Plymouth, Worthing, Barnet, Oxford, Nottingham, Merthyr Tydfil, Llandudno, Flint, Preston, Newcastle, and Dunbar. Others were in the countryside, like the tall obelisk with a gilded flame at its top, standing on Coombe Hill, the highest point in the Chilterns.

No sooner were these in place, than the government led its enlisted army into the bloodiest conflict in history, which was to leave 10 million Europeans dead and 30 million wounded or disabled. From Britain, three-quarters of a million soldiers died, about one seventh of those who had gone to war. The flow of memorials was to become a torrent. There was an official refusal to repatriate bodies, and every district began to collect funds for a suitable memorial. Most of Britain's 54,000 war memorials date from the period, 1919-27. Nearly all would be later adapted to include the names of 2nd World War dead.

To facilitate the link to art at this important time, the Royal Academy hosted a War Memorial Exhibition in 1919. It was strongly sculptural with exhibits of working drawings and plaster originals of sculpted figures, ready to be cast in bronze. Everything displayed was directly related to the experience of war.

On the very large scale, there were to be the mass memorials in France and Belgium. The Menin Gate at Ypres and the Memorial to the Missing of the Somme at Thiepval were designed respectively by two of the Imperial War Graves Commissioners, Sir Reginald Blomfield and Sir Edwin Lutyens. Both men were architects and garden designers who, at other times, utilised the obelisk feature in private gardens. It was Lutyens who designed The Cenotaph, and its Tomb of the Unknown Soldier, unveiled in temporary form in London's Whitehall on 11th November 1920, exactly two years after the armistice.

Even before the war had ended, discussions were opened in many circles as to which sort of memorial was wanted. In some cases, regions and towns opted for utilitarian memorials, such as additions to hospitals and new Memorial Parks. Darlington eventually raised enough money to have both a hospital and an obelisk in front of it. Throughout Britain's regions subscriptions for memorials were opened, as were local discussions about each proposal. At all levels there was the most sincere desire to 'honour their own' in the best possible way. The Gothic Revivalists, who had caused upheaval in the previous century, did not have their way with War memorials, although commissioners in Hereford, Warwick and Sledmere selected shrine-like structures, echoing Queen Eleanor's crosses.

Selection of memorial type by local committees was inevitably driven by finance. The British people gave heartily to the subscriptions. Large sums of money allowed most city and large borough committees to consider lavish memorials. The level of funding and an availability of talented artists caused the birth of a national collection of sculptural and architectural monuments. This wealth of public art is largely unsung, perhaps because of attitudes to war, and mostly omitted in Nikolaus Pevsner's *Buildings of England* county series. I hate to mention it, but the author and expert editor of the series, to whom English historians owe so much, was a German, and for him these monuments were actually new phenomena, coming as they did, in such large numbers.

Most memorials were a result of combining the arts. There are those which were chiefly architectural, such as the Welsh National Memorial and some fine examples in Aberdeen, Dundee,

Nottingham, Coventry and Kempston in Bedfordshire. There are notable sculptural treatments in Folkestone, Exeter, Colchester and elsewhere. Sculpture, poignant in grief, expressed great emotion, with iconic female figures of 'Death' and 'Victory' and, elsewhere, the stark realism of soldiers in battledress, overcoats, or kilts. Some of these figures carry rifles and bayonets and seem to advance, and these are less appreciated in the modern age.

After large structures and sculpted figures, the range of monuments at last narrowed to a choice between stone crosses, or obelisks. The obelisk could be seen as a very practical choice and would fit in with any budget. It might be huge, seen for miles, or it could be smaller, bought from a catalogue or mason's yard. Where possible, the committees preferred to use local stone.

Among the obelisk war memorials in cities and large towns, two of the finest are at Manchester and Northampton, with central features in between two obelisks. Both were by Lutyens, who was most influential in deciding the broadly classical manner in which the Great War Memorials would be made.

Edwin Landseer Lutyens,1869-1944, was born in London, the tenth of the thirteen children of Captain Charles Lutyens and his wife, Mary. His father was an artist and named him after the painter he admired. Edwin was critically ill in his childhood and was taught at home by one of his brothers. At the age of sixteen he entered the South Kensington School of Art, the present RCA, to study architecture. He progressed and signed up as an articled pupil to the architects, Sir Ernest George and Harold Peto. Two years later, in 1889, he set up his own practice.

Within months he had met Gertrude Jekyll and they struck up a collaborative rapport. Jekyll in turn, introduced him to Princess Louise and to Edward Hudson, editor of *Country Life*. He designed and built Munstead Wood for Gertrude Jekyll, and subsequently a number of country houses and gardens. Lutyens was commissioned to design the British Pavilion for the Paris Exhibition of 1900. He designed the *Country Life* office building in Fleet Street in 1904 and, in later years, added the Reuters and Press Association buildings nearby. Elected a member of the Delhi Planning Commission in 1912, he sailed on the first of numerous voyages to India to plan the new city and designs for the Viceroy's House, with its courts and fountains.

With the onset of the Great War, he was selected to the Imperial War Graves Commission. The architect was asked by Lloyd George to design a temporary catafalque for the peace procession of July 1919 in Whitehall: Lutyens provided The Cenotaph. A permanent structure in Portland stone was to follow in 1920. He was knighted in recognition of his work in Delhi and for his free services to the War Graves Commission. To cap it all he was elected to the Royal Academy in 1920 and awarded the Royal Gold Medal of the Royal Institute of British Architects in the following year.

It was during the early 1920s that Lutyens designed some of the finest memorials in England's cities. His works at Manchester, Northampton, Southend, Cowley and York used the obelisk with dignity and simple dramatic effect. His design for the memorial in St Peter's Square, Manchester was completed and unveiled in 1924: identical 23 feet tall obelisks stood on either side of a taller pylon cenotaph, itself topped by a stone figure of a soldier lying beneath his greatcoat. The view today is considerably altered by numerous lamps, signs and crosses in the same location. His design for Northampton was not completed until 1927 and featured a long altar-like stone mass connected by paths on either side to another twin pair of obelisks.

Using the same symmetry, but in the reverse order, the memorial at Southport in Lancashire featured a single 70 feet tall obelisk which was set on a central roundabout between two facing colonnades. Designers were being urged to add something to an obelisk. The Saddleworth memorial was designed by an ex-Serviceman, Gilbert Howcroft. It is a 52 feet tall obelisk, made of dressed blocks of local stone, with wreaths and inset crosses in the form of downward pointing swords on each stone flank. It has a stepped base and no pedestal. A line in the inscription implores, "Live thou for England – We for England died". The obelisk stands above the town of Oldham, on Pots and Pans Hill, where the moor reaches 1,400 feet above sea level. A crowd of five thousand had climbed up to the unveiling by Lord Lascelles in October 1923. The obelisk cost £1,985 to build, which appears to have been very good value. Typically, towns the size of Oldham would have raised more than twice that amount of money.

Only a month before, Lascelles had been with his father, the Earl of Harewood, as he unveiled another obelisk, this being in an urban setting in Harrogate. It was 75 feet tall with panels on the plinth and emblems carved by Gilbert Ledward. This esteemed sculptor, who had served as a soldier in the war, also made the decorative additions and plaques for Britain's tallest War Memorial obelisk, which stands 100 feet tall on Blackpool sea front.

The Scarborough obelisk on Oliver's Mount is exceptionally impressive. The site itself, 500 feet above the harbour, was named from Oliver Cromwell's occupation of the hill in order to threaten the royalist town with cannons. The obelisk, which was completed in 1923, is 75 feet tall, built of a light-brown moor stone, with a platform approached by steps from each direction. The views are extremely good from this high place, as is the view of the obelisk from the streets and seafront below. Apart from the seven hundred 1st World War dead and 2nd World War additions, are twenty names of Scarborough people killed in the town by the big guns of German battlecruisers off the coast. The architectural plan came from the municipal engineer, Mr H Smith, the building work from Bastiman & Sons of Scarborough.

Smaller than Scarborough's are a number of obelisk monuments between 35 and 60 feet tall, such as those at Bishops Stortford, Cowbridge and Accrington, Hebden Bridge, and the 'Departure Monument' at Stretton-on-Dunsmore near Coventry. Obelisks of a similar size were erected on coastal sites at Penzance, Southend, Hartlepool and Dunoon.

Memorials in which the obelisk was not the main feature, but provided background support, phyically or artistically, to a group of statues or emblems, are not necessarily listed in the gazetteer. However, the obelisk was chosen for about a thousand memorials as the sole or principal feature. Where memorial commissioners could not resist the temptation, they pushed for additional sculptural decoration. There are many examples: one such was Greenock's war memorial obelisk of 1924, a tall construction of granite sited above the Clyde Firth. From its base the prow of a viking ship emerges; above this a winged figure of 'Victory' offers wreaths of honour. Up the shaft are carved celtic patterns, Iona crosses, claymores and zoomorphic squirls.

Another instance of 'overegging' the design treatment in this way is Goscombe John's earlier obeliscal monument of 1916 to 'The Engine Room Heroes' of ss.Titanic, sited on Liverpool's Pierhead. As a monument (though not a war memorial), one might look and even marvel at its sculptural detail and gilding. As an obelisk, it is a disaster. From top to bottom you see a gilded torch, a coronet of figures in relief, the body of the obelisk with thick extruding jointing bands, and then the plinth, with its carved gods and lifelike engineers and wave patterns. The pure outlines of an obelisk are barely recognisable.

When memorial committees insisted upon 'christianising' obelisks, it oppressed the artist. Imagine the panic of an intelligent architectural designer being urged to produce an obelisk with a cross on its top. Discreet christian symbols to keep the vicar happy were one thing, but heavy-handed additions were open to ridicule. In context though, a high percentage of war memorials, including obelisks, were intended for erection on church land. In reality, obelisks belong to no religion, but this did not stop clergymen worrying about whether they were allowing an alien, heretical or pagan object on christian ground, as if they were a pope in Rome.[1]

Under pressure, the inventiveness of design to hide an obelisk as something else was remarkable. The architect Charles Armstrong, under the supervision of John Simpson, the RIBA president, almost succeeding in disguising the obeliscal war memorial at St Peters in Wolverhampton. It had an ornate plinth, additional ridges and recesses to its sides and, at the top, a truncated and stepped pyramidion. Paradoxically, even monumental crosses were by this time being cut with their upright in the shape of an obelisk, with four equal tapering sides. There are countless examples of this. Some of these are exactly like obelisks, so much so that the pyramidion (if it was an obelisk instead of a cross) forms the downward part of the cruciform enclosed within a circle at the top of the memorial.

Though all regions of Britain have obelisk war memorials, they seemed to have been favoured in certain districts. Yorkshire, Lancashire, Derbyshire, Wales and Scotland had relatively more, while Wiltshire, Berkshire, and Surrey had fewer. Durham has far more than Northumberland. The obelisks reach far out to the Isles, to Stornoway in the Hebrides, to the Shetlands and three of the Orkneys, including the little isle of Papa Westray. Lots of these war memorials are in the middle of villages, outside village halls, parish churches or non-conformist chapels. Most are to land forces, with a few to air crews, at Witchford in Cambridgeshire, Langar and RAF Beverley, for example. The Navy memorial obelisks standing in Portsmouth, Chatham and Plymouth are identical. There are also one or two unusual commemorations, such as the obelisk at Barton-on-sea in Hampshire, which was dedicated to Indian troops who served in Europe.

The Naval War Division Memorial commemorated 45,000 casualties, mostly at Gallipoli and the western Front. The Division disbanded after the Great War, having approached Edwin Lutyens for a design. The architect's response was unique, his design being a 10 feet tall obelisk of Portland stone which stood in an elegant bronze fountain bowl, an idea that could have been disastrous, but succeeded in practice. It was unveiled in 1925 at Horse Guards in central London and moved during World War II to the Royal Navy College buildings in Greenwich. Very recently the memorial has been restored and was returned to the corner of the Admiralty Building in Horse Guards at a rededication ceremony in November 2003. Behind it is the ivy-clad structure of Winston Churchill's 'bunker' and Britain's Command HQ.[2]

A few memorials were in schoolgrounds and honoured former pupils, like those at St.George's in Battersea, Wrexham's Lindisfarne College, or Daniel Stewart's in Edinburgh. Perhaps the finest of this sort was actually the 1903 Boer War Memorial outside Hailebury College in Hertfordshire, designed by Sir Reginald Blomfield. It was a very decorative treatment in marble, with ornate bronze plaques and Baroque flourishes on all sides of the obelisk. The work was carried out by Farmer & Brindley of Westminster and the original plan to have a figure of 'Valour' was dispensed with, having a small sphere instead. The memorial has beauty, though the author acknowledges a certain dual standard in noting this, having identified the 'overegging' of decoration to other obelisk memorials.

The obelisk was chosen for the memorials at Parkhurst prison, presumably for staff rather than inmates, and at London Zoo. Collieries at Doncaster, Garswood, Moira, and Park Hall put up memorial obelisks close to their premises to honour the many coalminers conscripted during the war. Preston Colliery near Newcastle commemorated their own with an obelisk at Preston Library. The memorial for workers at the Burlington Slate Company in Cumbria is a 6 feet tall obelisk of solid slate.

Even hobbies and social clubs were represented. Cycling was very popular before and after the war, and was well organised nationally in clubs. Saddle pals grieving the loss of companions gathered enough money to put a 30 feet tall obelisk memorial in the middle of England, on Meriden Green near Coventry. It has served since as a gathering point for cycle races and rallies.

Among employers were the railway companies, some of whom erected obelisk memorials at mainline stations at Euston, York and Motherwell. Euston's was in memory 3,719 LNWR railwaymen who died, and was unveiled by Field Marshall Earl Haig in 1921. Sited in front of the station, it is 30 feet tall with a bulky outline and an incised cross, standing on a pedestal with four bronze figures. York's was unveiled in 1924 and inscribed to 'The abiding remembrance of the 2,236 men of the North Eastern Railway who gave their lives for their country'. This too was designed by Edwin Lutyens. Up among the city walls above the station, a small stone cask on a stepped base was enclosed by a wall, from the centre of which an obelisk rose a total of 30 feet. Looming from parapets high above the platform, it has been a memorable sight for passengers.

A large proportion of Britain's war memorials were in country places, and unless there was a local patron, perhaps a squire who had lost a son, they were inevitably less well funded. It should be understood that there was extreme poverty in agricultural areas after the Great War. Among the poor, it was without doubt felt that any extra money in the parish should be directed to the immediate relief of the living, with hot food and warm housing. There were hamlets so small that their war memorials amounted to little more than an inscribed board on a post.

With a bit of money, village communities had enough to consider a stone cross, or, maybe, an obelisk. What meaningful debates there must have been, as valid as the arguments of architects or archbishops! Many country folk had never seen an obelisk before. Occasionally, there was a regimental scheme, where the county memorial was a large obelisk and the outlying towns and villages had lesser versions.

What was it in the obelisk that convinced the committees? Possibly it was the solid, Low-church simplicity of the thing which appealed; it was certainly more monumental and less grave-like than the cross. Britain had not fought the Great War for the cross. In a few cases, where committees were in dispute between a cross and a sculpture, a resolution was found by agreeing to an obelisk! In others, where an obelisk was finally chosen, agreements had only been reached by the promise of crosses on the obelisk. In the village of Durisdeer, in northern Dumfries, the dispute was about the siting of the memorial and the committee could not reach an agreement. In the end they had two memorials, one of which was an obelisk on the Edinburgh road.

A fairly typical memorial fund, in a village with two or three hundred people, might have reached £150-200. This was enough in

1920 for a small celtic cross in grey granite, including payment for its erection by a local builder's firm. A small polished granite obelisk could be obtained and installed for less than £150. In stoneworking regions the commission itself was often put to local firms, and these could be much cheaper. The obelisk at Mousehole in Cornwall was built of local granite blocks by Snells of Newlyn at a cost of just £50 with an extra eight shillings per dozen letters inscribed[5]. However, at Mousehole the workmen produced a quite ugly foreshortening near the top of their obelisk, which is stepped inwards, decreasing the height. For the most part, once the decision had been made to erect an obelisk, committees in outlying areas either contracted a local builder, or bought something from a monumental mason, who was himself supplied by quarries.

Of the hundreds of villages that raised obelisks after the Great War, some names, for instance, Holkham, or Bewcastle, are already familiar. The memorial commitee at Holkham, in Norfolk, made a considered choice as they were well acquainted with the monumental obelisk designed by William Kent in Holkham Park, which had been there for nearly two centuries. They chose a handsome 15 feet polished granite monolith, on a 4 ft plinth, with bronze wreaths at each side.

How intriguing it was that the memorial committee at Bewcastle, in Cumbria, should have selected the obelisk, instead of a cross or other treatment. Their village was famous for the Bewcastle Cross, dating from the 8th or 9th century. This once carried a cross on top, it is said, though it is very plain to see that the old stone, carved with runes and patterns, actually has the overall proportions and shape of an obelisk.

It may be fanciful, but I like to think that for so many small and remote country hamlets, the obelisk was chosen because an upright stone was a recognised placemarker in Britain from earliest times. The memorial committees of 1919 in Scotland and the Isles, in Wales, Cornwall and the northern England, had an historical affinity with standing stones in their neighbourhood. In a hill country place there is an outlying 1st World War Memorial obelisk, standing in a landscape with ancient upright stones, like another layer of British history.

So much changed in Britain with the war. The national psyche was troubled by the horror, damage and futility of it all. The war has been cited as an historical watershed in terms of politics, society, culture and art, and the period before the war, that brief decade from 1900-1914, is portrayed as the last few minutes of sunlight before the coming dark. Those few years, the shortlived Edwardian era, had in many ways been a continuation of the 1890s, with a flowering of literature and the the arts. It was during these years that the obelisk memorials from the Boer War were put up, and architects, sculptors and builders were busy.

Sculpture in 1900 was still in the ascendant, with a talented group of practitioners of 'New Sculpture'. Their finished pieces were of a very high standard, with technical advances in casting permitting better reproduction of detail and anatomical realism. An example of the quality of this new work to a traditional concept was the beautiful monument and drinking fountain of 1911, dedicated to King Edward VII, which stands opposite the Royal London Hospital in Whitechapel Road. It was by the sculptor, W Frith, and so superb are the Art Nouveau bronze figurines, cherubs and ornaments that one hardly notices that it is a blackened limestone obelisk.

When one of the new sculptors died, there was little question of a sculptural treatment by his peers. A small memorial obelisk was chosen instead for Edward Onslow Ford, raised in 1902 in Abbey Road in London's St Johns Wood. It was a golden era for literature, publishing and bookselling. A subscription was raised in 1911 for an obelisk in Wales, to David Williams, founder of the Royal Literary Fund. In Rochdale, a small obelisk was put up in 1900 in honour of four authors who made use of dialects in their writing. Every little history is part of the greater cavalcade of dates and facts and reminds us that it is the associations, inscriptions and anecdotes surrounding each obelisk that gives each of them extra meaning. Some are so trivial, yet add something: take the tale of Mr Brown the shoemaker, who had an obelisk put up as his memorial in Hampton Wick in 1900. It tells us that Brown had acted to preserve a public footpath across London's Bushy Park.

Obelisk monuments to relatively ordinary people could still be quite large, though within a few years, such grandeur would no longer be afforded to mere individuals in the way that it had been previously. An obelisk monument to Samuel Smith, a Liberal MP in Liverpool, was built of granite blocks in 1909 to a total height of 60 feet. By contrast, a small obelisk, akin to earlier memorials raised by charitable societies, was placed in 1901 on a lonely mountain in the Brecon

Beacons. It remembered the name of little Tommy Jones, aged five, who disappeared in the hills.

The recent tradition, with exceptions, of choosing an obelisk for Mining Disaster memorials was maintained. That there were many terrible accidents is a reflection on Britain's huge demand for coal and the working conditions of millions of miners. The 1913 Oaks Explosion Monument erected at Kendray, by Barnsley, is a limestone obelisk with bronze figures marking the memory of 334 miners killed in a pit explosion. Within the century the entire industry would be reduced to almost nothing and most Britons would never touch a piece of coal again.

One polished white granite obelisk of 1909 was an old-fashioned 'Martyrs memorial'. It was sited in Denmark Road in Exeter and bears two bronze plaques relating to protestant martyrs of 1531 and 1555. If one asks oneself why the protestant subscribers chose the obelisk and not the cross, the answer is surely that to erect a cross would have been glaring hypocrisy. Another obelisk to Marian martyrs was high up on Cliffe Hill, above Lewes in Sussex, and is even nowadays a place of religious hatred every Guy Fawkes Night. An obelisk and not a cross was chosen in 1915 to placemark the former site of Glasgow's 13th century Bishop's Palace.

After the Great War, when the hundreds of obelisk war memorials had been paid for by ordinary people and set up in their streets, the progress of the obelisk as a feature of the land and townscape appears to have slowed down. In fact, regarding the erection of new obelisks in Britain, the interwar and post WW2 period until about 1980 was relatively quiet. One reason, perhaps, was that within a few years of the war memorials being in place, the rise of Germany and Hitler's use of neo-classical architecture steered Britons away from classicism and associated items, such as the obelisk. The fascist leader Mussolini had an impressively large, marble obelisk erected at the entrance of his 1932 stadium in Rome.

Of course there were other reasons, one of which was that Britain was poorer, and that the thousand new obelisks of 1919 onwards were perceived to be enough for the time being. There was an inevitable association in people's minds between obelisks and war memorials; Britain wanted to look forward in the '30s, not to the past. All about was a modernistic zeal in civic and domestic architecture and a modern art movement in the making. Traditional public sculpture, previously in competition with the obelisk as far as commissions were concerned, would never be the same again. One exception to the trend was a 19 feet tall obelisk put up in 1930 in Burry Port in South-West Wales, which marks the landing of the transatlantic aviatrix, Amelia Earhart. Others, no more than a very few, were small private memorials, such as the 1936 obelisk in the sports field of Porthleven, dedicated to Mrs J Williams by her husband.

There would only be a few obelisks added to fine gardens and grand country houses. In fact, after the 1st World War there came a time of shortages, unemployment and depression. The great houses, the sort of places where obelisks used to be located, were in decline. Some old families quite suddenly ran out of money and their buildings were locked up and left, later to be demolished. It is quite probable that with the demolitions, some monuments were lost. Sometimes a house was lost and an obelisk in the grounds survived.

On the other hand, there was a great interest in the gardening movement started by Gertrude Jekyll and Lutyens in the early 1900s. There was even a garden city movement among town planners, with the new town of Letchworth in Hertfordshire, begun in 1903, serving as a model for post-war building in the 1920s and 1940s. Sir Edwin Lutyens himself, after more than ten years of work on war memorials, continued his list of architectural successes with works including the British Embassy in Washington, the fountains in Trafalgar Square and buildings at Oxford and Cambridge. He was knighted in 1930.

Lutyens became President of the Royal Academy in 1938 and in the same year designed a gateway pair of obelisks for Blagdon Hall in Northumberland. About 15 feet tall in smooth limestone ashlar, they are formal, formidable and not dissimilar to his earlier designs of twin obelisks for war memorials. The pair at Blagdon seem to be Lutyen's only obelisks in a civilian garden. Jane Brown, a very knowledgeable writer about Sir Edwin Lutyens, gave me the understanding that the architect, after his decade of war memorials, was never the same as he had been before, when working with Gertrude Jekyll in the early 1900s. Given the opportunity, I believe Lutyens would have created more obelisks. He was already at work planning the restoration of bombed areas of London when he died on New Year's day, 1944. Arguably the finest architect of the century, he was a man who used the obelisk feature carefully.

The Second World War provided another generation of dead soldiers. However, the long memorial procedures which had followed the Great War were avoided because, in practically all cases, the inscribed names of WW2 casualties were added to the existing WW1 memorials. There were a few additions, one of which was the Dover Patrol obelisk, 84 feet tall, on cliffs above the port, commemorating the Royal Navy Auxillary forces who had guarded the channel.

The twenty to thirty year period after the war was almost devoid of new obelisks. However, the idea of the gateway pairs of obelisks was used in the 1950s on a pair of outer gates at Okeover House in Staffordshire, by the architect Marshall Sissons. There were also a few centenaries to be commemorated with obelisks. One in 1975 at Pelsall church in Staffordshire is probably the last mining-related memorial, recalling an accident in 1872 in which twenty-two men had died. Another centenary was marked in 1960 with an obelisk erected outside Blaenavon Ironworks in South Wales, now a museum, to honour the industrial metallugist, S Gilchrist Thomas. On past form, this might have been made of metal, but it was not. On the other hand, an idealistic bicentennial memorial of Paine's *Rights of Man* was installed in Islington's Angel Square in 1991, and for some reason this obelisk was in bronze. Publicly subscribed, an obelisk was raised in North Shields in memory of a teacher, Mr T Haswell, who died a century earlier in 1889; it is rare that his profession be honored at all, still less by the obelisk feature.

In exactly the same way as maquettes or miniature sketch models of a sculpture have a value, both to the sculptor and to collectors, table models of obelisk monuments have been made by architects and model makers. They have been in existence for many years and, interestingly, a few are models of obelisks that were never made. Some may have been models of monuments in architectural competitions, others were remarkable and beautiful inventions, signed by the artists. In addition to this, marble craftsmen in Europe had for some time produced little obelisks which were purchased as ornaments. A pair of them do very well on a mantelpiece.

In the explosion of spiritual thinking originating from the 1970s, these obeliskettes, about one foot tall, took on new meaning. Placing one in the middle of a bare, sand coloured carpet and shining a torch on it from different angles, while listening to ethnic music, was a reasonable recreation. Year on year, the sales of these miniature stone obelisks have increased. They could be toys, but some owners will want real obelisks in times to come.

Returning to lifesize and its place in formal landscapes, an obelisk was made in a shady corner of the gardens at West Green House, Hartley Wintney, Hampshire, created by Sir Alistair MacAlpine in between 1950-80. Commissioning the work in the early 1980s, he dedicated the obelisk to the memory of his gardener. The deceased gardener, Tom Mann, had been a hardworking and integral part of the long project. It is known as 'The gardener's obelisk'. Most combinations of figurative sculpture and an obelisk are a mistake; here, in a most unusually successful union, a sculptor added the realistic and lifesize figure of Tom, leaning for a moment, against the base.

In a different capacity, though a memorial, was the placemarker obelisk on the Putney-Mortlake riverside path, London. It was put up in 1963 in memory of an Australian rower, Steven Fairbairn, 1862-1938. With a height of 11 feet, it has served as landmark adjacent to the riverside milestone used by the university boat race. In the same year an obelisk was installed by the Speech House at West Dean in Gloucestershire, its purpose to mark the centre of the Forest of Dean.

By the 1970s, though Britain had 'moved on' and put the war behind it, not everyone could lay events to rest. A number of Poles fleeing the partition of Poland in 1939 had formed a settled community in London. Some of their families were caught in negotiations between Stalin and Hitler on the Eastern Front, whereby Poles held as prisoners of war by the Russians were supposed to be handed over to the Germans. Stalin's attrocity was that the exchange did not take place and 14,500 Polish officers and men were put to death. He then accused the Germans of their murder, but contradictory proof and the remains of 4,500 of them were later found in a clearing in the Katyn forest. A memorial was proposed by London's Polish community, the Katyn Monument, which was to be an obelisk in Gunnersbury Cemetery. Unveiled in 1976, a sombre gravity was intended in the design of the obelisk, a hefty mass of three sections of black Nubian marble, standing 21 ft tall on a broad, dark plinth and three stepped base. It would seem any fascist overtones attached to the obelisk from the 1930s must have been forgotten by this time. In 1985, an obelisk and memorial seat were put in a small 'Peace Garden' in Doncaster to remember Tommy Jones and other British volunteers who went to fight against fascism in the Spanish Civil War in 1936.

33. The garden in 1910, Copped Hall, Essex; architect: Charles Eamer Kempe.

When E. Wythes took charge at Copped hall in 1883, he set about making additions to the old hall and creating a new garden. The ideas came from Kempe, an unusual architect best known for stained-glass work. Terraces were built around a square and retained by a balustrade, capped at intervals with obelisks, in all more than forty. Each was 6 feet tall, cut in a single piece on four small spheres. There were marble fountains and statues, two taller obelisks and two pavilions, or summerhouses carrying obelisk finials. Tragically in 1917, a fire destroyed the hall and the gardens were kept until the owner's death in 1949. Within a year or so, everything was sold and all the obelisks, fountains, and stonework torn away. To restore the house and grounds, great efforts are being made by another architect, Alan Cox, founder of the Copped Hall Trust, though to return the garden to its Edwardian condition would be to triumph against the odds.

photo © Country Life Picture Library.

33

34. The Corona, 1891-1899, Athelhampton House, Dorset; architect: F.I. Thomas.

Ringed by a wall with a series of stone obelisk finials, this was a circular enclosure at the centre of a new garden outside the 15th century house. In an old and formal style, it was designed by Francis Inigo Thomas, former assistant to the architect, Sir Reginald Blomfield, who wrote 'The Formal Garden in England'. The Corona has entrances at the four quarters and the obelisks are outlined to the West by several large pyramids of clipped yew in the adjacent garden.

35. Obelisk War Memorial, 1903, Hailebury, Herts; architect: Sir R. Blomfield.

A few war memorials were in schoolgrounds and honoured former pupils. The finest of this sort was the1903 Boer War Memorial outside Hailebury College, designed by Sir Reginald Blomfield. Unveiled by Lt General Sir J. French, it was a very decorative treatment in Portland stone and marble, with ornate bronze plaques and Baroque flourishes on all sides of the 29 feet tall obelisk. It has beauty, though there were instances of 'overegging' the decoration to other obelisk war memorials.

36. Obelisk, 1909, The Martyrs Memorial , Denmark Road, Exeter.

Less than a hundred years old, here is an old-fashioned memorial. An obelisk of polished white Devon granite in a single piece, it stands in a residential street upon a stepped base. Its plinth has a pronounced ledge protecting bronze relief plaques, which illustrate the execution of Exeter protestants in 1531 and 1555. The protestant subscribers chose to use the obelisk rather than a cross, because using the cross would have been glaring hypocrisy. Ecclesiastical authorities often chose the obelisk to placemark, as a cross might imply a burial.

Sculptural detailsof the Hailebury Memorial, 1903

Much as the connoisseur wishes to see the pure outlines of an unadorned obelisk, the Hailebury memorial is worth a second look (also see picture 35). All the sculpture, casting and construction was completed by Messrs Farmer & Brindley of Westminster, who had supplied details to the Albert Memorial and St.Paul's Cathedral, and at the time employed first rate sculptors like Chavalliaud and Harry Bates. The ball on the top was an afterthought; Blomfield's design had originally included a surmounted figure of 'Valour'.

37. Obelisk, 1923, War Memorial, Saddleworth Moor, West Yorkshire.

Designed by Gilbert Howcroft, who had served in the war, the 52 ft tall war memorial obelisk had a stepped base with no pedestal. Wreaths and inset crosses in the form of downward pointing swords were carved on each stone flank and a line in the inscription implores, 'Live thou for England – We for England died'. Known from afar, it stands above Oldham, on Pots and Pans Hill, where the moor reaches 1,400 feet above sea level. The obelisk cost £1,985 to build, which was very good value; typically, the memorial committees of towns the size of Oldham would have raised more than twice that amount of money.

Two obelisks, 1927, Memorial unveiling, Northampton; architect: Edwin Lutyens

Northampton's memorial was not completed until 1927 and featured a long altar-like stone mass which was connected by paths on either side to a twin pair of obelisks. A Garden of Remembrance around the memorial was added a decade later.

38. Obelisk War Memorial, Cowley, Oxford; architect: Edwin Lutyens
photo: ©John Robinson.

Obelisk War Memorial, 1924, N.E.Railway, York; architect: E Lutyens.

Shown in an old postcard, the obelisk has been a memorable sight for rail passengers, as it looms from parapets high above the platform. Up among the city walls above the station, a small stone cask on a stepped base was enclosed by a wall, from the centre of which the obelisk rose a total of 30 feet. Railway companies were among those who commissioned war memorials for their employees. York's was inscribed to 'The abiding remembrance of 2,236 men of the N.E.R who gave their lives for their country'.

39. Obelisk,1925, Naval War Div, Central London; architect: Edwin Lutyens

The Naval Division disbanded after the Great War, having approached Lutyens for a memorial to commemorate 45,000 casualties, mostly at Gallipoli and the western Front. His design was unique and successful in practice, a 10 ft tall obelisk of Portland stone in a bronze fountain bowl. Unveiled in 1925 at Horse Guards in central London and moved during WW2 to the R.N College buildings in Greenwich, it was recently restored and returned to the corner of the Admiralty Building in Horse Guards in 2003. Behind it is the ivy-clad hulk of Winston Churchill's wartime bunker building and Britain's Command HQ.

Sir Edwin Lutyens, 1869-1944

40. *upper* – **Obelisk, War Memorial, Blackpool, Lancashire.**

An old seaside postcard shows Britain's tallest 1st World War Memorial obelisk, standing 100 feet tall on the sea front. The esteemed sculptor, Gilbert Ledward, who had served as a soldier in the war, made decorative additions and plaques for this obelisk and the one at Harrogate in 1923.

lower – **Two obelisks,1924, War Memorial, Manchester; architect: Edwin Lutyens.**

Lutyens's design for the memorial in St Peter's Square was completed and unveiled in 1924. Identical 23 ft tall obelisks stood on either side of a taller pylon cenotaph, itself topped by a stone figure of a soldier lying beneath his greatcoat. The view today is considerably altered by numerous lamps and signs in the same location.

41. Obelisk War Memorial,1923, Scarborough, N Yorks; architect: H.Smith

Rising 75 feet above a stepped platform, the obelisk was well made, built of a light-brown moor stone. It is an impressive war memorial, partly because of the site, Oliver's Mount, 500 feet above the harbour, which Oliver Cromwell had once occupied in order to threaten the royalist town with canon. Apart from 700 1st World War dead and WW2 additions, are 20 names of people killed in the town by the guns of battlecruisers off the coast. The architectural plan came from the municipal engineer, Mr H.Smith, the building work from Bastiman & Sons of Scarborough.

42. Pair of obelisks,1938, Blagdon Hall, Northumberland; architect: Sir Edwin Lutyens.

Lutyens became President of the Royal Academy in 1938 and in the same year designed a gateway pair of obelisks for Blagdon Hall. About 15 feet tall in smooth limestone ashlar, they were formidable, dignified and not dissimilar to his earlier designs of twin obelisks for war memorials.

photo ©Jane Brown.

43. The Gardener s Obelisk, c1980, West Green House, Hartley Wintney, Hampshire.

In a modern re-instance of its place in formal landscapes, an obelisk was made in a shady corner of the gardens at West Green House created by Sir Alistair MacAlpine between 1950-80. Commissioning the work, he dedicated the obelisk to the memory of his hardworking gardener, Tom Mann. In a most unusually successful union of figurative sculpture with an obelisk, the sculptor added the realistic figure of Tom, leaning for a moment, against the base.

photo© Mike Cousins.

44. *left* – **Obeliscal monument,1999, Penarth Haven, Cardiff; Sculptor: M. Dan Archer.**

It is history now to reflect upon the Millennium, though in 1999 there was actually a hopeful air and opportunity for new public monuments and sculptures. Many artistic works went up, among them two obelisks by the sculptor, Michael Dan Archer,(1955-), who has used granite for twenty-five years and, as hands-on sculptor, rather than an architect, has been free to explore the material. His pieces are as much about the texture and massiveness of stone as they are about shape. The work in Cardiff Bay was a 28 feet tall granite upright with two of the sides tapering, or converging, while the other two diverge. The result appears like the blade of a mason's chisel.

right – **Obelisk, 1999, Wynyard Estate, Durham; Sculptor: M. Dan Archer**

Another Millennium Project, commissioned by Cameron Hall Estates, the 20 feet tall obelisk was construc of Cornish granite blocks with bands of green marble and bronze castings.

44

45. Tibetan Peace Garden, 1999, Imperial War Museum, London.

At the end of a century of war, the hopes of humankind in 1999 were expressed in a Tibetan Peace Garden created in the grounds the Imperial War Museum. Unveiled by the Dalai Lama, it featured a flat stone wheel, carved with symbols and, seen through a pair of obeliscal gateway uprights, a white limestone obelisk surmounted with a Tibetan symbol.

46. Obelisk and stone circle — a 20th century view, Ham Hill, Somerset.

Another arrival in 1999, was the stone circle made on the top of Ham Hill, the largest hillfort in Europe. It was in close view with the Stoke-sub-Hamdon war memorial obelisk unveiled by the Prince of Wales in 1923. This was not planned, but the action of Mr England, the quarryowner on the hilltop, using his machinery. An interesting and comparitive new view of England has been created on the quarried hilltop; in the foreground, a late 20th century stone circle and, behind it, a 20th century obelisk.

Obeliscal Jubilee marker, Roborough Down, Devon.

This rough marker on the edge of Dartmoor is visited by roaming cattle, ponies and deer. In order to prevent the short obelisk from being barged and toppled by livestock, the cube pedestal was bolted through to the base, then stabilised by a surrounding stone trough filling with rainwater. It could easily be mistaken for some older object, though the briefest inscription upon it states: V.R 1837-1897.   photo © F Kinmonth.

47. Obelisk, undated, Stoke Rochford, Lincolnshire.

This well-shaped obelisk in the churchyard cannot be explained. What can be seen is that it has been re-erected on the site, probably more than a hundred years ago. It is not a gravestone, and has no legible inscriptions on it apart from recognisable carved patterns in a Celtic, or Saxon manner. It has the patina of a very old Scottish stone that has been exposed to the elements or hard used in some way. There are no records of its arrival, let alone its origins. A monumental obelisk in proud memory of the Lincolnshire genius, Isaac Newton, is to be seen in the same village.

48. The Rudston Monolith, approximately 2,000BC, Rudston, N Yorkshire.

Many churchyards occupy former sacred sites following Pope Gregory's counsel to missionaries in Britain to convert pagan temples and megalithic sites into churches. Occupying part of the churchyard at All Saints, Rudston, the mighty obeliscal stone, about 45 feet tall, was raised to a perfect vertical 4,000 years ago. Today, 26 feet stand above ground. It is of a moor grit stone from the Cleveland Hills, at least thirty miles distant, and it was hewn, we are told, in the late Neolithic period, roundly 2,000-1,500BC and broadly contemporary with obelisks in Egypt. At some point in its long history, its top has been damaged, and it wears a copper formed hat.

Britain experienced right wing politics in the 1980s. Gorged on North Sea Oil revenue and European subsidies, the government proceeded to push for outward signs of modernisation. In cities, old housing and factories were removed to make way for a new era of property developments. This was inner city architecture, while out in the country, vast steel showroom sheds consumed thousands of acres of Britain. Already in progress was the long term redevelopment of a group of Buckinghamshire towns into one conurbation known as Milton Keynes. Numerous developments were enhanced with experimental architecture and Kinetic art pieces and a solid brick obelisk was built in 1984 in Great Holm, at the direction of Milton Keynes District Council.

The closure and redevelopment of London's old docklands, close to the City, was the most promininent sign of new construction. Sculptures and monuments were commissioned by property developers to 'humanise the empty spaces' in between the high rising office towers, in what what another writer has referred to as the 'capitalist ebullience of the eighties'[4]. Sculptures at the new Limehouse Link tunnel and London Bridge reflected modernism. In New Docklands itself, a development at Ambassador Gardens was attuned in 1987 with the addition of a 21 feet tall obelisk; its arrival met with no criticism.

Two or three miles away, in Finsbury Place, off Finsbury Circus, an unusual obeliscal structure was built in the street in 1998. A ventilation shaft was needed to underground workings, and this was clothed in the shape of an obelisk, formed by laying expanses of jointed limestone over a steel frame. Apertures near the top of the hollow structure allow air from below to escape. A nice touch to the project was the addition of a framed bust relief of George Dance jr, the architect of Finsbury Circus, whom readers may also recall as the builder of the 1771 obelisk in Kennington.

After a gap of over sixty years since the hilltop war memorials of the 1920s, a monumental obelisk was built in 1993 on high land at Bryn Pydew, near Llandudno. It was designed by the architect, Eric Throssell and commissioned by Richard Broyd of Bodysgallen Hall. It was solidly built of dressed stone blocks, with at least a third of its 64 feet height in the pedestal.

Mr Broyd's planning application had been fastened to his front gate for all to see, but curiously no-one objected to the application, which involved farm buildings and a folly tower as well as an obelisk. Then, when the building of the obelisk was nearly complete, residents over a large area reacted with complaints to Aberconwy council, which threatened to place a Discontinuance Order on the obelisk, possibly condemning it for demolition. Tempers were raised. The applicant enlisted the support of respected landowners, architects and writers in a published petition, but this only aggravated the local action group opposed to the obelisk. One objector, Mr I Williams declared that, 'Obelisks were erected to show domination over a subjugated populace. We are not pacified'.[5]

Unsurprisingly, the controversy gradually settled down and the obelisk remained. For architects and obelisk builders, however, there is something to learn from this. How quickly the Bodysgallen affair drew in the surrounding questions of land use, the rights of ratepayers, democracy, class war, environmental practice and the law. The whole affair declared that the view belongs to the people. It begged the question of how one should go about raising obelisks in modern Britain and whether people want obelisks on their horizon. The fact is that planning officers in regional councils hold sway these days; without their permission new obelisks will not be seen.

During my time of writing, I met the artist, Bruce Lacey, and mentioned my research with obelisks on hill tops. Without a second's pause, Bruce astonished me by saying that if he had his way he would knock them all down. He said that if he went up a hill, it would be to commune with nature, (though I know he is seldom in the hills). The last thing he wanted to see was a big obelisk which might seem to shout 'Look at me!' to the surroundings. This was the only time I heard anyone speak of obelisks in this way.

The Millennium celebrations are now history. In 1999 there was an atmosphere of hope, albeit shortlived. The occasion was also seen as an opportunity for new public monuments and sculptures. Many artistic works went up, among them a 28 feet tall obeliscal upright made of dressed granite at Penarth in South Wales. The sculptor, Michael Dan Archer,(1955-) made two of the sides taper or converge while the other two diverge: the result appears like the blade of a mason's chisel. Archer has used granite for twenty-five years and as a hands-on sculptor, rather than an architect, he has been free to explore the material he loves. His works are as much about the texture and massiveness of stone as they are about shape. A more traditionally shaped obelisk by Michael Dan Archer is the obelisk at

Wynyard Estate in Durham, made of Cornish granite with bands of green marble, completed in 1999.

Another story was told in 1999 in the raising of small obelisk at Trowell in Nottinghamshire. It bears the gold inscribed sign of the Festival of Britain and commemorates the fact that Trowell had been picked as The Festival Village in 1951, to represent all villages. A black marble obelisk with the air of a memorial reminds the viewer that the rapid changes in country life in our lifetimes are too recent to contemplate in a detached way.

Another arrival in 1999, was the stone circle made on the top of Ham Hill in Somerset, in view of the Stoke-sub-Hamdon war memorial obelisk unveiled by the Prince of Wales in 1923. This was not planned, but the generous offering of Mr England, the quarryowner on the hilltop, using his machinery. Mr England told the author that, 'It was just a bit of fun'. Whatever others may think about this, the stones are well arranged. What a strange view has been made on the quarried hilltop, actually the largest hillfort in Europe; in the foreground, a late 20th century stone circle and, behind it, a 20th century obelisk.

At the end of a century of war, the hopes of humankind in 1999 were expressed in a Tibetan Peace Garden created in the grounds of the Imperial War Museum. Unveiled by his Holiness, the Dalai Lama, it features a flat stone wheel, carved with symbols, and seen through a pair of obeliscal gateway uprights, a white limestone obelisk surmounted with a Tibetan symbol. It closed the 20th century.

The shortlived Millennium celebrations were an anti-climax and it was not long before those hopes for Peace dwindled. The story of the third millennium can be told by future historians. Here, my purpose is specific and the question of the 3rd millennium is: 'What is the obelisk's overall state of progress in Britain?'

The answer, I feel, is – 'Not bad'. The 20th century saw a massive increase of British obelisks following the Great War. After this, as mentioned, there was a decrease, but the upward trend began again in the last years of the century. Britain could experience a renewed period of obelisk raising. The feature has become a novelty again and to raise a new obelisk is unusual and a talking point, yet in a long tradition. They look as odd today as the first that came in the late 1500s.

To take stock of the progress of this feature in Britain, we can look at the large quantity of obelisks listed in this book's gazetteer, (far more than Egypt, or Rome, though doubtless of less worth) and all the reasons to raise them up, along with all their uses, different designs and co-incidental histories. There is variation in every respect, dispelling the first notion that, 'Once you have seen one, you have seen them all'.

Obelisks are not about to die out. They are objects of desire. Many readers would wish to have a fairly large obelisk and the house and garden to go with it. What has declined in Britain, maybe temporarily, is the strength of will to make larger obelisks. What has also disappeared is the granite industry, through reduced demands and foreign imports. This is a great loss and means that future obelisk makers will have to start from first principles, but perhaps this is the best way.

VII

The Purpose of Obelisks: The Theories

1. *Solely Solar*

2. *The One that knows*

3. *Phallicism or landscape philosophy?*

4. *On the wavelength.*

5. *Secret signs*

6. *The shape*

7. *'Books of History'*

8. *The return of an old friend*

For readers who have got this far and feel sated with so many places, names and dates, this is the occasion to examine speculative theories about the obelisk's purpose, or meaning. These are the views of others, apart from my own thoughts on contact between Mediterranean cultures and Ancient Britain. The views of others, even when deluded, or exaggerated, influence attitudes towards the obelisk.

The interpretative theories to be recounted cannot be dismissed, because it is unlikely, to say the least, that anyone will ever know the precise reasoning behind the first obelisks. As author, I might wish to be an effective guide, but like everyone else, I can only speculate.

This is the enigma of the obelisk. In the long run, not knowing the truths of Ancient Egypt need not detract from the enjoyment of looking at obelisks in Britain. If anything, it surely adds to the allure. Not knowing has needled numerous scholars for several centuries, and caused no end of speculation from persuasive sources. The texts which would have answered all these questions in full were contained in the library at Alexandria, all destroyed.

What follows are introductions to theories which assume knowledge and do not supply either sufficient evidence or source notes. They are ideas which will either accord or not with common sense, by which I mean the powers of reasoning available to anyone who applies their mind to aspects of the obelisk. For example, the question of why obelisks are four sided is answered by common sense.

If we are to wonder about the purpose of the obelisk, should we contemplate an Egyptian context, or consider its significance in Britain? It is an important distinction. Since many reasons behind the raising of obelisks in Britain have been noted in earlier chapters, it is necessary at first to turn to the original source of inspiration.

For some readers, the reason for making the first obelisk is the crux of the matter and the object of the quest. I fear they will be disappointed by these short expositions. It is a much travelled road and other writers, such as Erik Iversen, have marked the way quite satisfactorily. I have not been to Egypt and as author I am no authority regarding Egyptian rites and practices three and half thousand years ago.

Δ SOLELY SOLAR?

The first theory is the general Egyptological assumption that the obelisk in Ancient Egypt was exclusively a symbol of the sun. There is no questioning the obelisk's connection with the sun, but it seems that Egyptologists cannot go much further in their explanation, except to add that the obelisk's place was in pairs before the temple door.

The modern rule for Egyptology, the one absolute, is that very little can be stated with a high degree of certainty. So much that was taken as fact has been disproved lately and it has to be said that the accepted 'use', 'purpose', or 'significance' of the obelisk is not necessarily what Egyptologists have told us. There is no conclusive proof that obelisks are no more than solar symbols, intended for placing in pairs before a temple entrance, as at Heliopolis (as we are told again and again). The 'meaning' behind the obelisk could be a lot more than that, or a lot less. The experience of contemporary Egyptology has led to a situation in which it would be a mistake to accept as final the old passed-on notions.

Of course, everything in Egypt was linked to the sun. Ra, the sun god was also Re, at dawn the scarab known as Kephri, also Ra-Harakhte – the Sun Hawk, and Amun Re – patron of all Pharaohs and king of the gods, of which there were many. The fifth name of every Pharaoh was preceded by a cartouche of hieroglyphs which meant 'son of Ra'. They were themselves Sun-gods.

For eight years from 1352BC, the Pharaoh Amenhophis IV changed his name to Akhenaten and established a new era of sun worship, claiming that Aten the sun disc was the one and only god and that all the other gods were to be abolished. He built a new temple at Akhetaten, the present day Tell-el-Amarna, in Middle Egypt. A fine description is found in the Larousse Encyclopaedia of Mythology:

> 'The Pharaoh was his only priest, and his cult celebrated in a temple resembling the ancient solar temples of the Old Kingdom and called, like the celebrated sanctuary of Ra at Heliopolis, Het Benben, 'the Palace of the Obelisk'. There at the extremity of the courtyard, rose the obelisk of the sun. The ceremony consisted of an oblation of fruits and cakes and the recitation of hymns of great beauty, which were composed by the king himself, in honour of his god. In them the sun was glorified, as in olden days, as creator of mankind and benefactor of the world... All men, they proclaimed, were equally the children of Aten. In this modified attempt at monotheism we may suspect plans for an Empire-wide religion, especially if we remember that at this time Egyptian domination extended as far as Asia, where the Syrians worshipped Adonis and the Jews worshipped Adonai'.

In the time of the Pharaoh Akenhaten we see 'the obelisk of the sun' in a religious context as a part of the temple, as an instrument of the sun, the god Ra in all his divinations, and the possession of the personification of the sun-god (the Pharaoh). As a sundial it was an instrument of godly communication, by which the sun imparted knowledge to the Pharaohs priests. This I believe was its true purpose. If the obelisks had been solar symbols, they would have been worshipped, which was not the case.

But what about all the other obelisks in the temples of other gods, already in place before Akenhaten – and those that came after him?

Akenhaten's 'back to basics' dismissal of the pantheon was bound to have repurcussions. Within thirty years of his death, the priests of Amun managed to persuade the Pharaoh Tutenkhaten to reinstate all the other gods and their temples and to change his name back to Tutenkhamun. All the carved inscriptions on steles, obelisks and temple walls which had been changed to show Aten's name were changed back again a few years later.

Ancient Egyptian obelisks bear contradictory inscriptions, with erasures and re-inscriptions, naming more than one Pharaoh. Practically every obelisk of Ancient Egypt was taken from the country, often in different stages. The shifting locations of the obelisks, and conflicting chronology derived from their inscriptions have made them difficult to date exactly. The dating to years BC that I have followed is derived from Alun Buffry's Lists of the Pharaohs, its database cross-referring with many eminent sources.[1]

The very old city of On, not far from modern Cairo, became Heliopolis, meaning in Greek, 'City of the Sun'. The Pharaoh Seti I, ruling in 1294BC, claimed to have brought many obelisks to the place. Tuthmosis III, ruling in 1479BC brought obelisks to the temple of Ptah at Memphis, and also to Karnak. (Ptah was the god of inertia or stability, guardian of the *Tat* or *Djed* pillar of stability. Large obelisks also possessed this quality of immovable stability). Tuthmosis III was succeeded by Queen Hatshepsut who added four more obelisks to Karnak. Ramesses II, ruling from 1279-1184BC, brought two obelisks to the temple at Luxor, one of which is the one standing in Paris. It is said that he took fourteen obelisks to the city of Tanis in the Delta. For those who believe all obelisks were destined in pairs, that would be seven pairs.

Of an older vintage, though even less substantiated, are obelisks from much further South. Researchers have documentary evidence and fragments of obelisks put up at the Temple of Neurine at Absia by the Pharaoh Sahure in 2,458BC. The peak and top part of an obelisk known as Teti's Obelisk were found. The attribution to King Teti, 2,323BC, if true, would date the broken piece to the Old Kingdom. Other fragments have been linked with the Pharaoh Inyotef I, ruling in 2,074BC. These are inscribed with older hieroglyphs unknown to Champollion, or modern cryptographers. Among the oldest were *benben* which, although they were related to obelisks, were more akin to small pyramids raised on a tall bases and hardly qualify as obelisks in terms of the defining shape. They stood on taller bases and were much shorter and bulkier than the later 'proper' obelisks which date from approximately 1,500-500BC.

How many obelisks existed before Alexander the Great or the Caesars came to Egypt? Would that have been a hundred, or more? Surely many obelisks were removed or broken in earlier invasions when Egypt was attacked by Syrians, Hittites and Persians, the last of whom installed their king as Pharaoh and introduced the camel in 521BC. The Persians were particularly vexed by obelisks marked with the names of Tuthmosis III and Ramasses II, both of whom had treated them with no mercy in earlier times. They destroyed the Temple of the Sun at Heliopolis.

Smaller obelisks were easily moved, but larger ones required engineers. The Roman emperors held Egypt from the end of Julius Caesar and Cleopatra's time in 44BC, until roughly AD311 and removed as many as forty obelisks. After another 1,500 years, during which time others may have been taken, imperial France, Britain and the USA took the rest, a total of ten or more. And so it is that today there exists in Egypt no more than nine standing obelisks and ten fallen ones.

Their evidence, plus Greek and Roman accounts naming some of their previous locations, provide insufficient basis for the generalisation that obelisks were intended in pairs before the temple door. Prior to any of the pairs of obelisks, which were usually not pairs but separate obelisks brought from different places, the single upright was already the standard. Rather than being the rule, the use of dual obelisks, albeit frequent, was the exception. The dual obelisks tended to survive the ravages of invasion and destruction because they were protected by the temple and because some of them were very large and could not be removed easily. The obelisks associated with temples were nearly all made within the 18th and 19th dynasties of the New Kingdom, a period from about 1567BC to 1200BC. This was a period of temple building during which temples were built at Karnak, Luxor, Abu Simbel, Abydos and elsewhere. 'The period of obelisks', as it were, began a thousand years earlier and continued for a thousand years after.

I want to forget about 'meaning', (the word seems empty of itself in the present context) and concentrate on 'purpose'. There was a direct link to the sun and a purpose, held in the principle of the sundial. If the obelisk was the Pharaohs's priests' instrument of the sun, by which the sun provided knowledge to the priests, it was more likely to have been in a less confined space, such as a large courtyard, along with other scientific instruments.

Δ 'THE ONE THAT KNOWS'

The upright stick in the sand was the first instrument in mankind's search for measuring time. The first function of the obelisk – and I dare say its purpose – was as the supreme version of a 'shadow stick'. Casting a shadow which moved with the sun's angle, it served as the gnomon (Gr; 'The one that knows') at the centre of a piece of ground. It was seen that the shadow grew shorter when the sun was overhead, and since this was most of the day in Egypt, the taller the obelisk was, the better it defined the hours in the middle of the day. It is pleasing to think of an obelisk as a sort of Big Ben of the Nile, though to measure lesser periods of time, the temple priests also used waterclocks. After about 1,500BC smaller, more portable sundials, using a scribed plate and an inclined gnomon were used in Egypt.

Obelisks and the sundial principle promoted some of mankind's greatest discoveries. When it was seen that the shadows were inconsistent throughout the day and in the course of the year, the Pharaoh's mathematicians were forced to learn more about the earth's rotation and greater measures of time. A complete calendar could be calculated when it was seen that an obelisk at the Tropic of Cancer, which ran through Philae, cast no shadow at midday on the solstice. The circumference of the earth could be deduced by measuring the distance between two obelisks sited some way from each other, and then comparing the difference between the length of their shadows.

We can deduce from this that if the obelisks of ancient Egypt were solar timepieces in the control of the temple priests, their precise locations were critical. Thus when a pair of obelisks stood before the temple doors at Luxor or Heliopolis, they were placed at an exact point where the solstice sun would strike one and then gradually enter the door, penetrating the temple for a while before striking the other obelisk.

Thus we have measurements of time: 364 solar days plus some solstice hours, 13 lunar months and 28 days in the lunar cycle. We have measurements of great distances, and calculations for the curve of the earth, along with mathematics and geometry. Much of the progress of these sciences and discoveries was marked by watching the sun's arc in the sky in relation to obelisks located at different latitudes.

When the sun sank over the horizon, its last glows reflecting on the peak of the obelisk, there was another use. Charting the heavens was immensely important to the temple priests, who were men of science as well as superstition, making no division between astronomy and astrology. The same obelisks which marked the sun in the day were of essential astronomic use in positioning stars by the familiar method of measuring the angles and stellar movements in relation to the fixed obelisk. Whole books could and have been written about the advances in astronomy, mathematics and physics made by the Egyptians, all aided by 'the one who knows'.

Δ PHALLICISM OR LANDSCAPE PHILOSOPHY?

The obelisk's association with the sun gets complicated, because, in the minds of the temple priests of Ancient Egypt there was a connection between the sun and the phallus. In European cultures there has always been a link between the spring sun and fertility. Today, there is a tendency to see Freudian symbols everywhere.

The half-serious beliefs in phallicism as a motive or inspiration for erecting obelisks were put forward in England by Hargrave Jennings, briefly in his book about the obelisk in 1877, and extensively in his later book about phallicism. His texts on the worship of nature pointed out how much sexual imagery had been put into oblivion by witchfinders, churchmen and other puritans in Europe. (If priapic statues, herms and other obviously male attributes had still been in public places and among the crops, perhaps there would have been no need to look at towers, megaliths and obelisks in the same light).

There was a great deal of sexual imagery to be found in carvings and frescoes among the ruins and tombs of Ancient Egypt. Some were sanitised by christians, removing erect penises from paintings of Pharaohs and gods in order to avoid embarrassment. The symbolism of the Pharaoh's recurring erection was allied to the daily return of the sun. Both embodied the regenerating principle of fertility and life itself, and were celebrated by priests in the temple of Heliopolis. (Did Queen Nefertiti assist her husband Akhenaten in his auto-erogeny? Her correct title in the ceremony was 'The Divine Hand').

Although there was nothing to link obelisks directly to Jennings' wider phallicistic beliefs, (that all upright stones and structures had a sexual symbolism), there are graphic associations which cannot be dismissed. Obelisks rise from the earth and penetrate the sky. In the pantheon of Ancient Egypt, the earth-god Geb is depicted in paintings as a brown prone figure with an erect penis; arching over him is Nuit, the sky goddess, and at night her enveloping darkness sinks over the earth in a long coupling.

As a Rosicrucian, Jennings believed that the universe was ruled by the principle of light, or fire and this was represented by the sun, or in the physical world, the phallus. He used as his prime source and inspiration a privately published 18th century book, *Discourse on the Worship of Priapus*, of which only thirty-seven copies were printed in 1786. It was written by an unusual man, Richard Payne Knight,1751-1824, and was intended exclusively for the thirty-seven members of the Society of Dilettantes, none of whom were shocked by it. However, one of the Dilettantes showed the book to others outside the society, and before long there was a public outcry. One of the horrified was a man of letters, Thomas Mathias, who broadcast the 'Discourse' to a wider public in his own book, *The Pursuits of Literature – A Satirical Poem in Four Dialogues*, in 1794, which ran to sixteen reprintings.

Mathias wrote about his contact, the unknown Dilettante who showed him his copy of Payne Knight's private publication.

> 'He would insist on my perusing a long disquisition in quarto, on the Worship of Priapus with numerous and most disgusting plates... all the ordure and filth, all the antique pictures, and all the representations of generative organs, in their most odious and degraded protrusion, have been raked together and copulated (no other idea seems to have been in the mind of the author) and copulated I say, with a new species of blasphemy'.

Richard Payne Knight never lived this down. He admitted that the 'Discourse' had been unreasonably rushed and, apart from one or two stories from Naples and Sicily, not verified. He was a most widely self-educated man, a true dilettante who could understand issues which are difficult for today's single subject professionals to comprehend, and who wrote about landscape in a most enlightened way. A Classicist, poet, and planter of trees who was highly influential in the philosophy of landscaping, who opposed the works of Capability Brown and hated rules and the clergy, Payne Knight was also a trustee of the British Museum, an MP, and Deputy-President of the Society of Antiquaries. He was also author of *The Landscape* and *The Progress of Civil Society* and generally an ideological force to be reckoned with. Yet, as far as the public were concerned, he was a dirty old man because of his *Discourse on the Worship of Priapus*.

There is an anecdote about the founder of Surrealism, André Bréton, and his friends. As they came out of a doorway in Paris, Bréton glanced up to see the Egyptian obelisk at the Place de la Concorde. Apparently, he suggested a work of art depicting the huge monolith being licked like an ice-cream. That was a moment of surrealism. For Jennings and his Rosicrucian friends to have regarded obelisks and other stone uprights as phalli was unrealistic.

When a man or woman travels the land and begins to discern an upright stone on the horizon, he or she would have to be witless to think there was a phallicistic intention. That would be to miss the most obvious announcement of an upright stone, which is Life. We stand when we are alive. The upright tells us that somebody put the stone there, and if it is an obelisk, the hand of man is even more obvious. It declares that this stone matters to somebody and that if you challenge this stone or the declarations carved upon it, somebody will oppose you. And, if it is a large obelisk or stone, that somebody is going to be powerful. These are the fundamental reactions of homo sapiens. Ancient Egypt's obelisks demonstrated superhuman strength and the Pharaoh's supremacy. Even to illiterate desert tribesmen, the suspended mass of the upright stone contradicted universal laws and implied huge force. Those contemplating incursion would think twice before doing so.

There are, of course, stones of different sizes used in fertility rites in distant lands and some wonderfully blunt sexual objects like the Cerne Abbas Giant in the British landscape, fully intended to make the viewer recognise the phallic aspect instantly. Phallicism is a useful adjunct for writers pointing to the desecration of so many old stones by churchmen, but the the link with the obelisk is surely a red herring. As a way of viewing obelisks in Britain it is innaccurate, as the wish to put up a phallic symbol was not the intention.

Δ ON THE WAVELENGTH.

Coming from a different source are 20th century speculations that raised stones transmit signals between themselves, both through the air, and through the ground in which they stand. These theories derive from British geomancers and might apply to the obelisks of Egypt. Even the most reactionary of British landscape historians now acknowledge the presence of ley lines connecting a string of significant ancient sites over a long distance. Through these lines are channelled unseen forces, from one centre to another. Lines run through Europe towards Egypt, where the Pharaohs were geomancers of the first order and so it is quite possible that obelisks were linked in an old world web to similar sites some distance away.

Regarding unseen forces, obelisks in Ancient Egypt were capable of piezo-electric transmissions. Granite contains quartz crystal, the most sensitive conductor of piezo-electric currents. These are caused by positive and negative currents developing on alternate edges of its prismatic edges under differing conditions. If a tiny crystal in a crystal radio set can pick up transmissions from other continents, one wonders what sort of vibrations are moving between heavy granite monoliths cut in the shape of a crystal. How did the granite react to the great heat of the day and the cooling at night?

The science of ultrasound and molecular pulsation is still being discovered and my overall impression is that the theory may one day be proved. Even if it is, there is not the slightest indication that the obelisk makers of Ancient Egypt were even aware of the this type of energy.

On an audible level, I am reminded of the work of Mr J Richardson, buried beneath one of Britains largest monoliths in Kensal Green Cemetery (ch.IV). The experiments which Richardson had made in preparing the 'Rock Harmonicon' are yet to be absorbed. When he had held two identical rocks at a distance from each other, the striking of one was transmitted to the second stone. The unusual sounds made by striking pieces of different rocks had strong physical effects on his listeners.

Δ SECRET SIGNS

The obelisk as a covert symbol, or signal of something else, as discussed in earlier pages, has some basis in reality. However, the association between British obelisks and freemasonry needs to be kept in perspective. Freemasons were very numerous within the strata of society who created fine garden monuments, or who went on the Grand Tour.

Some obelisks have obvious masonic links, others are not linked at all. Take for example the obelisk in the beautiful landscape of

Wroxton Abbey. Readers may recall mention of this in an earlier chapter with reference to the commemoration of a visit from Frederick, Prince of Wales. Now add to this the facts that the Prince of Wales was a freemason, and that his chaplain, Reverend John Theophilus Desaguliers, Doctor of Law and Fellow of the Royal Society, had earlier been Grand Master and co-founder of the Grand Lodge in London. Desaguliers, who was part French, had already converted European kings and dukes to the brotherhood with missionary zeal. Wroxton's owner, the Earl of Guilford, was a mason and his son became Lord North, Britain's Prime Minister during the American War of Independence.

The year before his visit to Wroxton, Prince Frederick had visited Bath, where the obelisk which Beau Nash unveiled to celebrate the royal visit was intended to be in the Egyptian style, that is to say, without a Roman plinth. This bias was in line with freemasonry's interest in Ancient Egypt and it was intended to please the future king and Desaguliers. (In fact the designer had very little idea of what obelisks in Egypt looked like, and had constructed a sort of tapering pyramid – in those days another name for the obelisk – of the kind illustrated in early books about Egypt).

Compare the examples given, in which one can easily detect the hand of freemasonry, with the case of a later Prince of Wales, also an initiate: the future George IV. As king, he passed through Ramsgate and the town subsequently put up an obelisk to commemorate the event. Are we to regard the Ramsgate obelisk as a masonic phenomenon? The answer must be 'No', even if a mason in the town proposed the idea and raised the money.

It might be possible to see a masonic connection in every obelisk. Conspiracy theorists might think that those countless obelisks in cemeteries marked the graves of freemasons. Or that hundreds of obelisk war memorials from 1919 were the result of masonic influences among the officers and committees who chose the feature.

However, the masonic connection is not a viable research route because it is not consistent. Nor is there enough data to support or disprove the conspiracy theory: conclusions are impossible, even generalisations are difficult. As for cemeteries, obelisks mark the graves of masons and non-masons alike. With war memorials, there were many regional influences on the memorial committees, and while freemasonry may have been one of them, it was not to the fore. Even in the 18th century, when masonic and non-masonic landowners raised obelisks under the pretext that these were memorials to distant historical figures, we cannot be sure of their true purpose. Landscape philosophy, design and fashion, played their part, as did politics and status seeking.

Also discussed in earlier pages and even more tenuous were the underlying Roman catholic associations of some of Britain's earlier obelisks, from the 1590s until about 1730. Initially, these were in imitation of Rome, where the pope had symbolically mastered heresy by reraising the obelisks which had lain in the ground, surmounting them with his metal crosses. The story was much publicised as a catholic triumph, even in Britain, where catholicism was a proscribed religion. The link, when examined, comes to very little: there were far more obelisks of the period which had nothing to do with catholics.

Some of the catholics had friends and relatives among the Jacobite exiles in Rome. They dreamt of more than freedom of religion, and were in fact planning to return to Britain with King James and an army. However, it was one thing to build an obelisk on one's land to remind oneself of Rome, and quite another to join an armed rebellion. By the time the pope forbade the secret societies in 1738, those catholics who were freemasons had to leave the lodge, and presumably ended any relationship they may have had with the sign of the obelisk.

Δ THE SHAPE

Whatever the true meaning of the obelisk, either as an icon of sun worship, marked on the ancient coinage of Apollonia, or as an architectural monument with uses defined by Vitruvius, there is much that has never been said about the shape itself. Obelisks are defined by shape.

There is something peculiar about the obelisk shape. I have tried hard to discern exactly what this is, but remain unsure. No one has explained the outline: it is so simple, so recognisable. The uniform taper of the sides confounds the human eye with unidentifiable associations, not least of which is the appearance of dimininishing perspective. This is geometry, science and art in one and it affects the eye and recognition systems in the human brain. It seems to me that we can recognise the obelisk in a nano-second at a distance of up to thirty miles, yet cannot recognise what we have recognised. Such visual impressions seem to be operating on a subconscious level.

The obelisk has an elemental shape, yet contains other elements of vertical line, horizon, triangle, cube and cone. Its broadening base speaks of stability and the force of gravity; the regularity and evenness of its taper suggests the skilled and precise working of a large stone mass. The symmetry and perfection of the shape tells the viewer that it is not a natural occurrence, although in fact the shape can be seen in mineral crystals.

The shape of a monolithic obelisk from antiquity could not be copied at first by British architects and builders, because the structural strength of a monolithic obelisk is completely different from the strength of an obelisk made of blocks of stone. Thus, if the shape that an 18th century obelisk builder wanted to follow was copied from an ancient monolith, the result would be structurally weak and liable to partial collapse. This is what happened in several cases, and these obelisks needed rebuilding. To avoid such an outcome, obelisk builders learnt to bulk out the shape and employ taller pedestals to gain overall height. Later, after 1850 and the mechanisation of the granite industry, it became possible to hue colossal splinters of stone into monolithic obelisks. Even so, the bulked-out shape and tall plinth continued to prevail.

Another departure from the true shape was the suppression of the pyramidion. I can only conclude that this was for practical reasons, such as those mentioned above. The orthodox shape with its acute pyramidion was liable to weakness in an obelisk constructed of ashlar blocks, so the builders lowered it. The effect of lowering the pyramidion and bulking out the main outline was to alter the shape, making it more massive and less like a needle. The 'wrong' shape sticks out 'like a sore thumb'.

Whilst talking of shape, when is an obelisk not an obelisk? Shape is the only criterion and yet even an ill-made obelisk can work at a distance. For example, the Cook Monument on the North York Moors, when seen close, is not really an obelisk. A group of estate workers and builders climbed onto the ridge where the moors begin and built something obeliscal in outline from stone blocks cut from an outcrop a few yards away. At some point they must have run out of scaffolding, money, or patience because the overall shape is squat, bulky, and obtuse. It should have been taller. Yet this did not matter because the monument was intended to be viewed from afar, and at a distance it has has the appearance of an obelisk.

Δ BOOKS OF HISTORY

> 'We recall the appellation 'Books of History', and although this description was surely not the single purpose of the obelisks of Egypt, it was certainly one of its primary functions'.

Reading John Bell's summation of the accounts of Strabo we have a perceived purpose of the obelisk, unintended at first, but one which added associative meaning and increased its significance with each century. As a history book, 'Cleopatra's Needle' functions where it stands today. The history is invested in the form of inscriptions of proclamations and tributes to the Pharaoh, which the Egyptians carefully carved on the sides of the obelisk in ancient times.

As books of history, obelisks have served historians well, but their histories, legible to all, sometimes brought about their downfall, as in the Persian fury directed upon the obelisks marked with the hieroglyphs of Tuthmosis III and Ramesses II. Both Pharaohs were remembered for their merciless conquest of foreign lands.

This use of obelisks as permanent historical records invested them with language and writing; the form of the ancient Egyptian script, with its pictograms conjuring hybrid jackals and hawks, brought additional significance. Most of the interest devoted to the obelisks of Rome by the popes and the secret societies in the 16th and 17th centuries was in connection with the hieroglyphic inscriptions.

Whatever purposes the obelisks had in ancient times, the combination of indestructability and hieroglyphs ensured their worth as books of history, adding the quality of antiquity. Anybody in London seeing 'Cleopatra's Needle' and the hieroglyphs which confirm its age of about 3,500 years, is likely to experience a moment's reflection on the ephemerality of their own lives. The past gazes down on them, with the silence of a hundred generations.

The older inscriptions are, the more they are valued by historians. British obelisks, considerably younger, will one day be old enough to have a similar effect. As Books of History they are still slim volumes.

Δ THE RETURN OF AN OLD FRIEND

There is an appealing theory that the obelisks in Ancient Egypt were related in some way to the tapering megaliths of Ancient Britain. There is evidence for this contention, but historians will know that the relationship was not necessarily close or exclusive.

Were Britain's standing-stones and the Pharaoh's obelisks the same idea? They were certainly contemporary. If the link could be substantiated, it would explain why Britain, with its megalithic prehistory, welcomed the obelisk feature which appeared in Elizabethan England. It would be pleasing to think of the coming of obelisks over the last 400 years as a revival, like the return of an old friend, who has been abroad and returned in polished, foreign style.

From an Ancient Briton's perspective the obelisk is a very fine megalith, the standing stone of dreams, its shape made perfect by a degree of science which we are told our far ancestors never possessed. Perhaps the British view the obelisk in a slightly different way to other nations, because we dwell in a megalithic land. We have heel stones and sunken megaliths in these islands, some fairly close in shape to the obelisk.

Many British churchyards, founded in the 7th & 8th centuries occupy former sacred sites, dating from two thousand years earlier. The Christian church, already thriving before the Romans left Britain, prosecuted the destruction of such sites, despoiling the stones and issuing edicts forbidding the worshipping of them. Then, in 601, Pope Gregory counselled Abbot Mellitus to tell missionaries in Britain to convert such pagan temples and megalithic sites into churches. This was at least easier, as some of the megaliths were too large to destroy. Today they stand or lie within the churchyard.

Seven miles inland from Flamborough Head on the Yorkshire coast is the Rudston Monolith, occupying part of the churchyard at All Saints, Rudston. This mighty stone, about 45 feet long, was raised to a perfect vertical; 26 feet stand above ground today. It is of a moor grit conglomerate from the Cleveland Hills, at least thirty miles distant, and it was hewn, we are told, in the late Neolithic period, roundly 2,000-1,500BC.

At some point in its long history, the top of the monolith has been damaged, probably by someone trying to screw in a metal cross, and so it wears a copper formed hat. The building of the church on the actual site of the Ancient British temple associated with the monolith, a mere 10 yards away, illustrates the christian mission to convert earlier sacred sites. It must have been hard for the vicars of Rudston to explain in later years.

There are countless lesser examples in which old stones in the new churchyards of the 7th and 8th centuries were altered with symbols and carving and somehow accommodated within christianity's insistent tradition. Churchyard crosses and, indeed, later market crosses, were not necessarily crucixes, but marked a crossway, crossroads, or meeting place.

Even after the arrival of Christianity, large stones could be erected, and British and Early Saxon artisans were capable of carving elaborate patterns on a upright stone. An English example was the Bewcastle Cross, dating from the time of the Christian kingdom of Northumbria,c620-860, a very violent period. Carved in a local stone, the Bewcastle Cross is not a cross, though it is asserted that it once bore a cross on top. In 'Buildings of Britain: Cumbria', Pevsner states that the carving at Bewcastle has all the same sources as the Ruthwell Cross, thirty miles to the West. 'Iconography has been traced to Coptic, that is Egyptian, Early Christian sources – and Egypt was the country of origin of that branch of monasticism which via the South of France extended into Ireland and from there to Scotland and North England'.

If in iconography, why not in shape? As it stands, it is noticeable that the Bewcastle stone shares the same proportions and taper as an obelisk. The four sides of the fourteen and a half feet shaft are equal, covered with different runes and patterns and symbols.

To return to prehistory: many writers have gone before me in alluding to connections between Britain, Phoenicia, Assyria and Egypt. The great temples of Stonehenge, Avebury and Maes Howe in these islands were broadly contemporary with the building of pyramids and the raising of obelisks in Luxor and Karnak. In fact, and this may surprise, many of them are older. There is much evidence of trade between the eastern Mediterranean and Britain in the first and second millennium BC.

One line of enquiry is the mysterious Sanchoniathon's assertion that obelisks and sacred stones were erected in Phoenicia prior to their adoption in Egypt. The Phoenicians occupied a number of coastal sites in the Mediterranean from approximately 1400BC until about AD600. Seaborne traders who dealt in glass, precious metals, ivory and ceramics, they were a constant force of intercultural exchange. It was they who invented the alphabet in Byblos in about 1,000BC. Sanchoniathon, who came from Berytus (Beirut) and wrote in Beric (Phoenician), lived in the great age of Phoenicia, prior to the founding of Carthage in 814BC. Thinking of Sanchoniathon's claim that obelisks and *betulae* were in Phoenicia before Egypt, we should remember that Phoenicia was composed of ports and coastal sites around the Mediterranean. It touched on older cultures, such as the Minoan and Assyrian peoples, or even the dreaded Hyskos people who invaded Egypt in 1786BC, arriving from the sea.

Phoenician traders frequently visited the shores of Britain, bringing glass and pottery and taking away tin. Strabo stated that the Carthaginians traded for many years with the 'Tin islands', presumably the Scillies, and the nearby Cornish coast, where tin was mined. Phoenicians were certainly responsible for transplanting the idea of building dolmens and barrows on the North African coast. Any Mediterranean traders visiting the coasts of Spain, Portugal, France or Britain would have seen tall standing-stones.

History suggests that an obelisk from the Nile, though smooth and well defined, would not have appeared to the Ancient British as unfamiliar in itself. Doubtless, the hieroglyphs, granite smoothness and clean-cut pyramidion would have caused excitement, but not the shape. The four-sided aspect of the obelisk was the easiest to grind and cut; the taper made one end easier to lift into the air and the other stronger and more stable in the earth. My own speculation is that obelisks developed from other upright stones and then became the standard shape.

What made the Egyptians different from other cultures which may have had obelisks before them, was that they were engaged in quarrying and stone-cutting on an industrial scale. The real division between an obelisk from Egypt and a standing stone in one of Britain's sun temples was in technical expertise.

CHAPTER I

1. p.225 'The Monument Guide to England & Wales', Jo Darke, 1991 Macdonald & Co.

2. p.27 'Garden Sculpture', Michael Symes, Shire 1996.

3. Illus p.58 'Sculpture in Britain, 1530-1830' by Margaret Whinney, (revised John Physick, 1988) Pelican ,1964. Illustration in 'The History of St.Paul's', by William Dugdale/1658:photo: British Library.

4. A drawing from 1780 shows the former state with the obelisks when the tomb was sited at Midhurst. (see H.E Hinkley's 'Easebourne, Its Church and Priory', 1948. (Note:Ch.3,Note21: 'Sculpture in Britain, 1530-1830', Whinney/Physick.Pelican 1988.

5. 'Sculpture in Britain,1530-1830' by Margaret Whinney, (revised John Physick, 1988) Pelican, 1964, says of this tomb, 'A further new feature is the use of four tall obelisks standing at the corners of the base. This must surely be a borrowing from Du Cercau's 1562 'Second Livre d'architecture', where a tomb of this device is shown in conjunction with a single reclining effigy...'

6. Nikolaus Pevsner, Nottinghamshire, 2nd edition 1979, 'The Buildings of England' series

7. 'In Search of Shakespeare', Michael Wood, BBC 2003.

8. Viewed as a wholehearted borrower from others, he is described in the title of J.Godwin's biography as 'Kircher, A Renaissance Man and the Quest for Lost Knowledge'.

CHAPTER II

1. J.S Curl, 'The Victorian Celebration of Death', Sutton 2000)

2. This was the Kit-Kat club. p.276 'Enlightenment – Britain and the creation of the Modern World', Roy Porter, Penguin 2000 .

3. p.87- 'Hawksmoor', Kerry Downes, Thames & Hudson.

4. Blenheim Palace,David Green, Country Life 1951.

5. British Library- Additions/The Blenheim Papers, folios 240, 252-255B (letters around 1722)

6. British Library- Additions/The Blenheim Papers, folios 240, 252-255B (letters around 1722)

7. p.12 'The Victorian Celebration of Death', James Stevens Curl, Sutton 2000.

8. p.125 'Tomlinson's Comprehensive Guide to Northumberland', William Tomlinson, 12th Edtn, David & Charles 1968.

9. Devonshire Collection, Chatsworth, inventory reference W.C.154

10: 'The Correspondence of Alexander Pope', ed G.Sherborne, 1956.

11: p.406, 'The Biographical Dictionary of British Architects, 1600-1840', 3rd edtn, Howard Colvin, Yale 1995.

12: p.200 'The Monument Guide to England and Wales'. Jo Darke, Macdonald 1991.

13. p.209, 'Discovering London Statues & Monuments', Margaret Baker, Shire 2002.

14. This is an interesting subject, discussed in Alastair Laing's essay for the Symposium of the International Society of Church Monuments in 1982, subsequently a seminar at the Mellon Foundation for the Study of British Art. It was titled:'Fischer Von Erlach's Monument to Wenzel, Count Wratislaw Von Mitrowicz and its place in the Typology of the Pyramid Tomb'.

15: 'Farnborough Hall', G.Gervase Jackson-Stops 1981, revised Jeffrey Haworth, 1999, National Trust.

16. 'Sir John Soane: Enlightenment Thought and the Royal Academy Lectures', David Watkins, Cambridge University Press 1996.

17. Downing's map of 1740 does not show the obelisk, but it is shown on Warren's map of 1791 in its new location in Chequers Square. The author gratefully acknowledges the assistance of St.Edmundsbury Borough Council in this incomplete research.

18. Wiltshire Record Office 343.907.

19. 'Fitzwilliam Wentworth Estates', an article by Shirley Meek, 1992, Follies Magazine Vol 4, Issue No.3

CHAPTER III

1. All information and quotation relating to the Waithman obelisk are from Philip Ward-Jackson's text. p.389, 'Public Sculpture of the City of London', PMSA National Recording Project, 2003.

2. 'Victorian Taste – Some Social Aspects of Architecture', John Gloag, 1962. David & Charles 1972.

3. 'An Apology for the Revival of Christian Architecture', Weale, London 1843.

4. In acknowlegement of research in preparation for 'Public Sculpture of Bristol', by Professor Douglas Merritt and Janet Margrie, in the Public Monuments and Sculpture Association's National Recording Project series, 'Public Sculpture of Britain', published by Liverpool University Press.

5. p.214. 'The Monument Guide to England & Wales', Jo Darke, 1991.

6. The contestants for this title, in addition to the Helensburgh obelisk, are the two memorials in Kensal Green Cemetery in London, which are on taller

pedestals, but are monoliths of the same size and material and made in the same stone yards of Aberdeen.

7. 'The Monument Guide to England & Wales', Jo Darke, 1991.

8. 'Public Sculpture of Liverpool', Terry Cavanagh. University of Liverpool Press / PMSA.

9: PMSA National Recording Project.

10. From an unpublished coaching book, 'Waybilly – or Fifty Years Ago' , by G. Harrison, 1884.

11. Source – PMSA National Recording Project.

12: A quote of 7/- per dozen in 1875 equalled thirty-four letters to the pound. A stonemason of 1887 would earn about £1.50 a week; a skilled letter cutter would be paid a bit more than this.

13. Where did the Copped Hall obelisks go ? Two have turned up at Anglesey Abbey in Cambridgeshire.

CHAPTER IV

1. Henry Cole Diaries, notation Elizabeth Bonython, National Art Library, V&A Museum.

2. p.65, 'John Bell – The Sculptor's Life and Works', Richard Barnes, Frontier 1999.

3. John Selden, 1584-1654, Historian and Antiquary.

4. A mysterious Phoenician writer.

5. Joseph Bonomi jr,1796-1878, was the son of the anglicised Italian architect of the same name, who designed the pyramid at Blickling Hall, Norfolk. Young Bonomi studied sculpture in the Royal Academy Schools and then set off to Rome, and from there to Egypt, where he remained for twenty years, drawing and exploring the monuments. When he returned to Britain, he was commissioned to provide and set up the Egyptian Court of the Crystal Palace at Sydenham. This was his occupation at the time of Bell's lectures, though within a couple of years he was to become curator of the Soane Museum.

CHAPTER V

1. This information is to be found in J.S Curl's 'The Victorian Celebration of Death'.

2. p.131 'Churchyards of England & Wales', Brian Bailey, Hale 1987.

3. p.89 'The Rise and Progress of the Aberdeen Granite Industry', William Diack, 1948.

4. p.92. 'The Rise and Progress of the Aberdeen Granite Industry'.

CHAPTER VI

1. This sort of thinking has not entirely disappeared. As recently as 1999 a Norfolk resident prevented the placing of an artistic village sign in the form an upright mark stone, by claiming that he could not tolerate this heathen image within view of Berghapton church.

2. Restoration and repair costs of the Naval War Division Memorial was met partly by English Heritage and Friends of War Memorials.

3. 'At the Going Down of the Sun', Derek Boorman, Ebor Press 1988.

4. p.161. 'A Users Guide to Public Sculpture', PMSA, English Heritage 2000.

5. Follies Magazine, Vol 5, No.1, Spring 1993.

CHAPTER VII

1. Lists included in Alun Buffry's book 'From Dot to Cleo', Frontier 1997

In Acknowledgement

For their assistance, kindness and generosity to the author in his research, Richard Barnes wishes to thank the following:

Mike Cousins of the Folly Fellowship, who has been photographing obelisks for some years and provided photographs for this book (numbers 8,10a, 12b, 18a, 20a, 21b, 43) and invaluable assistance in checking details in the gazetteer; John Foster, Education Officer at Blenheim Palace, for design copies and valuable information about Hawksmoor's Explanation of the obelisk; Dr Pedro Gaspar, conservation officer of Friends of War Memorials; Nicola Grey, archivist at the Royal Society of Arts; Julian Lea-Jones of Bristol Historical Research & Temple Local History Group; Jane Furlong at National Inventory of War Memorials; Alan Cox at Copped Hall; Tim Skelton with his study of the War Memorials of Sir Edwin Lutyens; The Lutyens Trust and the author, Jane Brown, who gave me slides and helpful information about Lutyens; Henry Vivian-Neal of The Friends of Kensal Green Cemetery; Michael Dan Archer, sculptor; Susan Palmer, archivist & Librarian at the Sir John Soane Museum; J.J Hoare at Stourhead, Alastair Laing who provided the author with documentation covering the obelisk shape incorporated in church monuments; Martin Wood, for information on Boconnoc and Lord Camelford's letter to John Soane; Margaret Ball, archivist at Hailebury College; Michael Ames and the assistance of St Edmundsbury Council; the National Monument Record presently established by the Public Monument and Sculpture Association and English Heritage, RCHME; Siobhan McConnochie at RCAHMS, Edinburgh; Richard White, National Trust at Farnborough Hall; Andrew Martindale of the Society of Architectural Historians; Richard Robinson; and for his encouragement, the architect, Patrick Horsbrugh.

Initial subscriptions to this book were as follows:

1. H. Vivian-Neal.
2. Michael Brook.
3. Douglas Merritt.
4. Marquis of Lansdowne.
5. Hubert Chesshyre.
6. Prof James Stevens Curl.
7. Alastair Laing.
8. Terry Webster.
9. Dr.Eric Robinson.
10. Dr.Peter Freeman.
11. Dr.Anthony Henfrey.
12. Sir Roy Strong.
13. Andrew Patrick.
14. Anthony Pugh-Thomas.
15. Dr James Johnston.
16. Jo Darke.
17. Jennifer Johnson.
18. Dr A.Clarke.
19. Ray McKenzie.
20. Jo Stockdale.
21. John Harris.
22. Tracy Siggins.
23. Abi Rapley.
24. Dr Julian Litten.
25. National Art Library.
26. Simon Brown.
27. Susan Carter.
28. Guy Sinclair.
29. Paul Cockerham.
30. Phoebe Jane Smith.
31. Richard Graham.
32. John Agnew.
33. Piers Corke.
34. W.Fairbank.
35. J.A.T.Corke.
36. D.Squires.
37. National Trust Collection.
38. National Trust Collection.
39. Mike Cousins.
40. Mike Cousins.
41. Caroline Loughlin.
42. Peter Kent-Baguley.
43. Karen Lynch.
44. Martin Wood.
45. W.B.Sullivan.
46. R.T.Lowe.
47. A.Clayton.
48. D.A.Teale.
49. Stephen Upton.
50. Gilbert Addison.
51. R.G.Schofield.
52. D. Conway.
53. Stuart Smith.
54. David Martin.
55. R.Broyd.
56. R.Broyd.
57. N.T.G 'Pat' Patrick.
58. R.G Webber.
59. Nigel M. Waring.
60. T. Gwyn-Jones.
61. T.J.Fielding.
62. Geoffrey Ireland.
63. James C.Newcombe.
64. Julian Jeffs.
65. D.J.Foot.
66. Chloe Cockerill.
67. Peter Godfrey.
68. Ralfe Whistler.
69. Frank Kelsall.
70. Andrew Plumridge.
71. S.Stirling.
72. J.D. Lee.
73. Peter Dane.
74. E.Dunbartonshire Libraries.
75. Michael Pritchard.
76. A.R.Tavener.
77. B.J Rainbow.
78. Laurence Hunt.
79. Sir William McAlpine.
80. Patrick Horsbrugh.
81. Patrick Horsbrugh.
82. Curt DiCamillo.
83. The London Library.
84 Wim Meulenkamp.

85. T.M.Blackburn.
86. Iain Farrell.
87. Bradley Hale.
88. Bradley Hale.
89. Stephen Cook.
90. P.Barton.
91. Christopher Ridgway.
92. Christopher Ridgway.
93. Maxwell Craven.
94. Ann & Bruce Saunders.
95. Martin & Gillian Williams.
96. Richard Cocke.
97. T.S Hamaton.
98. T.S Hamaton.
99. John Clare.
100. Mrs Elizabeth Taylor.
101. J. Henderson.
102. David Lermon.
103. Roger Bowdler.
104. R.Prentis.
105. Stephen H. Johnston.
106. Paul Grinke.
107. Mrs S.F McGinn.
108. Anthony Tugnutt.

109. P.Dyson.
110. M.A.Cargill.
111. Paul Mellon Centre for Studies in British Art.
112. Richard Robinson.
113. Mr. M. Symes.
114. Mark Vidler.
115. Cuchullaine & Basha O'Reilly.
116. Jeremy James.
117. Malcolm Tempest Ltd,.
118. Mrs.J.Morgan.
119. Janet Hallett.
120. Miss Rat Riches.
121. Diana Reynell.
122. G.E Forster..
123. James Airy.
124. John L.Kynnersley.
125. Eric Throssell.
126. T.A.S. Jackson.
127. Geoffrey Wood.
128. Geraldine Beskin.
129. Dr Terry Friedman.
130. J.F. Ashby.

/500

BIBLIOGRAPHY

The Aberdeen Granite Industry, Tom Donnelly, Centre for Scottish Studies, Aberdeen Univ 1994

Architecture and the Afterlife, Howard Colvin, Newhaven/ Yale 1991

Architecture, landscape & liberty, Richard Payne Knight & the picturesque, A.Ballantyne, CUP 1997.

The Art and Architecture of Freemasonry, James Stevens Curl, Overlook Press, New York 2002

The Art of Remembering, Harriet Frazer, Carcanet 1998

At the Going Down of the Sun, Derek Boorman, Ebor Press 1988

Biographical Dictionary of British Architects,1600-1940, H.Colvin, Yale 1995

The Buildings of England. The county series, N. Pevsner (& others),Penguin 1991

Charles Bridgeman and the English Landscape Garden. Peter Willis, Zwemmer 1977

Church Monuments, Brian Kemp, Shire 1997

Churchyards of England & Wales, Brian Bailey, Hale 1987

Dictionary of Architecture, James Stevens Curl, OUP 1999

An English Arcadia, G.Jackson-Stops, National Trust 1992

The English Garden: Meditation and Memorial, David Coffin, Princeton 1994

Enlightenment - Britain and the Creation of the Modern World, Roy Porter, Penguin 2000

Follies, Grottoes & Garden Buildings, Gwyn Headley & Wim Meulenkamp, Aurum 1999

Garden Ornament, Gertrude Jekyll, Country Life / George Newnes Ltd 1918

Garden Sculpture, Michael Symes, Shire 1996

The Granite Industry of Aberdeen, P.J Enfield, 1951

Hawksmoor, Kerry Downes, Thames & Hudson 1970

Ivory Towers and Dressed Stones, vol I, Jim Jarratt, Cicerone Press 1994

London Cemeteries - An illustrated Guide and Gazetteer, Hugh Meller, Ashgate 1999

Lutyens and the Edwardians, Jane Brown, Viking 1996

The Magic of Obelisks, Peter Tompkins, Harper & Row, 1981

The Monument Guide to England and Wales, Jo Darke, MacDonald 1991

The Myth of Egypt and its Hieroglyphs in European Tradition, Erik Iversen, Princeton 1993

Neoclassical and 19th Century Architecture, vol I , David Watkin, Academy Editions 1980

Nicholas Hawksmoor - Rebuilding Ancient Wonders, Vaughan Hart, Yale 2002

Nostell Priory, G.Jackson-Stops, National Trust 1978

The Obelisk, Hargrave Jennings, 1877

Obelisks in Exile, Erik Iversen, 1968

Gli Obelischi de Roma, Cesare d' Onoforio

Obeliscus Pamphilis, Athanasius Kircher S.J, 1650

De gli Obelischi di Roma, Msnr Michele Mercati, 1589

Della Trasportatione dell Obelisco Vaticano, Domenico Fontana, 1590

De Origine et Usu Obeliscorum, Jorgen Zöega, 1796

Oedipus Aegypticus, 4 vols, Athanasius Kircher S.J, 1652

One Hundred English Gardens, Patrick Taylor, English Heritage / Headline 1995

The Polite Tourist -A History of Country House Visiting, Adrian Tiniswood, National Trust 1998

Public Sculpture of the City of London, Philip Ward-Jackson, Liverpool University Press/ PMSA 2003

Public Sculpture of Liverpool.Terry Cavanagh, Liverpool University Press/ PMSA 2001

Sir Edwin Lutyens - Designing in the English Tradition, E.Wilhide & C.Lutyens, Pavilion 2000

Sir John Soane - Enlightenment Thought and the RA Lectures, David Watkins, CUP 1996

The Stourhead Landscape, Kenneth Woodbridge, The National Trust 1982

Stowe, The Gardens and the Park, Michael Bevington, Capability Books 1994

The Ten books of Architecture, Leon Battista Alberti, 1755 Leon Edition. Dover Publications 1986

Tomlinson's Comprehensive Guide to Northumberland, 12th Edtn, David & Charles 1968

The Victorian Celebration of Death, James Stevens Curl, Sutton 2000

Wentworth Woodhouse, Marcus Binney, Country Life 24/01/1991.pps60-63

LIST OF PHOTOGRAPHS

SECTION 2 (in between pages 64-65)

17. Obelisk, Lansdowne Monument, Cherhill Down, Wiltshire, 1845.
18. a – Obelisk, Ickworth Park, Suffolk, 1804.
    b – Obelisk, detail, Captain Skinner's memorial, Holyhead, Anglesey, 1832.
19. a – Cook Monument, North York Moors, 1827.
    b – Painting of the Mail Coaching Monument near Llandovery, 1841.
20. a – Obelisk and church spire, Studley Royal, Yorkshire, 1805.
    b – Obelisk, The Melville Monument, Comrie, Perthshire,1812.
    c – 'To think that one should be buried in so sweet a place'.
21. a – Obelisk, Memorial to Admiral Nelson, Glasgow, 1806
    b – Wellington Monument, Somerset, completed 1892.
22. Model of obelisk for Great Exhibition Memorial, J.Bell, 1858.
23. a – J.Bell, sculptor, portrait.
    b – Obelisk, 1865, memorial to John Speke, Kensington Gardens, 1865.
24. Obelisk, 'Cleopatra's Needle', c1450BC. The Embankment, London.
25. Obelisk, 'The Philae Obelisk',c100BC. Kingston Lacy, Dorset.
26. Cemetery views.
27. Monolithic obelisk memorial to J.Richardson, Kensal Green, 1858.
28. Obelisk memorial to E.Willes, Jephson Gardens, Leamington Spa, 1875.
29. Monolithic obelisk memorial to Henry Bell, Helensburgh, Strathclyde, 1872.
30. a – Gurney Obelisk Drinking Fountain, Stratford Broadway, London, 1861.
    b – Gurney Obelisk Drinking Fountain, Tombland, Norwich, 1861.
31. a – Obelisk Drinking Fountain, Leamington Spa, 1880.
    b – Obelisk Drinking Fountain, Grand Parade, Brighton, 1871.
32. a – Obelisk memorial to J McGrigor, Aberdeen, 1858.
    b – Obelisk, graveyard and harbour; Peterhead.

GAZETTEER
of Obelisks
in England, Scotland & Wales

Derived from the PMSA National Recording project; Pevsner's 'Buildings of England Series'; Follies Magazine, 1988-2004; National Inventory of War Memorials.

BEDFORDSHIRE
Obelisk, 1771, m. 2nd Duke of Halifax, Appley Corner, Chicksands Priory, Beds.
Obelisk, 1815, resited 1976, 23 ft tall limestone, Napoleonic Wars, Chicksands Priory, Beds.
Obelisk, c1889, m. Henry Osborn, Chicksands Priory, Beds.
Obelisk, 1784, old pump and milepost at crossroads, arch: Wm Chambers, Ampthill, Beds.
Obelisk, 1864, m. William Whitbread, Whitbread Estate, Southill, nr Biggleswade, Beds.
Obelisk WM, Leagrave, Luton, Beds.
Obelisk WM, Stopsley, Luton, Beds.
Obelisk WM, St.Edmund's Ch, Blunham, Beds.
Obelisk WM, St.John's Ch, Flitton, Beds.
Obelisk WM, Felmersham, Beds.
Obelisk WM, All Saints Ch, Riseley, Beds.
Obelisk WM, St.Nicholas Ch, Barton le Clay, Beds.
Obelisk WM, m. Capt N.Robertson & 2nd Lieut Robinson, Dunstable Downs, WWI, Beds.
Obelisk WM, St.Leonard's Ch, Heath & Reach, Beds,
Obelisk WM, Sharpenhoe, Beds.
Obelisk WM, Sundon, Beds.
Obelisk WM, Toddington, Beds.

BERKSHIRE
Obelisk, 1745, m. Duke of Cumberland/ battle Culloden, Great Park, Windsor, Berkshire.
Obelisk, 18th C, Park Place, Remenham ch, nr Maidenhead, Berkshire.
Falkland Obelisk, 1878, 33 ft, granite, m. battle 1643, Andover Rd, Newbury, Berkshire.
'The Simeon Obelisk', 1804, des: J Soane, is not an obelisk. Market Pl, Reading, Berkshire.
Obelisk WM, 25 ft Portland stone, Leckhampstead, nr Newbury, Berkshire.
Obelisk WM, Clippenham, Slough, Berkshire.

BUCKINGHAMSHIRE
Obelisk, c.1710-1720, with carved garden tools, Hall Barn, nr Beaconsfield, Bucks.
Obelisk, 1735, m. Alexander Pope's mother, moved to Penn House, Amersham, Bucks
Obelisk, 1736, m. Wm Congreve, monument with bacchic heads and monkey, Stowe, Bucks.
Obelisk 1754, 100 ft, arch: Smith & Batchelor, later dedicated to Gen Wolfe, Stowe, Bucks.
Obelisk, c.1757, Arch: J.Gibbs, c.20 ft, globe finial, Hartwell House, nr Aylesbury, Bucks.
Obelisk, 1864, surmounting monument, m. 2nd Duke of Buckingham, Stowe NT, Bucks.
Obelisk, 1785, m. A hunt with George III, Micholls Ave, Chesham, Bucks.
Obelisk, c.1760, m. Hooton's cellar tombs,Tickford Abbey, Newport Pagnell, Bucks.
Obelisk, 1785, rough freestone, hilltop, Monument Lane, Chalfont St.Peter, Bucks.

Obeliscal Monument, (not an obelisk),1862, m. B Disraeli's father, Hughenden Manor NT.

Obelisk, 1984, Brickbuilt, Kensington Drive, Great Holm, Milton Keynes, Bucks.

Obelisk WM, 1904, Boer War, tall, prominent, Coombe Hill, Ellesborough, Wendover.

Obelisk WM, Bishopstone, Vale of Aylesbury, Bucks.

Obelisk WM, Cheddington, Aylesbury, Bucks.

Obelisk WM, Grendon Underwood, Aylesbury, Bucks.

Obelisk WM, Haddenham ch, Haddenham, Aylesbury, Bucks.

Obelisk WM, Long Crendon, Aylesbury, Bucks.

Obelisk WM, St.Faith's Ch, Newton Longville, Bucks.

Obelisk WM, Padbury, Buckingham, Bucks.

Obelisk WM, Stewkley, Vale of Aylesbury, Bucks.

Obelisk WM, Swanbourne, Aylesbury, Bucks.

Obelisk WM, Wingrave, Aylesbury, Bucks.

Obelisk WM, Holmer Green, Chiltern, Bucks.

Obelisk WM, 1903, Boer War,Latimer, Chiltern,Bucks.

Obelisk WM, Old Council School, Bletchley, Milton Keynes, Bucks.

Obelisk WM, Old Bletchley Bletchley, Bucks.

Obelisk WM, Castlethorpe, Milton Keynes, Bucks.

Obelisk WM, Parish Church, Simpson, Milton Keynes, Bucks.

Obelisk WM, St Mary Magdalene ch, Willen, Milton Keynes, Bucks.

Obelisk WM, 1904 - Boer War, Wolverton, Milton Keynes, Bucks.

Obelisk WM, Flackwell Heath, Wycombe, Bucks.

Obelisk WM, Wooburn, Wycombe, Bucks.

CAMBRIDGESHIRE

Wale Obelisk, c1739, m. Gregory Wale,'Maggots Mound'. Harston/ Little Shelford, Cambs.

2 Obelisks, (acquired in 1951 from Copped Hall), Anglesey Abbey, Arrington, Cambs.

Obelisk WM, Fen Ditton, Cambridge, Cambs.

Obelisk WM, Fen Drayton, Cambridge, Cambs.

Obelisk WM, Parish Ch, Great Chishill, Cambridge, Cambs.

Obelisk WM, Ickleton, Cambridge, Cambs.

Obelisk WM, Linton, Cambridge, Cambs.

Obelisk WM, Milton, Cambridge, Cambs.

Obelisk WM, All Saints ch, Teversham, Cambridge, Cambs.

Obelisk WM, Reach, Cambs.

Obelisk WM, St.Mary's ch, Guyhirn, Wisbech, Cambs.

Obelisk WM, Wicken, Cambs.

Obelisk WM, RAF, Witchford, Cambs.

Obelisk WM, Coates, Whittlesey,Cambs.

Obelisk WM, Murrow, Wisbech,Cambs.

Obelisk WM, St James Ch, Newton, Wisbech,Cambs.

Obelisk WM, Parson Drove,Wisbech, Cambs.

Obelisk WM, Easton Church, Easton, Huntingdon, Cambs.

Obelisk WM, Eaton Socon, Huntingdon, Cambs.

Obelisk WM, Ellington Church, Ellington, Huntingdon, Cambs.

Obelisk WM, Fenstanton, Huntingdon, Cambs

Obelisk WM, Overcote Lane, Holywell-cum-Needingworth, Huntingdon, Cambs.

Obelisk WM, Somersham, Huntingdon, Cambs.

CHESHIRE

Obelisk, 1714, Dunham Massey Hall NT, nr Altrincham, Cheshire.

Obelisk, c.1717, in woodland N. of Dunham Massey Hall, nr Altrincham, Cheshire.

Obelisk, c.1750, m. Legh family, 20 ft rustic, Norbury Booths Hall, Knutsford, Cheshire.

Obelisk, 1750, eagle at peak, raised by Sir E.Stanley, Old Hall, Nether Alderley, Cheshire.

Obelisk, 1858, 56 ft & 4 lions, m.Maj Barnston/ Indian Mut, Chester Rd, Farndon, Cheshire.

Obelisk, c.1865, m. Visc Combermere, Combermere Abbey, nr Nantwich, Cheshire.

Obelisk, 1860, m. Matthew Henry, Presbyterian Minister d.1714, Nicholas St, Chester.

Obelisk Drinking Fountain, 1861, m. J.Jackson, 16ft,Park Rd N, Birkenhead, Cheshire.

Obelisk, 1874, resting on 4 lions, High Warren, Appleton Thorn, nr Runcorn, Cheshire.

Obelisk, 1888, m. George Marsh, Marian martyr, d.1555, Boughton Road, Chester.

Obelisk, 1890, Belgrave Avenue, Eaton Hall, Eaton Park, Cheshire.

Obelisk WM, Village hall, Pulford, Chester, Cheshire.

Obelisk WM, St. Mary's ch, Thornton le Moors, Chester, Cheshire.

Obelisk WM, Threapwood, Chester, Cheshire.

Obelisk WM, Congleton edge, Cheshire.

Obelisk WM, St.Peter's ch, Swettenham, Congleton, Cheshire.

Obelisk WM, Bradfield Green, Crewe, Cheshire.

Obelisk WM, Tiverton,Tarporley, Cheshire.

Obelisk WM, Willaston,Crewe, Cheshire, Cheshire.

Obelisk WM, Macclesfield, Cheshire.

Obelisk WM, Styal, nr Macclesfield, Cheshire.

Obelisk WM, Sutton, nr Macclesfield, Cheshire.

Obelisk WM, 26 ft sandstone, Frodsham, Cheshire.

Obelisk WM, 20 ft Yorkshire stone, Overton Hill, Frodsham,Cheshire.

Obelisk WM, parish ch, Kingsley, nr.Frodsham, Cheshire.

Obelisk WM, Winsford, Cheshire.

Obelisk WM, Warrington, Cheshire.

Obelisk WM, Cheadle, Stockport, Cheshire.

Obelisk WM, St.James' ch, Gatley, Stockport, Cheshire.

Obelisk WM, St.Bartholomew's ch, Thurstaston, Wirral, Cheshire.

Obelisk WM, St.Hilary's ch, Wallasey, Wirral , Cheshire.

Obelisk WM, Methodist ch, Dukinfield, nr Hyde, Cheshire.

Obelisk WM, Godley Hill, Godley, Hyde, Cheshire.

Obelisk WM, 28 ft grey granite, hilltop, Werneth Low, Hyde, Cheshire.

Obelisk WM, Working Men's Club, Partington, nr Altrincham, Cheshire.

CORNWALL

Obelisk, 1737, m. Sir Peter Killigrew, Grove Place, Falmouth, Cornwall.

Obelisk, 1762, Dr.Martyn's Grave,12 ft tall in field by church, Botusfleming, Cornwall.

Obelisk, 1771, m. Sir Richard Lyttleton, 123 ft, Boconnoc, S. of Bodmin, Cornwall.

Obelisk, 1846, m. Victoria & Albert's visit, fell in harbour, recov' 1977, Fowey, Cornwall.

Obelisk, 1857, 144 ft, m. Sir W.R.Gilbert; Indian army, Beacon Hill, Bodmin, Cornwall.

Obelisk, Lanhydrock House NT, Cornwall.

Obelisk, 1889, Victoria Jubilee, Dennis Hill, Padstow, Cornwall.

Obelisk, 'Royal Mail Obelisk', outside library, Falmouth, Cornwall.

Obelisk, 1936, m. Josephine Williams, Recreation Ground, Porthleven, Cornwall.

Obelisk, Cremyll Playing Fields, Maker, Cornwall.

Obelisk, 'Dunstanville Monument', Carn Brea, Redruth, Cornwall.

Obelisk, 1917, m. Lt.Col A.Thynne, 12 ft, rough granite, Kilkhampton, Bude, Cornwall.

Obelisk WM, 1922, 35 ft, on sea front, Battery rocks, Penzance, Cornwall.

Obelisk WM, Hall Walk,Bodinnick, Caradon, Cornwall.

Obelisk WM, Cawsand, Caradon, Cornwall

Obelisk WM, Naval trainees, St.Mylor Churchtown, Falmouth, Cornwall.

Obelisk WM, St.Wynwallow ch, Lizard, Lizard Point, Cornwall.

Obelisk WM, St.Michael's ch, Ponsanooth, nr.Penrhyn, Famouth, Cornwall.

Obelisk WM, Victoria Park, Redruth, Redruth, nr St.Ives, Cornwall

Obelisk WM, The Post Office, Fore st, Boscastle, N.Cornwall.

Obelisk WM, Wadebridge, N.Cornwall.

Obelisk WM, Lostwithiel, Cornwall.

Obelisk WM, Castle st, Liskeard, Cornwall.

CUMBRIA

Obelisk, 1788, centenary dedication 'to liberty', Castle Howe Hill, Kendal, Cumbria.

Obelisk, c.1790, 'The Greystoke Pillar', Greystoke Castle, nr Penrith, Cumbria.

Obelisk, c.1790, rough freestone, Spire Wood, Finsthwaite, Windermere, Cumbria.

Obelisk, c.1808, 20 ton, cast-iron, m. John Wilkinson, Ironmaster; Lindale, Cumbria.

Obelisk, 1810, m. George III's jubilee,Market, Broughton-in-Furness, Ulverston, Cumbria.

Obelisk, 1814, comm. William Pitt, Tolson Hall, Burneside, nr Kendal, Cumbria.

Obelisk, 1851, m. Charles II on remote moor at Black Dub, Lyvennet Vale, Cumbria.

Obelisk WM, Abbey Town, nr Aspatria, Maryport, Cumbria.

Obelisk WM, Underskiddaw, Applethwaite, nr Keswick, Cumbria.

Obelisk WM, Ennerdale Bridge, nr Whitehaven, Cumbria.

Obelisk WM, Christchurch, Waverton, nr Carlisle, Cumbria.

Obelisk WM, Wigton, nr Carlisle, Cumbria.

Obelisk WM, Newton, Carlisle, Cumbria.

Obelisk WM, St. Cuthbert's church, Bewcastle, Carlisle, Cumbria.

Obelisk WM, Ref ch, Bewcastle, Carlisle, Cumbria.

Obelisk WM, St.Cuthbert's ch, Carlisle, Cumbria

Obelisk WM, Harraby, Carlisle, Cumbria.

Obelisk WM, St.Mary's ch, Stapleton, Carlisle, Cumbria.

Obelisk WM, Cleator, St.Bee's, Cumbria.

Obelisk WM, Distington, nr Workington, Cumbria.

Obelisk WM, Gosforth, nr Whitehaven, Cumbria

Obelisk WM, Meth ch,Lowca, nr.Workington, Cumbria.

Obelisk WM, 1904, St.George's ch, Millom, nr Duddon Bridge, Cumbria.

Obelisk WM, Silecroft, nr Duddon Bridge, Cumbria.

Obelisk WM, Whicham, nr Duddon Bridge, Cumbria.

Obelisk WM, Alston, Penrith, Cumbria.

Obelisk WM, Hunsonby, Penrith, Cumbria.

Obelisk WM, Langwathby, Penrith, Cumbria.

Obelisk WM, St.John's, Melmerby, Penrith, Cumbria.

Obelisk WM, St.John's ch, Murton, Appleby, Cumbria.

Ravenstonedale Obelisk WM, St.Oswald's ch, Ravenstonedale, Cumbria.

Obelisk WM, Warcop, Appleby, Cumbria.
Obelisk WM, Slate 6ft, Burlington Slate Co, Kirkby-in-Furness, Cumbria.

DERBYSHIRE
Obelisk, 19th C, m. A favourite horse, moved to Oakerthorpe, Ripley, Derbyshire.
Obeliscal monoliths, 1991,Stone Island, des.Lewis Knight, Carsington Water, Derbyshire.
Obelisk WM, Belper, Derby, Derbyshire.
Obelisk WM, Memorial Park, Heanor, Derby, Derbyshire.
Obelisk WM, roadside, Kilburn, nr Belper, Derby, Derbyshire.
Obelisk WM, 25 ft, local stone, Church st, Holloway, Derby, Derbyshire.
Obelisk WM, Stainsby Heath, Ault Hucknall, Bolsover, Derbyshire.
Obelisk WM, Palterton, Bolsover, Derbyshire.
Obelisk WM, Hollingwood, Chesterfield, Derbyshire.
Obelisk WM, Burbage, Derby, Derbyshire.
Obelisk WM, St Helen's House, Derby School, Derby, Derbyshire.
Obelisk WM, St.Thomas ch, Biggin, Dovedale, Derbyshire.
Obelisk WM, Dethick, Lea, Matlock, Derbyshire.
Obelisk WM, Kniveton, Ashbourne, Derbyshire.
Obelisk WM, St.Andrew's ch, Stanley, Derby, Derbyshire.
Obelisk WM, St.Michael's ch, Stanton by Dale, Derby, Derbyshire.
Obelisk WM, Roadside, Ockbrook, Derby, Derbyshire
Obelisk WM, Burbage, Buxton, Derbyshire.
Obelisk WM, Charlesworth, nr Glossop, Derbyshire.
Obelisk WM, St.George's ch, New Mills, Debyshire.
Obelisk WM, Peak Dale, High Peak, Derbyshire
Obelisk WM, Trinity ch, Brackenfield, Matlock, Derbyshire.
Obelisk WM, Village Square, Unstone, nr Chesterfield, Derbyshire.
Obelisk WM, Castle Gresley, nr High Cross, S.Derbyshire.
Obelisk WM, Church Gresley, nr High Cross, S.Derbyshire.

DEVON
Obelisk, 1742, 100 ft, sandstone, coastal landmark, Mamhead Castle, Dawlish, Devon.
Obelisk, 1747, 70 ft, Bicton Park Gardens, East Budleigh, Budleigh Salterton, Devon.
Obelisk, 1803, site where King William arrived in 1688, Newquay,nr Paignton, Devon.
Obelisk, c.1816, m. French prisoners, Lydford, nr Tavistock, Devon.
Obeliscal Tower, 1818, commem Waterloo, above river in Gt Torrington, Devon.
Obelisk, 1860, m. Lt Col W.Morris, Crimea; Hatherleigh Down, Okehampton, Devon
Obelisk, c.1860, m. Dr Herbert Chilcote, Babbacombe, Devon.
Obelisk, 1864, m. William Wills, centre of road, The Plains, Totnes, Devon.
Obelisk, 1887, 15 ft, freestone, Arlington Court NT, nr Barnstaple,Devon.
Obelisk, c.1887, ' VR -Jubilee Obelisk, village crossroads, Zeal Monachorum, Devon.
Obelisk, 1897, m. VR- 60 yrs, 10 ft & round trough, Roborough Down, Yelverton, Devon.
Obelisk, 1902, m. Prince Christian Victor, granite; Citadel, Hoe Rd, Plymouth, Devon.
Obelisk, 1909,'Martyrs Memorial', bronze plaques, Denmark Road, Exeter. Devon.
Obelisk, Berry Head Road, Brixham, Devon.
Obelisk, 1855, broken (lightning 1932) m.A.Cleveland,Tapeley Pk House, Westleigh, Devon.
Obelisk, m. William Rock; Taw Vale Road, Barnstaple, Devon.

Obelisk, 1976, Gorwell House, Barnstaple, Devon.
Obelisk WM Boer War, red granite, tall, Plymouth Hoe, Plymouth. Devon.
Obelisk WM Naval Division, 10 ft, Portland stone, with statues, Plymouth Hoe, Devon.
Obelisk WM, Higher Tale, Honiton, Devon.
Obelisk WM, Culmstock, Devon.
Obelisk WM, Rackenford, N.Devon.
Obelisk WM, Swimbridge ch, Swimbridge, Barnstaple, N. Devon.
Obelisk WM, St.Peter's ch, Harbertonford, Totnes, Devon.
Obelisk WM, Loddiswell, Kingsbridge, Devon
Obelisk WM, 1944, m. D Day preparations, The Causeway, Slapton, nr Dartmouth, Devon.
Obelisk WM, Church Row, Modbury, nr Plymouth, Devon.
Obelisk WM, Kenton, Newton Abbot, Devon.
Obelisk WM, Teignmouth, Devon.
Obelisk WM, Paignton, Torbay, Devon.
Obelisk WM, Appledore, Torridge, Devon.
Obelisk WM, Sheepwash, Torridge,Devon.
Obelisk WM, Monkleigh, Torridge,Devon.
Obelisk WM, North Tawton, Crediton, Devon.
Obelisk WM, American PoWs, HMP Dartmoor, Princetown, Devon.
Obelisk WM, Church Gn, High Street, Newton Poppleford, Devon.

DORSET
'The Philae Needle'. Ancient Egyptian Obelisk at Kingston Lacy Hall, Wimborne, Dorset
Obelisk, c1730, in SW of park, Kingston Lacy Hall, Wimbourne, Dorset
Obelisk, 1887, in honour of Queen Victoria at Kingston Lacey, Wimborne, Dorset.
Obelisk, 1727, to George II's accession, rebuilt 1836, Thornhill House, Stalbridge, Dorset
Obelisk, 1761,'Pleydell Monument'; 60 ft, brick; Weatherby Castle, Milborne St.Andrew.
Obelisk, 1784, on site of the old Town Pump, South st, Dorchester, Dorset.
Obelisk, 1784, old town pump site, moved 1990 to Cove Close, Weymouth, Dorset.
Obeliscal pillar, 1785-6, 'Frampton Monument', 75 ft, Moreton House, Dorset.
Obelisk, 1835, 40 ft, m. Lord Stowell, Encombe House, Corfe Castle. Dorset
Obelisks, 1892, as finials to walls of Corona Gdn, Athelhampton Hall, Dorchester, Dorset.
'Ulwell Obelisk, c20ft, moved from London in 1892, Ballard Down, Swanage, Dorset.
'Look Out Point', Obelisk WM, 1920, 30 ft stone on 3 step pedestal, Portland, Dorset
Obelisk WM, Durweston, Blandford Forum, Dorset.
Obelisk WM, Glanvilles Wootton, Sherborne, Dorset.
Obelisk WM, Pimperne, Blandford Forum,Dorset.
Obelisk WM, Tarrant Monkton,Blandford Forum, Dorset.
Obelisk WM, Winterbourne Kingston, Blandford Forum,Dorset.
Obelisk WM, St.Michael's ch, Broadmayne, Dorchester, Dorsct.
Obelisk WM -Indian Frontier,15 ft tall, base encircled, Borough Gdns, Dorchester.
Obelisk WM, Maiden Newton, Dorchester, Dorset.
Obelisk WM, All Saints ch, Wyke Regis, Weymouth, Dorset.
Obelisk WM, Whitelackington, nr Dorchester, Dorset.

DURHAM
Egyptian Obelisk, 7ft 3 inches, red granite, 1400BC, Oriental Museum, Durham University.
Obelisk, 1827, 127 ft, to Duke of Wellington, Wynyard Park, Stockton-onTees, co.Durham.

Obelisk, 1999, by m. Dan Archer Sc, Wynyard Estate, Stockton-on-Tees, co. Durham.
Obelisk, 1850, 99 ft, meridian marker for Observatory, Obelisk Lane, Durham, co.Durham
Obelisk, 1882, commemorating a day's grouse shooting, Barningham Moor, co.Durham.
Obelisk WM, 40 ft, Victory Square, Hartlepool, Durham.
Obelisk WM, 1904, 22 ft, red granite, Albert Park, Middlesborough, Durham.
Obelisk WM, parish ch, Egglescliffe, nr Stockton-on-Tees, Durham.
Obelisk WM, Egglescliffe & Preston, nr Stockton-on-Tees,Durham.
Obelisk WM, Haverton Hill, nr Billingham, Durham.
Obelisk WM, Boer War, 20 ft, Shap granite, Chester- le-Street, Durham.
Obelisk WM, 1919, Chester- le-Street, Durham.
Obelisk WM, Joyce brothers, Aviators; Anfield Plain, Derwentside, Durham.
Obelisk WM, Burnopfield, nr Stanley, Durham.
Obelisk WM, Castleside, nr Consett, Durham.
Obelisk WM, Greencroft, nr Anfield Plain, Durham,
Obelisk WM, Prince Bishop Inn, Brandon, Durham, co Durham.
Obelisk WM, WW2, The Greyhound PH, Kelloe, Durham, co Durham.
Obelisk WM, Sherburn Hill, Durham, co Durham.
Obelisk WM, Bowes Museum, Barnard Castle, Teesdale, Durham
Obelisk WM, High Etherley, Barnard Castle, Durham.
Obelisk WM, Middleton in Teesdale, Barnard Castle, Durham
Obelisk WM, Stainton, nr Darlington, Durham.
Obelisk WM, All Saints ch, Eastgate, Crook, Durham, co Durham.
Obelisk WM, Howden le Wear, Crook, Durham, co Durham.
Obelisk WM, Greenside, Gateshead, co Durham.
Obelisk WM, m. Pte Finlay, Swalwell, Gateshead, co Durham.

ESSEX
Castle Obelisk, early 18th C, m. to garrison command, Inner Bailey, Colchester Castle.
Obelisk, c.1820, 18 ft, m. General Grosvenor' s horse,The Warren, Loughton, Essex.
Boudicca's Obelisk 1, late 18 C?; - "Where she took poison"; Warlies Pk, Upshire, Essex.
Boudicca's Obelisk 2 - "Where she died", a mile away, Obelisk Farm, Upshire, Essex.
Crowstone Obelisk 1, 18th C, Prittlewell, Southend-on-sea, Essex.
Crowstone Obelisk 2, 1836, Port of London marker, on Thames, Southend-on-sea, Essex.
Greenwich Meridian Obelisk,1824, not a true obelisk, Pole Hill Pk, Chingford, Essex.
Obelisk, 1825, Woodham Mortimer Hall, Woodham Mortimer, Chelmsford, Essex.
Obelisk m. Lt.Gen J.Brown, St John's ch, Layer de la Haye, Colchester, Essex.
Obelisks, c.1905, as finials to garden terrace, mostly destroyed, Copped Hall, Epping, Essex.
Obelisk WM, Portland stone, 40 ft tall on 35 ft pedestal, Southend-on-sea, Essex.
Obelisk WM, Braintree, Essex.
Obelisk WM, Stoke-by-Clare, nr. Halstead, Essex.
Obelisk WM, to Glider Pilots, Marks Hall estate, Coggeshall, Essex.
Obelisk WM, Boer War, Essex Regiment, Chelmsford, Essex.
Obelisk WM, St.John's ch, Ford End, Chelmsford, Essex.
Obelisk WM, St.Mary's ch, Woodham Ferrers, Chelmsford, Essex.
Obelisk WM, St.Margaret's ch, Aldham, Colchester, Essex.
Obelisk WM, St.Mary's ch, High Ongar, Epping, Essex.
Obelisk WM, St.Thomas' ch, Bradwell on Sea, nr Maldon, Essex.
Obelisk WM, Burnham on Crouch, nr Maldon, Essex.

Obelisk WM, All Saints ch, Purleigh, nr Maldon, Essex.
Obelisk WM, St. Leonard's ch, Southminster, nr Maldon, Essex.
Obelisk WM, St.Lawrence's ch, Bradfield, nr Manningtree, Essex.
Obelisk WM, Great Oakley, nr Harwich, Essex
Obelisk WM, 'Wix Cross', Wix, nr Harwich, Essex.
Obelisk WM, m. Coalhouse Fort, St.Catherine's ch, East Tilbury Village, Essex.
Obelisk WM, Stanford le Hope, nr Basildon, Essex.
Obelisk WM, 18 ft, Main Rd, South Ockendon, nr Havering, Essex.
Obelisk WM, St. Mary's ch, Stifford, Thurrock, Essex.
Obelisk WM, Reform ch, Clavering, nr Saffron Walden, Essex.

GLOUCESTERSHIRE - (for near Bristol see SOMERSET)
Obelisk, 1721, m. A favourite horse, Nether Lypiatt Manor, nr Bisley, Gloucestershire.
2 obelisks at North front, Badminton House, Chipping Sodbury, Gloucestershire.
Obelisk, 18th C. near Cotswold Avenue in Cirencester Park, Gloucestershire.
Obelisk, 18th C, 'Fairford Column', Fairford Park, Fairford, Gloucestershire.
Obelisk, c.1852, m. G.Dowdeswell, The Down House, Redmarley d'Abitot, Glos.
Obelisk, 1957, marking centre of Forest of Dean, Speech House, West Dean, Glos.
Obelisk WM, 29 ft Portland stone on 6 ft base, Cheltenham, Glos.
Obelisk WM, Aldsworth, nr Burford, Glos.
Obelisk WM, Down Ampney, nr Cirencester, Glos.
Obelisk WM, Paxford, nr Moreton-in-marsh, Glos.
Obelisk WM, Awre, nr Cinderford, Gloucester, Glos.
Obelisk WM, Little Dean, Forest of Dean, Glos.
Obelisk WM, Eastcombe, Stroud, Glos.
Obelisk WM, Frocester, Stroud, Glos.
Obelisk WM, Brockworth, nr Tewkesbury, Glos.
Obelisk WM, St.Lawrence's ch, Swindon, nr Tewkesbury, Glos.

HAMPSHIRE
4 black marble obelisks, 1594, around Southampton tomb,Titchfield Church, Hampshire.
Obelisk, 1759, The Plague Memorial, Upper High st, Winchester, Hants.
Obelisk, 1799, Borough boundary, Torrington Road, Hilsea, Portsmouth, Hants.
Obelisk, 1810, m. Charles J.Fox, Weston Lane, Southampton, Hants.
Obelisk, c.1815, m. Battle of Waterloo, South Garth, Romsey, Hampshire.
Obelisk, 1840-1, 80 feet, m. Adm H.Burrard Neale, Walhampton, Lymington.Hants.
Obelisk, c.1930 Hinton Ampner Garden NT, Bramdean, Alresford, Hants.
Obelisk, c.1975 & sculpture of Tom the gardener, Westgreen House, Hartley Wintney, Hants
Range of small obelisks, 1879-1904, Sea Front and Clarence Gardens, Portsmouth
          m. HMS Active- Kaffir War & Zulu wars.
          m. HMS Powerful- Boer War.
          m. HMS Royal Sovereign - 1901 accident.
          m. HMS Shah - Pacific & Zulu War.
          m. HMS Victoria - disaster.
Obelisk WM Naval War Division, 10 ft, Portland stone, with statues, Portsmouth,Hants.
Obelisk WM, 1862, m. HMS Racer, Kingston, Portsmouth, Hampshire.
Obelisk WM, m. HMS Thunderer & Engineers, Kingston, Portsmouth, Hampshire
Obelisk WM, Crimean War, tall, Clarence Esplanade,Southsea,Portsmouth,Hampshire.

Obelisk WM, m. HMS Trident, Southsea, Portsmouth,Hampshire
Obelisk WM, HMS Boadicea, Gosport, Portsmouth, Hampshire.
Obelisk WM, St.Mary's ch, Hayling Island, Havant, Hampshire
Obelisk WM, St.Peter's ch, Northney, Havant, Hampshire.
Obelisk WM, Indian Troops, Barton-on-sea, Hampshire.
Obelisk WM, Brockenhurst, nr Lymington, Hampshire.
Obelisk WM, Thorney Hill, nr Lymington, Hampshire.
Obelisk WM, Totton, New Forest, Hampshire
Obelisk WM, Ashmansworth, nr Basingstoke, Hampshire.
Obelisk WM, Liss, nr Alton, Hampshire
Obelisk WM, Rowlands Castle, Havant, Hampshire.
Obelisk WM, m. Volunteer Ambulance Corps, Southampton, Hampshire.
Obelisk WM, West Tytherley, nr Winchester, Hampshire.
Obelisk WM, Wherwell, nr Andover, Hampshire.

HEREFORDSHIRE
Obelisk, 1758, m. J.Cocks - French wars, churchyard, Wigmore, Leominster, Herefordshire.
Obelisk, 1771, m. J. Cocks. Somers Chapel, St John's ch, Eastnor, Ledbury, Herefordshire.
Obelisk, 1812, m. Hon E.C. Cocks, 40 ft, stone blocks, Eastnor Castle, Ledbury, Herefs.
Obelisk, 1838, c.30 ft,arch: G. Manners, Moor Park, Clifford, Hay-on Wye, Herefordshire.
Obelisk WM, parish ch, Brilley, Leominster, Herefordshire.
Obelisk WM, parish church, Kinnersley, Leominster, Herefordshire.
Obelisk WM, Marden, S.Herefordshire.

HERTFORDSHIRE
Nell Gwynn Obelisk, 18th C, Tring Park, Tring, Hertfordshire.
Obelisk, 1879, 7 ft tall,m. T.Clarkson, Slave Abolitionist, Wadesmill, nr Ware, Hertfordshire.
Obelisk, 18th C, Newsells Park, Barkway, nr Royston, Hertfordshire.
Obelisk WM, 1903, 29 ft, ornate, Arch:Sir R.Blomfield, Hailebury Coll, nr Hoddesdon.
Obelisk WM, The Common, Berkhamsted, Hertfordshire.
Obelisk WM, 38 ft, Town Park, The Causeway, Bishops Stortford, Hertfordshire.
Obelisk WM, parish ch, Datchworth, nr Stevenage, Hertfordshire.
Obelisk WM, Richard Hale School, Hertford, Hertfordshire.
Obelisk WM, Dove Cottage, Markyate, Hertfordshire.
Obelisk WM, St.Catherine's ch, Sacombe, nr Hertford, Hertfordshire.
Obelisk WM, Borehamwood, Hertfordshire.
Obelisk WM, Haberdasher Askes School, Elstree, Hertfordshire.
Obelisk WM, m. Willian Air Crash, Willian, Letchworth, Hertfordshire.
Obelisk WM, Pirton, Hitchin, Hertfordshire.
Obelisk WM, Park st, St.Albans, Hertfordshire.
Obelisk WM, Redbourn, St.Albans, Hertfordshire.
Obelisk WM, Stevenage, Hertfordshire.
Obelisk WM, m. The Cuffley Zeppelin, Cuffley, Cheshunt, Hertfordshire.

ISLE OF WIGHT
Obelisk-seamark, 1849, m. Earl of Yarborough, RYC Commodore, Culver, Bembridge, IoW.
Obelisk, 1774, m, to Sir R. Worsley, broken by lightning in 1831, Stenbury Down, IoW.
Obelisk, 1830, small memorial to Valentine Gray, Church Litten Park, Newport I.o.W.

Obelisk WM, HMP Camp Hill, Parkurst, Cowes, IoW.
Obelisk WM, Porchfield, Cowes, IoW.
Obelisk WM, Totland, nr The Needles, IoW.

KENT
Obelisk, c.1835, lightning-struck 1967, m. Sir William Cosway, Bilsington, Romney, Kent.
Obelisk, c1764, commem Lord Amherst, Montreal, Riverhead, Sevenoaks, Kent.
Obelisk, c.1833, m. C.Larkin, Telegraph Hill, Higham, nr Rochester, Kent.
Obelisk, 1822, m. George IV's passage by boat, arch: J.Shaw, Harbour st, Ramsgate, Kent.
Obelisk gateway, 1847, Egyptian temple, Kings Street, Canterbury
Dover Patrol Obelisk WM, 84 ft on square base, Leathercote Point, overlooking sea, Dover.
Obelisk WM Naval War Division, 10 ft, Portland stone, with statues, Chatham, Kent.
Obelisk WM, 1917, m. Lord Kitchiner, Brompton Barracks, Brompton, Gillingham, Kent.
Obelisk WM, m. Boxer Rising Incident - HMS Barfleur, Gibraltar Hill, Chatham, Kent.
Obelisk WM, Molash, Ashford,Kent.
Obelisk WM, parish ch, Westwell, Ashford, Kent.
Obelisk WM, Kent Cricket Club, Canterbury, Kent.
Obelisk WM, Darenth Hospital, Dartford, Kent.
Obelisk WM, Headcorn, Maidstone, Kent.
Obelisk WM, Boer war, Tonbridge Castle, Tonbridge, Kent.
Obelisk WM, St.Lukes ch, Chiddingstone Causeway, Penshurst, Kent.
Obelisk WM, m. HMS Vulture, Halfway Houses, Sheerness, Kent.
Obelisk WM, m. R.Marchand, Nouds Farm, Lynsted, Faversham, Kent.
Obelisk WM, Queenborough, nr Sheerness, Kent.

LANCASHIRE
Obelisk, 18th C, Churchtown Green, Southport, Lancashire.
Obelisk, c.1770, was at Allerton Hall, now in Allerton Road, Allerton, Liverpool
Obelisk, 1781, 22 ft, fluted, S. of church, Atherton, Wigan, Lancashire
Obelisk, c.1805, m. Horatio Nelson, Springfield Park, Knotty Ash, Liverpool
Obelisk, 1815, ball finial, m. Wellington, Bispham Hall, Billinge, Orrell, Wigan, Lancashire.
Obelisk, 1828, 28ft, Earlestown Market Place, Newton-le-Willows, Lancashire.
Obelisk, c.1830, near entrance, Hall-i'-th'-wood, nr Bolton, Lancashire.
Obelisk, 1842, m. Henry Hunt, statue atop, 32 ft stone,Every St, Ancoats, Manchester.
Obelisk, 1844, Bushell Hospital, Goosnargh, nr Preston, Lancashire.
Obelisk, 1858, m. Richard Yates, 15 ft in two granite blocks, Princes Park, Liverpool.
Obelisk, 1859, c.25 ft tall, flute edged, sandstone, Old Market, Leigh, Wigan, Lancs.
Obelisk, 1867, marks height of flood of 1866, c.10 ft, The Crescent, Salford, Lancs.
Obelisk, 1874, base only, m. Jethro Tinker,'Our local Linnacus', Ashton-under-Lyne, Lancs.
Obelisk, 1877, m. Sam Bamford, writer & reformer, Middleton, Rochdale, Lancashire.
Obelisk, 1888, m. Joseph Rayner, d.1879, Stamford Park, Stalybridge, Manchester.
Obelisk, 1888, m. 1886 Lifeboat disaster, above tabernacle, Southport, Lancashire.
Obelisk, 1891, m. Mark Addy, lifesaving swimmer, 24 ft, Central Drive, Salford, Lancs.
Obelisk, 1893, m. Oliver Heywood: banker, philanthropist, Broad St, Salford, Lancs.
Obelisk, 1900, m. Four Dialect Writers, Rochdale, Lancashire.
Obelisk, 1909, m. Samuel Smith, 60 ft inc granite plinth, Sefton Pk, Liverpool.
Obelisk, 1916, m. SS.Titanic Engine Room Heroes, Goscombe John, Pier Head, Liverpool.

Obelisk, 1928, Bishops Park, Wotherhead Hill, Ripponden Rd, Oldham, Lancashire.
Obelisk, 1937, m. Marshall Stevens MP, red granite, Trafford Wharf Rd, Manchester.
Obelisk WM, 1923, 100 ft, statuary by Gilbert Ledward, Blackpool, Lancashire
Obelisk WM, London Square, Southport, Lancashire.
Obelisk WM, King Edvard VII School, Lytham St,Anne's, Lancashire.
Obelisk WM, Lower House Wesleyan Sunday School, Burnley, Lancashire.
Obelisk WM, Brinscall, nr Chorley, Lancashire.
Obelisk WM, tall, statue of 'Grief', Accrington, Lancashire.
Obelisk WM, Methodist ch yard, Ribchester Road, Blackburn Lancashire.
Obelisk WM, Blackburn Cathedral, Lancashire.
Obelisk WM, Great Harwood, via Blackburn, Lancashire.
Obelisk WM, Methodist ch,Wilpshire, Whalley, Lancashire.
Obelisk WM, Low Moor Club, Clitheroe,Lancashire.
Obelisk WM, 1858, Crimean War, 24 ft monolith, Quernmore Rd Cem, Lancaster.
Obelisk WM, Roman Road at Lowgill, (remote),Tatham Fells, Lancaster.
Obelisk WM, Boer war, 25 ft red granite, Avenham Park, Preston, Lancashire.
Obelisk WM, Ribbleton Av Methodist ch, Preston, Lancashire.
Obelisk WM, Freckleton, nr Preston, Lancashire.
Obelisk WM, Methodist ch, Lostock hall, Preston, Lancashire.
Obelisk WM, Knowl Green, Longridge, Preston, Lancashire.
Obelisk WM, Aughton, nr Ormskirk, Lancashire.
Obelisk WM, Newburgh, nr Ormskirk, Lancashire
Obelisk WM, 15 ft sandstone,Crimean war,Victoria Park, Ormskirk, Lancashire.
Obelisk WM, 20 ft tall on 12ft pedestal, Up Holland, nr Ormskirk, Lancashire.
Obelisk WM, Nateby, Garstang, Preston, Lancashire.
Obelisk WM, Trinity Chapel, Farnworth, Bolton, Lancashire.
Obelisk WM, Lancs Fusiliers, Wellington Barracks, Bury, Lancashire.
Obelisk WM, St.James' ch, Westhoughton, Bolton, Lancashire.
Obelisk WM, St.Peter's ch, Blackley, Manchester.
Obelisk WM, St.Thomas' ch, Crumpsall, Manchester
Obelisk WM, Belle Vue, Gorton, Manchester
Obelisk WM, All Souls ch, Heywood, Rochdale, Lancashire.
Obelisk WM, Littleborough, Rochdale, Lancashire.
Obelisk WM, All Saints ch, Rhodes, Rochdale, Lancashire.
Obelisk WM, Broughton House, Broughton Park, Salford, Lancashire.
Obelisk WM, 22 ft Portland stone, Clifton, Salford, Lancashire.
Obelisk WM, British Legion, Ordsall, Salford, Lancashire.
Obelisk WM, Parrfold Park, Worsley, Salford, Lancashire.
Obelisk WM, Garswood Collieries Inst, Ashton-in-Makerfield, Wigan,Lancashire.
Obelisk WM, Atherton, Wigan, Lancashire.
Obelisk WM, St.Peter's ch, Hindley, Wigan, Lancashire.
Obelisk WM, Obelisk WM, St Catherine's ch, Davyhulme, Eccles, Lancashire.

LEICESTERSHIRE
Obelisk, 18th C, 80 ft, brick & cement render, Garendon Park, Loughborough, Leicestershire.
Obelisk, m. George Fox, crossroads, Fenny Drayton, Hinckley, Leicestershire.
Obelisk, Stanford Hall, Lutterworth, Leicestershire.
Obelisk WM, Blaby, nr Leicester, Leicestershire.
Obelisk WM, St.Helen's ch, Sharnford, Blaby, nr Leicester, Leicestershire.

Obelisk WM, Rothley, Charnwood nr Leicester, Leicestershire.
Obelisk WM, Thrussington, Charnwood, nr Leicester, Leicestershire,
Obelisk WM, Thurmaston, nr Leicester, Leicestershire.
Obelisk WM, St.Peter's ch, Leire, Market Harborough, Leicestershire,
Obelisk WM, Barlestone, nr Hinckley, Leicestershire.
Obelisk WM, Botcheston, nr Hinckley, Leicestershire.
Obelisk WM, m. to A.Kettleby, St.James ch, Melton Mowbray, Leicestershire.
Obelisk WM, St.Luke's ch, Gaddesby, nr Melton Mowbray, Leicestershire.
Obelisk WM, Plungar, nr Melton Mowbray, Leicestershire.
Obelisk WM, m. Moira Colliery, 20 ft sandstone, Moira Nat Forest Visitor Cent, Leics.

LINCOLNSHIRE
Obelisk, 1763, High Bridge, Lincoln, Lincolnshire.
Obelisk, c.1780, 45 ft tall, m. A favourite horse, Belwood, Belton, Axholme, Lincolnshire.
Obelisk, 1835, m. R.Wharton Myddleston, Rookery Lane, Leasingham, Lincolnshire.
Obeliscal Monument, 1844, to D of Wellington, Waterloo Wood, Woodhall Spa, Lincs.
Obelisk, 1847, 60 ft tall, m. Isaac Newton, Stoke Rochford Hall, nr Grantham, Lincolnshire.
Obelisk, very old, unknown origin, 8 ft, Stoke Rochford Church, nr Grantham, Lincolnshire.
Obelisk, 1862, m. William Smith, d.1845, Barnoldby-le-Beck, Cleethorpes, Lincolnshire.
Obelisk WM, 18 ft on 5 ft pedestal, Kirton in Lindsey, Lincolnshire.
Obelisk WM, Memorial Gdns, Boston, Lincolnshire.
Obelisk WM, m. Burma Star Assoc, Boston, Lincolnshire,
Obelisk WM, Frampton, Boston, Lincolnshire.
Obelisk WM, South Ekington, nr Louth, Lincolnshire.
Obelisk WM, Birchwood Centre, Skellingthorpe, Lincoln, Lincolnshire.
Obelisk WM, Bassingham, nr Lincoln, Lincolnshire.
Obelisk WM, Potterhanworth, nr Lincoln, Lincolnshire.
Obelisk WM, Holbeach St.Johns, Holbeach, South Holland, Lincolnshire.
Obelisk WM, St.Mark's ch, Holbeach St.Marks, Hobeach, South Holland, Lincolnshire.
Obelisk WM, Long Sutton, South Holland, Lincolnshire.
Obelisk WM, Ropsley, nr Grantham, Lincolnshire.
Obelisk WM, Blyton, nr Gainsborough, Lincolnshire.
Obelisk WM, Coates, West Lindsey, Lincolnshire.
Obelisk WM, St.Peter's ch, Normanby, nr Market Rasen, Lincolnshire.
Obelisk WM, Scotter, nr Scunthorpe, Lincolnshire.
Obelisk WM, Thorpe le Fallows, nr Lincoln, Lincolnshire.
Obelisk WM, St. Andrew's ch, Willoughton, nr Gainsborough, Lincolnshire.

LONDON - The City, E & S.E
Obelisk, 1721, 14 ft, stone, on 4 globes, suburbia, Monument Gdns, Lewisham, SE13.
'The Obelisk', 1771, Arch: G.Dance Jr, comm Brass Crosby,St.George's Circus, SE11.
Obelisk, 1904, m. Royal Arsenal Explosion, Plumstead Cem, E.Wickham, London SE2.
Obelisk, 18C-replaced 1970s, 10 ft, 4 globes, Broomhill Wlk,Woodford Gn.London E4.
Obelisk, 1855, 35 ft granite,m. J.Bellot, lost in search Franklin exp, Greenwich Pier, SE8.
Obelisk, 1864, 20 ft, in 4 blocks, Wm. Maori Wars NZ, Riverside, Greenwich, SE8.
Obelisk, c.1806 m. Admiral Lord Nelson, Guildhall, City of London, EC1.
Gurney Obelisk Drinking Fountain, 1861, 42 ft, Sc:John Bell,Stratford Broadway, E.15.
Obelisk, 1833, m. R.Waithman MP,18 ft granite & 6ft plinth, Salisbury Square, EC4.

Obelisk in Leman St/Commercial Rd, Whitechapel, London EC3.
Obelisk Drinking Fountain, 1861, m. R.J.Little, stone,Grand Depot Rd, Woolwich SE18.
Obelisk & Drinking Fountain,1866, 15 ft limestone,Lewisham Road / Hill,London SE13.
Obelisk Drinking Fountain,1878, raised Rev H.Pincott, Christchurch Gdns, LondonSE18.
Obelisk-Coal Tax Post,1861,(1 of many)30 yds Whalebone Br, Chadwell Heath, London E
Obelisk, 1870, m. Daniel Defoe,10 ft marble shaft on 4 ft plinth, Bunhill Fields, EC1.
Obelisk, 1955, m. George Lansbury MP, small, granite, 39 Bow Road, London E3.
Obelisk, 1987, 21 ft tall, Ambassador Gdns, Newham, Docklands, London E16.
Obelisk, 1998, steel ventilation shaft, Finsbury Place, London E5 -
Obelisk with finial, 1999, Tibetan peace Gdn, unv by Dalai Lama, I.War Mus, SE11.
Obelisk WM, Upper Norwood, London, SE27.
Obelisk WM, Promenade de Verdun, 25 ft, Woodcote, London SE25.
Obelisk WM, Afghan & Zulu wars, Woolwich Artillery, Woolwich, London SE18.
Obelisk WM, Bexleyheath, Bexley, South-East of London.
Obelisk WM, St.Paul's ch, Sandford Est, Deptford, London SE14.
Obelisk WM, Camberwell, East Dulwich, London SE22
Obelisk WM, m. Commonwealth war graves, Nunhead Cemetery, London SE15
Obelisk WM, Lewisham Borough, London SE4.
Obelisk WM, St.George's ch (Hawksmoor), Shadwell, Tower Hamlets, London E1.
Obelisk WM, Hackney Wick, London E3.
Obelisk WM, Stonebridge Common, Haggerston, Hackney, London E3.
Obelisk WM, m. Tramway employees, LT Bus Garage, West Ham, London E13.

LONDON -W & S.W
Obelisk, 1718 m. Earl of Derwentwater, moved 1904 to E.Churchfield Rd, Acton, W3.
'Orange Tree Obelisk' c.1730, 16 ft, by Classical temple, at Chiswick House, London W4.
Obelisk, 1732, 18 ft, limestone, frieze, Burlington Lane Gate, Chiswick House, London W4.
Obelisk, 1751, A lady's grave, urn finial, c.13 ft, Chelsea Square, London SW3.
'Cleopatra's Needle', Ancient Egyptian Obelisk, The Embankment , SW3.
Obelisk,1865, m. to explorer John Speke, 3 part granite shaft, Kensington Gdns, W8.
Obelisk, 1858, m. Charles Wesley, St.Mary's, Marylebone High st, London, W1.
Fire Plates Obelisk, 1788, Arch: G.Dance Jr, Tibbet's Cnr, Putney Heath, SW15.
Obelisk, 1889, 10 ft tall, Victoria Jubilee, marble, Latewood Rd, Brentford,London W4.
'Katyn Monument', 1976, m. Polish P.o.W, 21 ft, black marble, Gunnersbury Cem, W5.
Obelisk, 1900, m. T.Brown, Sandy Lane, Hampton Wick, Middlesex.
Obelisk, 1963, m. S.Fairbairn, Univ boat race milestone, Putney, London SW15.
Obelisk 1863 'Chillianwallah Monument', WM -Sikh Wars, Kings Road, London SW3.
Obelisk WM fountain, 1925, rededicated 2003, m. RN Division, Horse Guards, SW1.
Obelisk WM, St George's School, Battersea, London SW11.
Obelisk WM, East Sheen, Richmond-on-Thames.
Obelisk WM, Chiswick, London W3.

LONDON - N & N.W
2 Obelisks, 18th C, m. Shakespeare and Garrick, Hendon Hall, Ashley Lane London NW4.
Obelisk, 1740, Hadley Highstone, com. Battle of Barnet, Monken Hadley, Barnet, London.
Obelisks, early 18 C, 60 ft, removed from Wrest Pk, to Trent Pk, nr Barnet, N.London.

Obelisks, early 18 C, c.15 ft, removed from Wrest Pk, to Trent Pk, nr Barnet, N.London.

Catvellauni Obelisk, 1750, 25ft, W.of RNO Hospital, Brockley Hill, Harrow, N.London.

Obelisk, 18th C, m. Julius Caesar, Stanmore Park, Harrow,N.London.

Obelisk, 1879, with drinking fountain, m. Mrs Smithies, Bounds Green Road, London N11.

Obelisk, 1902, M. E.Onslow Ford, Abbey Rd, London NW8.

Obelisk, 1991, M. Tom Paine, sc. K.Jordan, Angel Sq, Islington, London N1.

Obelisk WM, Jack Straw's Castle, West Heath, Hampstead, NW3.

Obelisk WM, Zoo keepers, Inside London Zoo, Regents Park, London NW1.

Obelisk WM, 1921, m. LMS Railwaymen, 30 ft, limestone, Euston Station, London NW1.

Obelisk WM, Upper st, Islington, London N1.

Obelisk WM, South Tottenham, London N15.

Obelisk WM, St. Mary's ch, Harefield, Hillingdon, NW London.

Obelisk WM, Cranford, Hillingdon, NW London.

Obelisk WM, Boer War, Christchurch,Barnet, North of London.

NORFOLK

Obelisk, 1729, 70 ft, designed Wm Kent, on avenue in grounds of Holkham Hall, Norfolk.

Obelisks, 18C on island at Reffley Temple, destroyed 1984, S.Wootton, Norfolk.

Obelisk, 1814, m. Admiral Nelson, erected: J.Drestier, Little Dunham, Norfolk.

Obelisk, 1861, Gurney Drinking Fountain, 12 ft granite, Tombland, Norwich, Norfolk.

Obelisk WM, 32 ft granite, St.George's Park, Great Yarmouth, Norfolk.

Obelisk WM, Norwich Boys Model School OB, Norwich Cathedral, Norfolk.

Obelisk WM, 25 ft, Vicar Street, Wymondham, Norfolk.

Obelisk WM, Colkirk, nr Fakenham, Norfolk

Obelisk WM, St.Mary's ch, East Bilney, nr Fakenham, Norfolk.

Obelisk WM, Foxley, nr Fakenham, Norfolk.

Obelisk WM, St.Andrew's ch, Guist, nr Fakenham, Norfolk.

Obelisk WM, Necton, nr Swaffham, Norfolk.

Obelisk WM, North Lopham, Diss, Norfolk.

Obelisk WM, Sts.Peter& Paul ch, Wendling, nr East Dereham, Norfolk.

Obelisk WM, Foulsham, nr Fakenham,Norfolk.

Obelisk WM, Flitcham, nr Sandringham, Norfolk.

Obelisk WM, Holkham Hall, WW1 and WW2, Holkham, Wells-next-sea, Norfolk.

Obelisk WM, St.Lawrence's ch, Harpley, nr Sandringham, Norfolk.

Obelisk WM, Methwold, nr Downham Market, Norfolk.

NORTHAMPTONSHIRE

Triangular Lodge, 1597, with three-sided obelisk finials, Rushton Northamptonshire.

Obelisk, 1764, m. 4th Duke of Devonshire, Boughton Park, nr Northampton, Northants.

Obelisk, Deene Park, Corby, Northamptonshire.

Naseby Obelisk, 1823, 20 ft tall, a mile from battlefield, Clipton Rd, Naseby, Northants.

Obelisk WM, with 2 obelisks, arch. E.Lutyens, St.Mary's ch, Northampton, Northants.

Obelisk WM, Weldon, Corby, Northants.

Obelisk WM, 1921, 6 ft obelisk in avenue planted by Earl Spencer, Althorp, Northants.

Obelisk WM, Clipston, nr Daventry, Northants.

Obelisk WM, Spanhoe USAAF, nr Kettering, Northants.

Obelisk WM, Kings Sutton, nr Brackley, Northants.

Obelisk WM, St.Mary's ch, Stoke Bruerne, nr Northampton, Northants.

Obelisk WM, parish ch, Bozeat, Wellingborough, Northants.
Obelisk WM, made of wood, Hartwell, nr Northampton, Northants.

NORTHUMBERLAND
Obelisk, 1723, base only,maybe by Vanbrugh, Seaton Delaval,Whitley Bay, Northumberland.
Obelisk, 1737, 60 ft, sandstone blocks, Seaton Delaval, Northumberland.
Obelisk, 1788, m. centenary William III, Kirkley Hall, Ponteland, Northumberland.
Obelisk, 1805, m. Lord Nelson, Acton, nr Felton, nr Alnwick, Northumberland.
Obelisk, 1808, to private friendship/Ld Nelson, Old Swarland Hall, Northumberland.
Obelisk. 1828, m. father & brother of Sir W Davison, Lanton Hill,Wooler, Northumberland.
Obelisk, 1862, m. Hartley Mining Disaster, Hartley, Earsdon, Whitley Bay.
Obelisk, 1882, m. R.Gardner,1625-1687,12 ft , Chirton Gn, N.Shields, Northumberland.
Obelisks - a pair, 1938, arch:Lutyens, Blagdon Hall, Seaton Burn, Morpeth.
Obelisk, 1989, m. T.Haswell,1807-1889, teacher, N. Shields, Northumberland.
Obelisk, 1997, as Market Cross, coarse cut blocks, Bedlington, nr Morpeth.
Obelisk, 1908, WM.Boer War, with bronze figures, Percy Street, Newcastle.
Obelisk WM, Trinity ch, Cambo, Alnwick, Northumberland.
Obelisk WM, Seahouses, nr Bamburgh, Northumberland.
Obelisk WM, Spittal, across bay from Berwick-on-Tweed, Northumberland.
Obelisk WM, Longhirst, nr Morpeth, Northumberland.
Obelisk WM, Ponteland, nr Newcastle, Northumberland.
Obelisk WM, Humshaugh, nr Hexham, Northumberland.
Obelisk WM, West Woodburn, nr Otterburn, Northumberland.
Obelisk WM, Backworth, nr Tynemouth, Northumberland.
Obelisk WM, m. Preston Colliery, Preston Public Library, North Shields, Newcastle.

NOTTINGHAMSHIRE
Obelisk, Vincent Lodge, Forest Lane, Papplewick, Hucknall, Nottinghamshire.
Obelisk , Howe Plantation, Woodland Grange, Papplewick, Nottinghamshire.
Obelisk 1999, m. Festival of Britain 1951, 9 ft, black marble,Trowell, Nottinghamshire.
Obelisk WM, City & County Boer War, 25 ft granite, City Park, Nottingham, Notts.
Obelisk WM, Afghan War, Nottingham, Notts.
Obelisk WM, St. Peters ch, Hayton, nr East Retford, Notts.
Obelisk WM, Laneham, nr East Retford, Notts.
Obelisk WM, Lound, nr Worksop, Notts.
Obelisk WM, St.Matthew's ch, Normanton-on-Trent, Tuxford, Notts.
Obelisk WM, St.John's ch, Awsworth, Nottingham, Notts.
Obelisk WM, Crimean War, St.John's ch, Beeston, Nottingham, Notts.
Obelisk WM, m. Munitions Explosion, Ordnance Depot, Chilwell, Nottingham, Notts.
Obelisk WM, St.Catherine's ch, Cossall, Nottingham, Notts.
Obelisk WM, Eastwood, Nottingham, Notts.
Obelisk WM, Gedling, Nottingham Notts.
Obelisk WM, Village Green, Bilsthorpe, Newark, Notts.
Obelisk WM, Lowdham, Arnold, Nottingham, Notts.
Obelisk WM, RAF,Langar, Rushcliffe, Notts.

OXFORDSHIRE
Obelisk, c.1730, arch: Wm Kent, Shotover House, Wheatley, Oxon.

Obelisk, 1742, commemorating Prince of Wales' 1739 visit, Wroxton Abbey, Banbury, Oxon.
Obelisk, 18th C, Northfield End, Marlow Rd, Henley-on-Thames, Oxon.
Obelisk, c.1820, m. A favourite foxhound, 1 mile S. of church, Stoke Lyne, Oxon.
Obelisk, 1843, m. John Hampden 1643, Old Watlington Rd, Chalgrove, Oxon.
Obelisk WM, 30 ft Portland stone,Oxon & Bucks Light Inf, Oxford. Oxon.
Obelisk WM, 1900, 25 ft Bath st, m. 62 infantry at Tirah, India, in 1898. Bonn Sq, Oxford.
Obelisk WM, m. East African wars, Queen st, Oxford, Oxon.
Obelisk WM, Warborough, nr Oxford, Oxon.
Obelisk WM, Easton Hastings, nr Oxford, Oxon.
Obelisk WM, Ducklington, Witney, Oxon.
Obelisk WM, Swerford, nr Chipping Norton, Oxon.

SHROPSHIRE
Obelisk Milestone, c.1823, 20 ft, handsome, distances inscribed, Craven Arms, Shropshire.
Obelisk, 1835, 70 ft, m. 1st Duke of Sutherland, Lilleshall, nr Newport, Shropshire.
Obelisk, 1842, m. Sir A. Corbet from tenantry, 15 ft, Lee Brockhurst, Wem, Shropshire
Obelisk, 1874, (previously at Station),The Quarry, Shrewsbury, Shropshire.
Obelisk, Shirlett Hall, Willey, Much Wenlock, Shrewbury, Shropshire.
Obelisk, m. retriever fell into coal-shaft, 50 ft, Shirlett Rd, Bridgenorth, Shropshire.
Obelisk WM, Iron, roadside, Paradise, Coalbrookdale, Shropshire.
Obelisk WM, Loppington, Wem, Shropshire.
Obelisk WM, Whitchurch, Shropshire.
Obelisk WM, Whixall, Wem, Shropshire.
Obelisk WM, St.James' ch, Morton, nr Oswestry, Shropshire.
Obelisk WM, Oswestry,Shropshire.
Obelisk WM, All Saints ch, Berrington, Shrewsbury, Shropshire.
Obelisk WM, All Stretton, nr Church Stretton, Shropshire.
Obelisk WM, parish ch, Bishop's Castle, nr Church Stretton, Shropshire.
Obelisk WM, parish ch, Knowbury, Ludlow, Shropshire.
Obelisk WM, Ticklerton, Church Stretton, Shropshire.

SOMERSET- including Bristol
Obelisk, 1734, put up by Beau Nash, to Prince of Orange, Orange Grove,Bath, Somerset.
Obelisk, 1738, 50 ft, put up by Beau Nash to Prince of Wales, Queen Sq, Bath, Somerset.
Jubilee Obelisk, 1838, Royal Avenue / Marlborough Lane, Bath, Somerset.
Obelisk, 1762, virtually destroyed, m. Elizabetha Somerset d.1760, Stoke Pk, Bristol.
Obelisk, 1766, 25 ft, m. William Pitt, d.1788, moved 1883 to Clifton Green, Bristol.
Obelisks, a pair of vermiculated ashlar pillars, c.1790, entrance to Cotham Park, Bristol.
Princess Charlotte Obelisk, 1818, Queen Victoria House, Redland Hill, Bristol.
Obelisk, c.1790, 25ft freestone, G.Messiter's old estate, Barwick Park, Yeovil, Somerset.
Obelisk, c.1790, forshortened on large pedestal, town centre, Yeovil, Somerset.
Obelisk, 'Nempnett Needle', Rookery Farm, Nempnett Thrubwell, Cheddar, Somerset.
Obelisk, 1801, m. King Alfred of Wessex, d.899, Athelney, Lyng, Taunton, Somerset.
Obelisk Drinking Fountain, concrete, foreshortened shape, Vivary Pk, Taunton, Somerset.
Wellington Monument, 1892, 175 ft w.stairs, only 3 sided, Wrangway, Somerset.
Obelisk, 1852, m. H.Colston, d.shooting accident, 10 ft, Breach Wood, Butleigh, Somerset.
Obelisk WM, hilltop with new stone circle, Ham Hill, Stoke-sub-Hamdon, Yeovil, Somerset.

Obelisk WM, Crimean War, Abbey Cemetery, Bath, Somerset.

Obelisk WM, Freshford, Bath, Somerset.

Obelisk WM, Clifton RFC,Playing fields, Henbury, N. Bristol.

Obelisk WM Westbury-on-Trym, N. Bristol.

Obelisk WM, The Scouts' obelisk, Downend, near Bristol.

Obelisk WM Downend & Southwell, prominent on Staple Hill, Kingswood, near Bristol.

Obelisk WM m. H.Holvey and Sgt Tune, All Saints Church, Dunkerton, Somerset.

Obelisk WM m. Maj F.Savage, Somervale Sec School, Midsomer Norton, Somerset.

Obelisk WM, Pilton, Shepton Mallet, Somerset.

Obelisk WM, Ansford, nr Shepton Mallet, Somerset.

Obelisk WM, parish ch, Babcary, nr Glastonbury, Somerset.

Obelisk WM, Barton St.David, nr Glastonbury, Somerset.

Obelisk WM, St.John's ch, Brewham, nr Shepton Mallet, Somerset.

Obelisk WM, Henstridge,nr Yeovil, Somerset.

Obelisk WM, West Buckland, Taunton, Somerset.

Obelisk WM, Cutcombe, nr Minehead, Somerset.

Obelisk WM, USAF crash site, Porlock, nr Minehead, Somerset.

Obelisk WM, Wheddon Cross, nr Minehead, Somerset.

STAFFORDSHIRE - (for Birmingham see Warwickshire).

Obelisk, c.1735, m. Craven Kynnersley, gundog accident, Loxley Hall,Uttoxeter, Staffs.

Obelisk, 1776, milepost, at crossroads in Tixall, nr Stafford, Staffordshire.

Obelisk, c.1770, 35 ft, sandstone, Knoll Hill, Weston Hall,Weston-under-Lizard, Staffs.

Obelisk, 1811, raised by Lord Bagot, nr Abbots Bromley, Staffordshire.

Obelisk, 1839, m. John Wedgwood, Audley, nr Stoke-on-Trent. Staffordshire.

Obelisks, c.1955, a pair on outer gate piers, Okeover House, Okeover, Staffordshire.

Obelisk, 1894, m. Timothy Trow, London rd, Stoke-on-Trent, Staffordshire.

Obelisk, 1975, m. 1872 Mining disaster, 22 men lost, parish ch, Pelsall, Staffordshire.

Obeliscal topiaries, 'Little Egypt', Biddulph Grange Gardens, Staffordshire.

Obelisk WM, Bridgetown, Cannock, Staffs.

Obelisk WM, Rugeley, Cannock, Staffs.

Obelisk WM, Wimblebury, Cannock, Staffs.

Obelisk WM, Yoxall, Staffs.

Obelisk WM, Shenstone, nr Lichfield, Staffs.

Obelisk WM, Audley, nr Newcastle-under-Lyme, Staffs.

Obelisk WM, Halmerend, nr Newcastle-under-Lyme, Staffs.

Obelisk WM, Knutton, nr Newcastle-under-Lyme, Staffs.

Obelisk WM, Newcastle-under-Lyme, Staffs.

Obelisk WM, Cheslyn Hay, Cannock, Staffs.

Obelisk WM, Kinver, nr Amblecote, Staffs.

Obelisk WM, Wombourne, nr Sedgley, Staffs.

Obelisk WM, Moddershall, nr Stone, Staffs.

Obelisk WM, Stafford GrammarSchool, Staffs.

Obelisk WM, Weston, nr Stafford, Staffs.

Obelisk WM, m. Park Hall Colliery,Ferguson-Wilde Wks, Dillhorne, Stoke-on-Trent, Staffs.

Obelisk WM, Farley Hall, Farley, nr Cheadle, Stoke-on-Trent, Staffs.

Obelisk WM, St.Mark's ch, Foxt, nr Cheadle, Stoke-on-Trent, Staffs.

Obelisk WM, parish ch, Sheen, Dovedale, nr Leek, Staffs.

Obelisk WM, Bucknall, Stoke-on-Trent, Staffs.
Obelisk WM, Tunstall, Stoke-on-Trent, Staffs.
Obelisk WM, Blackheath, nr West Bromwich, Staffs.
Obelisk WM, 32 ft, Powke Lane cem, Rowley Regis, nr West Bromwich, Staffs.

SUFFOLK
Obelisk, c.1750, 15 ft, Portland stone, Chequer Square, Bury St.Edmunds, Suffolk.
Obelisk, c.1790, 10 ft, inscr milestone & ball finial, White Hart Inn, Nayland, Suffolk.
Obelisk, 1804, m. Frederick Hervey, 4th Earl Bristol, c.40 ft, Ickworth Park, Suffolk.
Obelisk, 1819, m. Dr.Taylor, martyred in 1558, obtuse, c.15 ft,Hadleigh, Suffolk,
Obelisk, c1825, bricks & mortar, Helmingham Hall, Stowmarket, Suffolk.
Obelisk, demolished,18th century, fluted, solar orb finial, Woolverstone, Ipswich, Suffolk.
Obelisk WM, Field of Honour, Ipswich cemetery, Ipswich, Suffolk.
Obelisk WM, m. Ransome & Rapier, Ipswich, Suffolk.
Obelisk WM, parish ch, Stoke Ash, Stowmarket, Suffolk.
Obelisk WM, parish ch, Barningham, nr Ixworth, Suffolk.
Obelisk WM, Barrow, nr Bury St.Edmunds, Suffolk.
Obelisk WM, Culford, nr Bury St.Edmunds, Suffolk.
Obelisk WM, Hawkedon, Bury St. Edmunds, Suffolk.
Obelisk WM, Higham, nr Bury St.Edmunds, Suffolk.
Obelisk WM, parish ch, Hopton, nr Ixworth, Suffolk.
Obelisk WM, Withersfield, nr Wickham Street, Bury St.Edmunds, Suffolk.
Obelisk WM, Recreation ground, Bawdsey, nr Felixstowe, Suffolk.
Obelisk WM, Cretingham, nr Stowmarket, Suffolk.
Obelisk WM, Wetheringsett, nr. Eye, Suffolk.
Obelisk WM, parish ch, Knoddishall, Suffolk.
Obelisk WM, Wickham Market, nr Saxmundham, Suffolk.
Obelisk WM, 15ft, Halesworth, Suffolk.
Obelisk WM, 20 ft, end of promenade, Lowestoft, Suffolk.
Obelisk WM, Beck Row, nr Mildenhall, Suffolk.
Obelisk WM, 20 ft Portland stone, Lakenheath, Suffolk.
Obelisk WM, West Row, nr Mildenhall, Suffolk.
Obelisk WM, Worlington, nr Mildenhall, Suffolk.

SURREY
Obelisk, 1777, 10 ft, Inscribed Milestone, by bridge, Richmond-on-Thames, Surrey.
3 obelisks, 1778, Royal Society time markers, separate, Deer Park, Richmond, Surrey.
Obelisk, 1809, George III Jubilee, Shirleychurch Rd,Addington, Croydon, Surrey.
Obelisk, 1822, com. borough water supply, Mitcham Common, Surrey.
Obelisk, m. Prince Leopold and Princess Charlotte, Claremont, Surrey.
Obelisk WM, RAF, 1991, 23 ft surm bronze eagle, Purley Way, Croydon, Surrey.
Obelisk WM, Wallington, Sutton, Surrey.
Obelisk WM, St.Nicholas' church, Compton, Guildford, Surrey.

SUSSEX
Obelisk, 1794, for Gen Murray, arch: J.Soane; Beauport Pk, Baldslow, Hastings, E.Sussex.
Obelisk, 'Martyrs Monument'-m. Sussex executions of 1555- Cliffe Hill, Lewes, E.Sussex.
Obelisk, c.1808, 'Mad Jack Fuller's needle', 65 ft, roughbuilt, Brightling Down, E.Sussex.
Obelisk Drinking Fountain, 1871,18ft, granite, N.end Grand Parade, Brighton, E.Sussex.
Obelisk, m. Richard Cobden - Free Trader, c.20 ft, Cocking Causeway, Midhurst, W.Sussex.
Obelisk WM, Royal Sussex Regt, Brighton.
Obelisk WM, 1886, Egypt Campaign,Victoria Fountain Gdns, Brighton, E.Sussex.
Obelisk WM, Hampden Park, Eastbourne, Sussex.
Obelisk WM, Crimean War-Finnish prisoners, St.John's ch, Lewes, Sussex.
Obelisk WM, Brazen Memorial, St.Michael's ch, Newhaven, Sussex.
Obelisk WM, Newhaven Patrol, Aux RN, Newhaven, Sussex.
Obelisk WM, St.Giles' ch, Dallington, nr Battle, Sussex
Obelisk WM, Micheldene, Birling Gap, nr Seaford, Sussex.
Obelisk WM, All Saints ch, Crowborough, Sussex.
Obelisk WM, m. Lancing Carriage Works, Lancing, Sussex.
Obelisk WM, Southwick, nr Brighton, Sussex.
Obelisk WM, Slindon, near Arundel, Sussex.
Obelisk WM, St.M. Magdalen ch, Rusper, Horsham, Sussex.
Obelisk WM, Boer war, Worthing, Sussex.

WARWICKSHIRE
Obelisk, c1746- rebuilt 1828, 55 ft tall, ashlar, Farnborough Hall NT, nr.Banbury, Warwicks.
Obelisk, 1749, built by 1st Lord Archer, Umberslade Pk, Tamworth-in-Arden, Warks.
Obeliscal Milestone, 1813, inscribed, 16 feet tall, restored 1953, Dunchurch, Warwickshire.
Obelisk, m. Battle of Edge Hill, Edge Hill, Warwickshire.
Obelisk, 1846, m. Mediaeval chapel site, bulky, Grendon Rd, Polesworth, Warwickshire.
Obelisk, 1854, m. D.of Wellington/Waterloo, 20 ft, Edgehill Wood, Radway, Warwicks.
Obelisk, 1856, m. Lt.Col Unett, St.Philip's Sq, The Cathedral, Birmingham.
Obelisk, 1875, m. E.Willes; 25 ft (15 ft monolith); Jehpson Gdns, Leamington Spa, Warks.
Obelisk Drinking Fountain, 1880, m. H.Bright, 32 ft, Parade, Leamington Spa, Warwicks.
Obelisk, 1876, m. M.Philips MP,120 ft, granite,Welcombe Hills,Stratford,Warwickshire.
Obelisk, 1885, m. F.Burnaby, soldier and writer, 56 ft, St.Philip's Sq, Birmingham.
Obelisk, c.1890, m. George Eliot (Marian Evans),Eliot Mem Gdns,Nuneaton, Warwicks.
Obelisk, 1921,Departure Monument/ Gallipoli troops,50 ft,Stretton-on-Dunsmore,Warks.
Obelisk, 1932, m. Gregory family, 8ft, Stivichall Rd, Coventry, Warwicks.
Obelisk WM, m. Cannon Hill Pk Boy Scouts, Birmingham,
Obelisk WM, St.Mary's ch, Pype Hays, Birmingham,
Obelisk WM, Triumph Co, Coventry, Warwickshire.
Obelisk WM, m. Cyclists, 30 ft granite, Meriden Green, Coventry, Warwickshire.
Obelisk WM, Radford, nr Leamington Spa, Warwickshire.
Obelisk WM, St.Augustine's ch, Dudley, Warwickshire.
Obelisk WM, m. Men & Women of Dudley, 14 ft, Dudley,Warwickshire.
Obelisk WM, ch of Ascension, Wall Heath, Dudley,Warwickshire.
Obelisk WM, St.Nicholas ch, Baddesley Ensor, nr Nuneaton, Warwickshire
Obelisk WM, parish church, Hurley, nr Nuneaton, Warwickshire
Obelisk WM, Reading Room, Church Lawford, Rugby, Warwickshire

Obelisk WM, Sts Peter&Paul ch, Long Compton, Stratford-on-Avon, Warwickshire.
Obelisk WM, Lower Shuckburgh, Stratford-on-Avon, Warwickshire.
Obelisk WM, St.Lawrence's ch, Napton on the hill, Stratford-on-Avon, Warwickshire.
Obelisk WM, Prior's Hardwick, Stratford-on-Avon, Warwickshire.
Obelisk WM, Sutton-under-Brailes, Stratford-on-Avon, Warwickshire.
Obelisk WM, Wormleighton, Stratford-on-Avon, Warwickshire.

WILTSHIRE
Lansdowne Obelisk, 1845, total 125 ft, prominent on iron age fort, Cherhill Down, Wilts.
Obelisk, 1839-40, total 105 ft + sundisc, replacing 1746 obelisk, Stourhead NT, Wiltshire.
Obelisk, 1781, Silver st, Warminster, Wiltshire.
Obelisk, 1814, com. Peace of 1814, was at Bremhill Court, Bremhill, Calne, Wiltshire.
Obelisk, 'The Sabbath Drowning Obelisk', Devizes, Wiltshire.
Obelisk WM, St.Mary's ch, Collingbourne Kingston, nr Ludgershall, Wiltshire.
Obelisk WM, Marlborough, Wiltshire.
Obelisk WM, St.Mary's ch, Bradenstoke, nr Chippenham, Wiltshire.
Obelisk WM, Old School House, roadside, Silver st, Minety, nr Malmesbury, Wiltshire
Obelisk WM, Boughton Gifford, nr Warminster, Wiltshire.
Obelisk WM, Westbury House, Bradford on Avon, Wiltshire.
Obelisk WM, Ham Green, nr Marlborough, Wiltshire.

WORCESTERSHIRE
Obelisk, a wooden replica, Hanbury Hall NT, near Redditch, Worcestershire.
Obelisk, 1764, 70ft, in disrepair, grounds of Hagley Hall, Stourbridge, Worcestershire.
Obelisk, 18C, 14ft tall, limestone blocks, St.Oswald's Gdns, Worcester, Worcs.
Obelisk, 1834, m. Henry Windsor, Earl of Plymouth, Monument Lane, Lickey, Worcs.
Obelisk, 1841, m. Battle of Evesham 1265, Abbey Manor, Evesham, Worcestershire.
Obelisk, 1880, m. R.Baxter, 50 ft, Drakelow Rd,Wolverley, Kidderminster, Worcestershire.
Obelisk Milestone, 10 ft tall, distances inscribed, nr church, Bredon, Worcestershire.
Obelisk WM, All Saints ch, Bromsgrove, Worcestershire.
Obelisk WM, Somers family, Eastnor, Malvern Hills, Worcestershire.
Obelisk WM, St.Egwins ch, Church Honeybourne, Wychavon, worcestershire.
Obelisk WM, 20 ft Portland stone, Severn Stoke, Wychavon, Worcestershire.
Obelisk WM, Village Hall, Wyre Piddle, Wychavon, Worcestershire.
Obelisk WM, Hoobrook, Wyre Forest, Worcestershire.

YORKSHIRE
Aislabie Obelisk, 1702, arch:Nicholas Hawksmoor, Market Place, Ripon, N.Yorkshire.
Marlborough Obelisk,1714, 100 ft, Hawksmoor & Vanbrugh, Castle Howard, N.Yorkshire.
Obelisk, 1717, m. Elizabeth Dalton, Hauxwell Hall, W. Hauxwell, nr Richmond, N.Yorks.
Obelisk, 1771, short bulky re-erection, Market Place, Richmond, N.Yorkshire.
Obelisk, c.1780, c.18 ft, to West of house Baldersby Pk, nr Ripon, N.Yorkshire.
Obelisk, c.1780, c.18 ft, before ornamental lake, Baldersby Pk, nr Ripon, N.Yorkshire.
Obelisk, 1827, 'Cook Monument', 70 ft tall, prominent, Easby Moor, Gt.Ayton N.Yorks.
Obelisk, 1805, Studley Royal, nr Ripon, N.Yorkshire.
Obelisk, 1820, Village green, West Burton, nr Leyburn, Richmond, N.Yorkshire.
Obelisk, m. Battle of the Standards in 1138, roadside, Northallerton, N.Yorkshire.

Obelisk, 19 C, m. R. Evans, Crow Lane, Newton-le-Willows, nr Catterick, N.Yorkshire.

Obelisk, c.12 ft, gardens of Burton Agnes Hall, Bridlington, N.Yorkshire.

Obelisk, Newton House, Ugglebarnby, nr Whitby, N.Yorkshire.

Obelisk, 1906, m. Willance's Leap in 1606, 14 ft, Richmond, N. Yorkshire.

Obelisk, 1873, m. Brig Gen Palmer, Cave Road, Brough, N.Ferriby, E.Yorkshire.

Obelisk, 1747, m. Lady Mary Montague, Wentworth Castle, Rotherham S.Yorks.

Queen Anne's Obelisk, 1734, Rockley Lane, Hood Green, Rotherham S.Yorkshire.

Obelisk, 1775, inscribed '3 miles to Wentworth', Birdwell, Barnsley, S.Yorks,

4 Obelisks, 1793, 35 ft,Rockingham Mausoleum,Wentworth Woodhouse,Doncaster, S.Yorks.

Obelisk, 1913 'Oaks Explosion Monument'-mining disaster, Kendray,Barnsley, S.Yorks.

Obelisk, 1985, m. British in Spanish Civil War, Peace Gdn,Wharncliffe St, Doncaster.

Obelisk, c.1841, m. Sir Francis Chantrey RA, Norton, Sheffield, S.Yorkshire.

Obelisk, c.1778, m. Mrs Beaumont, Darton, Barnsley, S.Yorks.

Obelisk at Sutton Moor, nr Keighley, S.Yorkshire.

'The Needle's Eye', Obelisk-Pylon Gate,1776, Arch: R.Adam, Nostell Priory, S.Yorkshire.

4 Obelisks, c.1720, each 8 ft, in forecourt at Bramham Park, Wetherby, W.Yorkshire.

Obelisk. c1763, m. 2nd Lord Bingley's son, Bramham Park, Wetherby, W.Yorkshire.

Stoodley Pike Obelisk, 1815 / rebuilt 1856, 120 feet, 1st fl gallery, Todmorden, W.Yorkshire.

Obelisk, c1815, demolished, 65 ft, 'The (leaning) Waterloo Monument,Pontefract, W.Yorks.

Obelisk WM, m. NER Railway, 30 ft Portland stone, Station Road, York, N.Yorkshire.

Obelisk WM. Boer war, 20 ft granite, Tower street, York, N.Yorkshire.

Obelisk WM, 59 ft, Harrogate, N.Yorkshire.

Obelisk WM, St. Mathews ch, Keasden, Settle, N.Yorkshire.

Obelisk WM, 'The Cracoe Cairn', obtuse 25 ft, local stone, Cracoe, Skipton, N.Yorkshire.

Obelisk WM, Lothersdale, Skipton, N.Yorkshire.

Obelisk WM, Easingwold, nr. Boroughbridge, N.Yorkshire.

Obelisk WM, Helperby, nr. Boroughbridge, N.Yorkshire.

Obelisk WM, Hutton Rudby, nr. Northallerton, N.Yorkshire.

Obelisk WM, Osmotherley, nr Northallerton, N.Yorkshire.

Obelisk WM, St.Mary's ch, Gt.Ouseburn, Harrogate, N.Yorkshire.

Obelisk WM, Private W.Short VC, parish ch, Grangetown, Redcar, N.Yorkshire.

Obelisk WM, Lazenby, Wilton, nr.Guisborough, N.Yorkshire

Obelisk WM, Kettlesing Bottom, Harrogate, N.Yorkshire.

Obelisk WM, m. 'Twiggy' Short, Emston Cemetery, Middlesborough, N.Yorkshire.

Obelisk WM, Ramsgill, Pateley Bridge, Harrogate. N.Yorkshire.

Obelisk WM, St. Thomas' ch, Scotton, Harrogate, N.Yorkshire.

Obelisk WM, Upper Poppleton, nr York, N.Yorkshire.

Obelisk WM, Reeth, nr Richmond, N.Yorkshire.

Obelisk WM, St.Nicholas' ch, North Grimston, Malton, N.Yorkshire.

Obelisk WM, Eden Camp Monument, Eden Camp Museum, Malton, N.Yorkshire.

Obelisk WM, Flixton, Filey, N.Yorkshire.

Obelisk WM, Gristhorpe, nr Filey, N.Yorkshire.

Obelisk WM, Hunmanby, nr Filey, N.Yorkshire.

Obelisk WM, 70 ft on 18 ft base, Oliver's Mount, Scarborough, N.Yorkshire

Obelisk WM, Snainton, Scarborough, N.Yorkshire.

Obelisk WM, Trinity ch, Barkston Ash, nr Selby, N.Yorkshire.

Obelisk WM, Brayton, nr Selby, N.Yorkshire.

Obelisk WM, Beech Tree House, Burn, Selby, N.Yorkshire.
Obelisk WM, St. James ch, Fairburn, Selby, N.Yorkshire.
Obelisk WM, Selby, N.Yorkshire.
Obelisk WM, RAF, Beverley, E.Yorkshire.
Obelisk WM, Little Weighton, Beverley, E.Yorkshire.
Obelisk WM, St. Michael's ch, Skidby, Beverley, E.Yorkshire.
Obelisk WM, Woodmansey Park, Woodmansey, Beverley, E.Yorkshire.
Obelisk WM, North Newbald, Beverley, E.Yorkshire.
Obelisk WM, Hotham, nr Boothferry, E.Yorkshire.
Obelisk WM, parish ch, Snaith, nr Boothferry, E.Yorkshire.
Obelisk WM, St.Mary's ch, Huggate, E.Yorkshire.
Obelisk WM, Aldbrough, Holderness, E.Yorkshire.
Obelisk WM, Great Hatfield, Holderness, E.Yorkshire.
Obelisk WM, Holy Apostle ch, Kingston-upon-Hull, E.Yorkshire.
Obelisk WM, Blacker Hill, Barnsley,S.Yorkshire.
Obelisk WM, Hoyland, Barnsley, S.Yorkshire.
Obelisk WM, South Yorkshire Aircraft Museum, Doncaster, S.Yorkshire.
Obelisk WM, Blaxton, Doncaster, S.Yorkshire.
Obelisk WM, Doncaaster Wire Co, Doncaster, S.Yorkshire.
Obelisk WM, Yorkshire Colliery, Edlington, Doncaster, S.Yorkshire.
Obelisk WM, St.Cuthbert's ch, Fishlake, Doncaster, S.Yorkshire.
Obelisk WM, St.Thomas' ch, Kilnhurst, Doncaster, S.Yorkshire.
Obelisk WM, Tinsley Infants School, Tinsley, Sheffield, S.Yorkshire.
Obelisk WM, Barnoldswick,nr Skipton, W.Yorkshire.
Obelisk WM, Salterforth, nr Barnoldswick, W.Yorkshire.
Obelisk WM, 1923, 52 ft, Pots & Pans Hill, Saddleworth Moor, Uppermill, W.Yorks.
Obelisk WM, Methodist ch, Blackshaw Head, Todmorden, W.Yorkshire.
Obelisk WM, Crossley Heath Sch, Crossley Heath, Halifax, W.Yorkshire.
Obelisk WM, 30 ft, Wakefield Road, Lightcliffe, Halifax, W.Yorkshire.
Wadsworth Obelisk WM, 40 ft stone, Pecket Well, Hebden Bridge,W.Yorkshire.
Obelisk WM, Rastrick Library, Rastrick, Brighouse, Leeds, W.Yorkshire.
Obelisk WM, Brotherton, nr Castleford, Leeds, W.Yorks.
Obelisk WM, Cross Stone, Todmorden,W.Yorkshire.
Obelisk WM, Clayton West, Kirkburton, Huddersfield, W.Yorkshire.
Obelisk WM, St.Mark's ch, Longwood, nr Holmfirth,W.Yorkshire.
Obelisk WM, m. Bowers Allerton, Great Preston, Leeds,W.Yorkshire.
Obelisk WM, St.Michael's ch, Headingley, Leeds,W.Yorkshire.
Obelisk WM, Meth School Rooms, Otley, Leeds,W.Yorkshire.
Obelisk WM, Pool, Otley, Leeds,W.Yorkshire.
Obelisk WM, Crigglestone, Wakefield, W.Yorkshire.
Obelisk WM, Crofton, Wakefield,W.Yorkshire.
Obelisk WM, Community Centre, Ferrybridge, Wakefield, W.Yorkshire.
Obelisk WM, Kirkhamgate, Wakefield,W.Yorkshire.
Obelisk WM, Normanton, Wakefield, W.Yorkshire.
Obelisk WM, West Bretton, Wakefield,W.Yorkshire.
Obelisk WM, Tong Park, Baildon, Bradford, W.Yorkshire.
Obelisk WM, Bolton Woods, Bradford,W.Yorkshire.
Obelisk WM, Clayton, Bradford,W.Yorkshire.
Obelisk WM, m. Horse Artillery Servicemen, Low moor, Bradford,W.Yorkshire.

Obelisk WM, Ukrainian Comm, Low Moor, Bradford,W.Yorkshire.
Obelisk WM, Reform ch, Saltaire, Bradford,W.Yorkshire.
Obelisk WM, Silsden, Bradford, W.Yorkshire.
Obelisk WM, Stanbury, Bradford,W.Yorkshire.

WALES
Obelisk, 1736, m. 429 Celtic victory over Picts & Saxons,16 ft, Rhuallt, Holywell, Clwyd.
Obelisk, 1830, marking forestry plantations by Lord William Bagot, Clocaenog, Clwyd
Obelisk, 1898, m. John Parry, 16 ft, land reformist,Llanarmon-yn-Ial, Ruthin, Clwyd.
Obelisk, Briggs Memorial, Tredegar House, Newport, Gwent.
Mail Coach Obelisk,1841, near Pentre-bach, Llandovery, Dyfed.
Obelisk, 1844, m. W&H.Crawshay, 12 ft, stone,Treforest House,Caerphilly,Glamorgan
Obelisk, c.30 ft, limestone ashlar, Colby Woodland Gardens NT, Amroth, Narbeth, Dyfed.
Picton Obelisk, 1847, m. Gen Picton, 1988 restored & reduced to 60 ft, Carmarthen, Dyfed.
Obelisk, 1864, m. John Mirehouse from tenantry, Angle, Pembrokeshire, Dyfed.
Obelisk, 1803, m. 5th Duke of Bedford, Devil's bridge, Aberystwyth, Dyfed
Obelisk, 1887, m. Sir R. Green Price, 15 ft, fell down 1976, Hengwm Hill, Norton, Powys.
Obelisk, 1885, m. J.Y.Lloyd from his tenantry, 20 ft, Llangurig, Powys.
Obelisk, 1832, m. Captain J.m. Skinner, 30 ft total, overlooking Holyhead, Anglesey.
Obelisk, 1850, m. Britannia Bridge workers killed, 25 ft, Llanfair Pwllgwyngyll, Anglesey.
Obelisk, 1866, m. to Mari Jones, Llanfihangel-y-Pennant, Bala, North Wales.
Obelisk, 1882, m. Sir Richard Bulkeley, 90 ft tall, Beaumaris Castle, Anglesey,
Obelisk, 1894, m. Robert Griffith, minister, Baptist chapel, Llanddeiniolen, Gwynedd.
Obelisk, 1993, 64 ft, arch: Eric Throssel; Bryn Pydew, Bodysgallen, Llanrhos, Gwynned.
Obelisk, 1901, m. Tommy Jones, Pen-y-fan, northern Brecon Beacons, Powys.
Obeliscal seamark, very dramatic location on exposed coast, Pen Anglas NT, Dyfed.
Obelisk, 1930, m. Amelia Earhart's flight, 19 ft tall,Stepney Rd, Burry Port, Dyfed.
Obelisk Monument, 1933, stepped 80 ft, surmounted statue, Aberystwyth, Dyfed.
Obelisk, 1960, m. S.G.Thomas,19C metallurgist;Ironworks Mus, Blaenavon,Glamorgan.
Obelisk, 1911, m. D.Williams,d.1816,founder R.Lit Fund,Castle Pk,Caerphilly,Glamorgan
Obelisk, 1999, 20 ft tall, dressed stone blocks, sc: Dan archer, Penarth, S.Glamorgan.
Obelisk WM, Llwydcoed, Cynon Valley, Mid Glamorgan.
Obelisk WM, Tregibbon, Cynon Valley, Mid Glamorgan.
Obelisk WM, Boer War, Merthyr Tydfil, Mid Glamorgan.
Obelisk WM, Boer War, Thomastown, Merthyr Tydfil, Mid Glamorgan.
Obelisk WM, Blackmill, Mid Glamorgan.
Obelisk WM, St.Bride's Major, Mid Glamorgan.
Obelisk WM, Blaenrhondda, Mid Glamorgan.
Obelisk WM, County School, Porth, Rhondda, Mid Glamorgan.
Obelisk WM, Brynna Llanharan, nr Pontypridd, Mid Glamorgan.
Obelisk WM, Pontypridd, Mid Glamorgan.
Obelisk WM, Parish ch, Rhydyfelin, Pontypridd, Mid Glamorgan.
Obelisk WM, Old St.Mellons, Cardiff, South Glamorgan.
Obelisk WM, 38 ft, m. Glamorgan Yeomanry, Cowbridge, South Glamorgan.
Obelisk WM, 22 ft granite, Pontardawe Arts Centre, Lliw Valley, West Glamorgan.
Obelisk WM, Resolven, Neath, West Glamorgan.
Obelisk WM, Risca, Islwyn, Gwent.

Obelisk WM, St.Mary's ch, Port Skewett, Monmouth, Gwent.
Obelisk WM, Griffithstown, Torfaen, Gwent.
Obelisk WM, Pontnewydd, Torfaen, Gwent.
Obelisk WM, Hundred House, nr Builth Wells, Brecon, Powys.
Obelisk WM, parish ch, Buttington, Montgomery, Powys.
Obelisk WM, parish ch,Dolanog, Montgomery, Powys.
Obelisk WM, parish ch,Forden, Montgomery, Powys.
Obelisk WM, parish ch, Llandrionio, Montgomery, Powys.
Obelisk WM, parish ch,Llanerfyl, Montgomery, Powys.
Obelisk WM, St.Mary's ch, Llanfair Caereinion, Montgomery, Powys.
Obelisk WM, Llanbister, Radnor, Powys.
Obelisk WM, Crimean War, 32 ft Portland stone, plume of feathers finial, Carmarthen.
Obelisk WM, Newcastle Emlyn, nr Carmarthen, Dyfed,
Obelisk WM, Welfare Hall, Pontyates, Carmarthen, Dyfed.
Obelisk WM, Red Roses, nr Carmarthen, Dyfed.
Obelisk WM, Bwlch chapel, Bwlch y Groes, Cardigan, Dyfed.
Obelisk WM, Cellan, Cardigan, Dyfed.
Obelisk WM, Llanfarian, Cardigan, Dyfed.
Obelisk WM, Rhydyfelin, Cardigan, Dyfed.
Obelisk WM, Milford Haven, Pembroke, Dyfed
Obelisk WM, Carew, Pembroke, Dyfed.
Obelisk WM, Pembroke Dock Memorial, Pembroke Dock, Pembroke, Dyfed.
Obelisk WM, St. Florence's ch, St.Florence, Pembroke, Dyfed.
Obelisk WM, Municipal Offices, Conwy, Aberconwy, Gwynedd.
Obelisk WM, Dolgarrog, Aberconwy, Gwynedd.
Obelisk WM, Boer war, St.Tudnos ch, Llandudno, Aberconwy, Gwynedd.
Obelisk WM, Parish ch, Penmachno, Gwynedd.
Obelisk WM, Jerusalem ch, Penmaenmawr, Aberconwy, Gwynedd.
Obelisk WM, Penrhyn-side, Aberconwy, Gwynedd.
Obelisk WM, The Red Lion Inn, Tyn y Groes,Aberconwy, Gwynedd.
Obelisk WM, Llanerchymedd, Anglesey, Gwynedd.
Obelisk WM, Bangor city, Gwynedd.
Obelisk WM, m. R.Evans, Blaenau Ffestiniog, Merioneth, Gwynedd.
Obelisk WM, Llandecwyn chapel, Llandecwyn, Merioneth, Gwynedd.
Obelisk WM, Christ ch, Talsarnau, Merioneth, Gwynedd.
Obelisk WM, Hawarden, Deeside, Clwyd,
Obelisk WM, parish ch, Gwytherin, Colwyn, Clwyd.
Obelisk WM, Alms Houses, Llansannan, Colwyn, Clwyd.
Obelisk WM, Boer War, Flint, Clwyd.
Obelisk WM, Picton, Delyn, Clwyd.
Obelisk WM, Chirk, Llansantffaud Glyn Ceiriog, Glyndwr, Clwyd.
Obelisk WM, Nantglyn, Glyndwr, Clwyd.
Obelisk WM, Dyserth, Rhuddlan, Clwyd.
Obelisk WM, All Saints ch, Ffynnongroyw, Rhudlan, Clwyd.
Obelisk WM, Holt, Wrexham, Clwyd.
Obelisk WM, m. Lindisfarne College, St.Mary's ch, Ruabon, Wrexham, Clwyd.

SCOTLAND

Obelisk, 1794, 12 ft, recessed figures James I & II, Dryburgh Abbey, St.Boswell's, Borders.

Obelisk, c.1748, m. James Thomson, poet, Ednam Road, Kelso, Borders.

Obelisk, 1779, m. Linnaeus, Arch: James Craig, Edinburgh.

Obelisk, 1883, red granite, 72nd Highland Regiment, Edinburgh Castle.

Obelisk, 1844, m. political martyrs of 1793, Calton Burial ground, Waterloo Pl, Edinburgh.

Ramsay's Monument, 1759, Pierced obeliscal tower, m. Allan Ramsay, Penicuik, Lothian.

Newhall obelisks, 1810, m. Allan Ramsay & T.Dunsmore, Carlops, nr Penicuik, Lothian.

Obelisk, 1856, m. Earl of Haddington, d.1835. Tyningham House, Broxburn, Lothian.

Obelisk, 1788, 100 ft, m. G.Buchanan,(1506-1582), Arch: James Craig, Killearn, Stirling.

Obelisk, 1806, rebuilt 1810, m. Lord Nelson, 144 ft, arch: D.Hamilton, Glasgow Green.

Obelisk, 1836, m. Henry Bell, steamship builder, Dunglass Rock, nr Dunbarton, Glasgow.

Obelisk, 1872, m. Henry Bell, 25 ft granite monolith, Helensburgh, Dunbarton, Strathclyde.

Blantyre's Obelisk, Erskine Ferry, Strathclyde.

Obelisk, m. David Hutcheson, North end, Isle of Kerrera, Oban, Strathclyde.

Obelisk, 1915, site of 13C Bishop's Palace, nr Livingstone monument, Glasgow.

Obelisk, 18 C, m. S.Rutherford, Anwoth, nr Wigtown, Dumfries & Galloway.

Deer Obelisk, 19 C, Carsphain, Dumfries and Galloway.

Obelisk, 1835, m. A.Murray, Clatteringshaws, Galloway Forest Pk, Dumfries and Galloway.

Obelisk, 18 C, overlooking sea, Girvan, Strathclyde.

Obelisk-Sundial, 1630, Drummond Castle, Muthill, Crieff, Perth, Tayside.

Obelisk, 1850, comm. Presbyterian church anniversary, Gairneybridge, Perth, Tayside.

Obelisk, 1755, 'Balvenie Pillar', small ,Tom na Croiche hill, Blair Atholl, Tayside.

Obelisk, 1812, m. Viscount Melville, 72 ft, granite, Dunmore Hill, Comrie, Tayside.

Obelisk, 18th c, hilltop, New Scone, Tayside.

Obelisk, 1837, m. Robert Nicholl, poet, Tullybelton, Perth, Tayside.

Obelisk, 19C, m. Sir David Baird, c.50ft, Trowan, Quoig, Comrie, Tayside.

Lamont Obelisk, Inverey, Grampian

Obelisk, 1816, m. brother of Earl of Aberdeen,Haddo House, Methlick, Grampian

Obelisk, 1858, m. Sir J. McGrigor, 72 ft, polished granite blocks, Duthie Park, Aberdeen.

Obelisk, c1714, 65 ft, leaning, removed c1910, m.1st Earl of Cromartie, Dingwall, Cromarty.

Obelisk, c1920, small replica of the 1714 obelisk, nr Dingwall parish church, R & Cromarty.

Murchison Obelisk, Balmacara, near Kyle of Lochalsh, Ross & Cromarty.

Obelisk, c.1815, m. Col J.Cameron, Corpach, nr Fort William, Inverness.

Mackintosh Obelisk, 19 C, Moy, Inverness

Obelisk comm General Wade,(1673-1748), Wade Road, Fort William, Inverness.

Obelisk WM, 24 ft granite, Main st, Berwick-on-Tweed, Borders.

Obelisk WM, Memorial Park, Station Road, Duns, Berwickshire, Borders.

Obelisk WM, parish ch, Roberton, Roxburgh, nr Kelso, Borders.

Obelisk WM, roadside, Yarrow, Selkirk, Borders.

Obelisk WM, Broughton, Tweedale, nr Peebles, Borders.

Obelisk WM, 20 ft, granite, Ecclefechan, nr Dumfries, Dumfries & Galloway.

Obelisk WM, Kirkpatrick Fleming, nr Gretna Green, Dumfries & Galloway.

Obelisk WM, Collin, Nithsdale, Dumfries & Galloway.

Obelisk WM, Dunscore, nr Dumfries, Dumfries & Galloway.

Obelisk WM, Gelston, Nithsdale, Dumfries & Galloway.

Obelisk WM, Balmaclellan, nr Dumfries, Dumfries & Galloway.

Obelisk WM, parish ch, Corsock, nr Dumfries, Dumfries & Galloway.

Obelisk WM, Glasserton, Wigtown, Dumfries & Galloway.

Obelisk WM, Leswalt, Wigtown, Dumfries & Galloway.

Obelisk WM, Glebe Cemetery, Stranraer, Wigtown, Dumfries & Galloway.

Obelisk WM, 22 ft, Daniel Stewarts College, Edinburgh, Lothian.

Obelisk WM, Lothians Boer War, Dunbar, East Lothian.

Obelisk WM, parish ch, Glencorse, Midlothian.

Obelisk WM, Bathgate, nr Edinburgh, West Lothian.

Obelisk WM, West Calder, nr Edinburgh, West Lothian.

Obelisk WM, 40 ft, Dunoon Castle, Argyll, Strathclyde.

Obelisk WM, Queen's Hall Gardens, Dunoon, Argyll, Strathclyde.

Obelisk WM, Kilchrenan, Argyll, Strathclyde.

Obelisk WM, Tarbert, Argyll, Strathclyde.

Obelisk WM, 15 ft granite, at school, overlooking sea, Achafolla, Isle of Luing, Argyll.

Obelisk WM, 27 ft, municipal cemetery, Hamilton, nr Glasgow, Strathclyde.

Obelisk WM, Great Cumbrae Island, Firth of Clyde, Strathclyde.

Obelisk WM, Darvel, nr Kilmarnock, nr Glasgow, Strathclyde.

Obelisk WM, Ayr, Ayrshire, Strathclyde.

Obelisk WM, Girvan, Ayrshire, Strathclyde.

Obelisk WM, 20 ft granite, Railway Station, Omoa Rd, Cleland, Motherwell, Strathclyde.

Obelisk WM, Morningside, Motherwell, Strathclyde.

Obelisk WM, Carnock, Culross, Dunfermline, Fife.

Obelisk WM, parish ch (demolished), Mossgreen, Coaledge, Dunfermline, Fife.

Obelisk WM, Cowdenbeath, nr Dunfermline, Fife.

Obelisk WM, Culross, Dunfermline, Fife.

Obelisk WM, 22 ft, celtic carving on front face,parish ch, Lochgelly, Dunfermline, Fife.

Obelisk WM, United Free ch (redundant), North Queensferry, Dunfermline, Fife.

Obelisk WM, Saline, Dunfermline, Fife.

Obelisk WM, Leven, Kirkcaldy, Fife.

Obelisk WM, Scoonie Kirk, Scoonie, Kirkcaldy, Fife.

Obelisk WM, Giffordtown, N.E Fife.

Obelisk WM, Bonnybridge, Falkirk, Central Scotland.

Obelisk WM, Bannockburn, Stirling,Central Scotland.

Obelisk WM, Doune, Stirling, Central Scotland.

Obelisk WM, Carmyllie, nr Dundee, Angus, Tayside.

Obelisk WM, Edzell, nr Brechin, Angus, Tayside.

Obelisk WM, Friockheim, nr Arbroath, Angus, Tayside.

Obelisk WM, parish ch, Rescobie, Angus, Tayside.

Obelisk WM, Boer War, Market Sq, Alyth, nr Blairgowrie, Perth, Tayside.

Obelisk WM, Madderty, nr Perth, Tayside.

Obelisk WM, Milnathort, nr Perth, Tayside.

Obelisk WM, m. Polish soldiers, Perth, Tayside.

Obelisk WM, Strathtay, Perth, Tayside.

Obelisk WM, Parish ch, Auchterlees, Banff & Buchan, Grampian.

Obelisk WM, 32 ft, parish ch, Gamrie, Gardenstown, Banff , Grampian.

Obelisk WM, Kirkhill Transfer Station, Kininmouth, Buchan, Grampian.

Obelisk WM, Parish ch, Maud, nr Peterhead, Buchan, Grampian.

Obelisk WM, Village hall, Mulben, Banff & Buchan, Grampian.

Obelisk WM, 22 ft granite, parish ch, Savoch, Banff & Buchan, Grampian.

Obelisk WM, Parish ch, Tyrie, Banff & Buchan, Grampian.

Obeliscal WM, 40 ft Peterhead granite, by Chas MacDonald Ltd, Peterhead, Aberdeen.

Obelisk WM, Parish ch, Nigg, Aberdeen.

Obelisk WM, Parish ch, Daviot, nr Huntly, Aberdeen.

Obelisk WM, Drumblade, nr Huntly, Aberdeen.

Obelisk WM, 35 ft granite, Huntly, Aberdeen.

Obelisk WM, parish ch, Methlick, Old Meldrum, Aberdeen.

Obelisk WM, Auchenblae, Drumtochty, Kincardine, Grampian.

Obelisk WM, Birse, nr Ballater, Aberdeen.

Obelisk WM, Durris, nr Banchory, Aberdeen.

Obelisk WM, Gourdon, nr Stonehaven, Kincardine, Grampian.

INDEX
(See Gazetteer for locations of obelisks)

192